Writing about Literature:

Step by Step

Seventh Edition

Pat McKeague
Moraine Valley College

KENDALL/HUNT PUBLISHING COMPANY
4050 Westmark Drive Dubuque, Iowa 52002

BOOK TEAM
Chairman and Chief Executive Officer   Mark C. Falb
Vice President, Director of National Book Program   Alfred C. Grisanti
Editorial Development Supervisor   Georgia Botsford
Developmental Editor   Angela Willenbring
Assistant Vice President, Production Services   Christine E. O'Brien
Prepress Editor   Jenifer Chapman
Permissions Editor   Colleen Zelinsky
Cover Design Manager   Jodi Splinter
Cover Designer   Suzanne Millius

Editor's Note: Many of the literature selections highlighted in this book are published in their entirety in The Kendall/Hunt Anthology © 2003 by Kendall/Hunt Publishing Co., ISBN 0-7575-0195-8. To order, call (800) 247-3458, ext. 6.

"I have often thought how interesting a magazine paper might be written by an author who would—that is to say who could—detail, step-by-step, the processes by which any one of his compositions attained its ultimate point of completion."

Edgar Allan Poe
The Philosophy of Composition

Writing about Literature: Step by Step is a companion to another Kendall/Hunt text entitled *Writing Step by Step* by Randy DeVillez.

Cover images © 2002 PhotoDisc, Inc.

Copyright © 1982, 1986, 1989, 1992, 1995, 1999, 2002 by Kendall/Hunt Publishing Company

ISBN 0-7872-9013-0

Printed in the United States of America
10 9 8 7 6 5 4 3 2 1

For my parents, Michael and Selma,
who always believed in all their children.

Contents

Chapter 12   Tone Analysis

Chapter 13   Writing an Extended Literary Analysis Essay

Chapter 14   Writing Literary Research Papers

Chapter 15   Taking Essay Examinations in Literature

Chapter 16   This Is Not the End

Index   321

Preface

Writing about Literature: Step by Step can be used effectively in a variety of classes:

- composition classes that use literature as the basis for essay assignments;
- literature classes where students are expected to write about what they have read;
- humanities classes that include a study of literature.

To introduce students to the elements of fiction, poetry, and drama—character, theme, setting, point of view, symbolism, imagery, structure, and tone—each chapter contains the following learning activities:

- a thorough, easy-to-understand discussion of a literary concept;
- step-by-step instructions on how to choose a topic and organize an essay;
- a diagram of the structure of a typical essay, including instructions on how to produce an effective introduction, a well developed body, and a logical conclusion;
- student-written model essays that illustrate the suggested structure;
- a plan sheet and an evaluation form to guide the writer through the drafting process;
- a group exercise to actively involve students in the learning process.

The intent of the step-by-step approach is to take the mystery out of the writing process. By following guidelines and structural patterns, students learn the basics of good writing: focus, structure, organization, and development based on the literary analysis pattern. Mastering these skills will prepare them to write about any material they must analyze in college or on the job.

Writing about Literature: Step by Step can be used with any literature anthology in any class that deals with literature and composition. Each model essay can stand alone since it contains quotations from the work it analyzes to illustrate and support the writer's thesis. **In fact, each chapter offers at least three different model essays for students to study and imitate—more than other current textbooks on writing about literature.**

New material in the Seventh Edition includes

- **additional information on how to read and think critically about literature;**
- **updated models for documentation entries, including electronic sources;**
- **new student-written model essays in many chapters;**
- **additional information on using electronic research tools and on writing the research paper;**
- **an updated CD-Rom that includes Acrobat Reader 5.0 as the platform for additional exercises on composition and literature.**

All of the revisions and additions have one major goal: to increase student learning.

Students at Moraine Valley College have worked with these materials while they were being written and revised, and they have found them helpful; I have found that their essays improved significantly. I hope that you will also benefit from the seventh edition of *Writing about Literature: Step by Step*.

Acknowledgments

I especially want to thank all of my colleagues for their support and for all of the things I've learned from them;

all of my students, especially those whose essays appear in this book, for all the things they have taught me;

all of my family and friends for their encouragement and support;

and

Randy DeVillez, Allan Monroe, Sandy Bryzek, Anne Reagan, Louann Tiernan, Margaret Lehner, Bill Muller, Rod Seaney, Len Jellema, Betsy Teo, Nahid Shafiei, Jay Noteboom, John Sullivan, Jean McAllister, and Carol Garlanger for their help in preparing the revised editions.

To the Instructor

Since I have been teaching students how to write, I have probably learned as much as or more than they have. One of the things I've learned is that most students have strong doubts about their ability to write. As you know, they tend to believe that writing is some magical act or some miraculous experience in which a power greater than themselves moves the pen along the page. And, of course, this great skill is given only to a chosen few—certainly not to them.

To take writing out of this highly mystical, abstract world, I began teaching students specific patterns for writing by drawing diagrams of the different types of paragraphs and essays and by developing general formulas for the different analytical approaches to writing. Making the process more concrete seemed to help my students understand the concept that there is a way to write clear, well organized essays in which they can effectively convey their ideas to their reader.

The material in the following pages has helped my students learn to write effective essays about literature. By understanding the literary concepts involved, by analyzing works of literature in class, by studying model student essays, and by carefully planning their own writing, students can master the process of writing.

Each chapter is a self-contained unit, so you can introduce the literary elements in the order that best meets your approach to teaching. That's why *Writing about Literature: Step by Step* can be used successfully with **any** literature anthology. I think you'll find that the supplementary material included with the Instructor's Guide is general enough to blend effectively with most teaching styles. The transparency masters can be used to visually reinforce important concepts, and the extra exercises and class handouts give students a chance to practice what they've learned.

It is my sincere hope that using this text will help make your students even better writers and that it will help make your teaching just a bit easier. May all your semesters be filled with good grammar, good paragraphs, good essays, and good students.

To the Student

Studying literature is one of the best ways to learn about human beings and the ways they deal with life. As you read works in the three genres or types of literature—prose fiction, poetry, and drama—you will encounter all types of human personalities dealing with all types of human problems. As you come to understand the characters' motives, actions, and reactions, you will surely come to understand your own behavior and that of others better.

After you analyze a work of literature, you can clarify your thinking even further and share your insights with others by writing them down. As you return to the work to look for supporting quotes to back up the main point or thesis in your essay, your understanding of the work will increase, and you will come to appreciate the craft of the author and the unique way he managed to produce certain responses in you as a sensitive and informed reader. And when you write, you will be synthesizing your ideas and those of the author to produce an organized, well supported essay, one that can be appreciated and understood even by those who have not read the work of literature on which the paper is written.

Being able to write about what you've read is a skill that is invaluable in any college course, for you will often be asked to analyze in writing such things as journal articles, essays, reports, or experiments to demonstrate your understanding of them. It is my hope that this book will help you develop this important skill. The explanations, exercises, plan sheets, and model essays have helped my students at Moraine Valley College, and I am confident that if you use them as they are intended, you, too, will discover that there is a formula for writing that anyone can master.

And so the ability to write is not a gift given only to a select few; it is a skill that can be developed by learning and practicing certain organizational principles that hold true whether you are writing for a teacher, a supervisor, a customer, or even the chairperson of the board. Mastering these principles will pay off no matter what career you plan to enter, so let's get started right now.

The Elements of Literature

Overview

The creator of literature is an artist whose main tool is words. Through them and with them, he creates a "mini" world of people living out a "limited" experience. We can see its beginning, middle, and end. To fully understand the art of literature, you should be able to identify the elements—the parts, the supporting structures—that work together to produce the overall effect a literary work has on its audience. By reading thoughtfully and thinking critically, you can learn to appreciate the relationship of literature to life.

The Creative Process and the Elements of Literature

Writers are people, sensitive, aware, and intelligent, whose thoughts and experiences produce definite reactions—usually pleasurable, sometimes painful—in them. The desire to share these reactions generally leads them to create a literary work that they hope will produce the same effect on the audience. As authors begin to write, they determine what particular causes will produce the desired effect, and they work them into a world of their own making. Now this world will, in most instances, be similar to the "real" world, but the writers have total control over what events will happen to what people at what precise moments. They are "gods," eliminating chance and establishing connections between and among the events in the work.

As the author plans the work, he or she may decide to write a poem, a form of literature sometimes distinguished from prose by its intense, compact use of language, by its unique appearance on the printed page, and by its use of devices like rhyme, rhythm, figurative language, and imagery. Perhaps the author will choose to share his or her ideas by writing a piece of prose fiction, either a short story, a novella, or a novel, depending on the length of its plot. If the author wants to present the plot by having actors perform on stage before a live audience, he or she will be writing a drama. These three literary forms—poetry, prose fiction, and drama—comprise the major types or genres of literature.

When writers create their worlds by using the medium of words, they use language in their own unique way, thereby illustrating their unique **style**. And whether these writers choose to write poetry, prose fiction, or drama, they will be using many of the same elements of literature. For example, a writer usually begins with a series of related actions—**a plot**—and then creates people—**characters**—to carry out these actions. The central character, the character whose will moves the action of the plot, is called **the**

protagonist. The characters or forces that work against the protagonist are called **the antagonists** or **the antagonistic forces**. These opposing forces—the source of **conflict** in the story—may be another human being, nature, the supernatural, society, technology, or even the protagonist himself.

In attempting to achieve a particular goal or objective, the protagonist—through his actions and those of others—learns significant things about himself, other people, and life. As he gains this knowledge, he experiences what is called an **epiphany**. This insight into life, which most often occurs at the climax of the work, changes the protagonist. He will never be the same because of the events which have occurred in his life. Because of this change, the protagonist is a **dynamic or round character**, one who is growing while responding to life's challenges. Characters who help in this growth process but who do not change themselves are called **static or flat characters**. They may be antagonists working against the protagonist, or they may be minor characters who sometimes function as **foils**, contrasting with the protagonist to reveal his or her qualities more clearly.

In deciding how to most effectively tell their story, writers choose an appropriate **point of view**. They may want one of the characters in the story to narrate in the first person, or they may wish to create a third person narrator, perhaps an objective one who reports only the words and actions of the characters or possibly an omniscient one who can describe the characters' thoughts and emotions as well as their words and actions. The method of narration is important because it directly influences the **theme** of the work, the idea or meaning writers wish the audience to gain from sharing this experience. In developing the theme, authors may also use **symbols**—characters, objects, actions, colors, or places with two levels of meaning—to underscore their point about life.

As readers, we come to this world of the writer willing to believe in everything he or she has created. As the plot pattern begins, **the exposition** introduces the characters, and we learn about their situation and their setting in time and place. In the next part of the pattern, **the complication**, we watch their conflicts or problems develop, study their responses to these difficulties, and pick up hints of the outcome through the author's use of **foreshadowing**. When **the climax**—the third part of the pattern—occurs, we reach the turning point in the story and learn whether the protagonist will or will not achieve his goal. The last part of the pattern is the **resolution or dénouement**, where we share the characters' insights into life and either glory with them in their success or weep with them in their failure. If we do our part by participating imaginatively and creatively in the characters' world, if we are willing to get involved, we are entertained as we wonder what will happen next, and we are instructed as we experience the message of the work; it has meaning for us.

And meaning is one of the primary reasons for reading literature. Through their works, writers hope to share their vision, their view of the human experience, and while we may not always agree with their ideas, writers help us to clarify our own values and attitudes toward life. We can also learn from a work by seeing it as the product of a certain period in history (the historical approach), as the product of a certain set of social standards and conventions (the social approach), or as the product of the writer's personal attitudes, conflicts, and concerns (the biographical approach). We can even analyze the motivation of the characters or the author by applying specific psychological theories (the psychological approach) or by noting the recurrence of certain types of characters, situations, or symbols that appeal to our unconscious minds in an instinctive and intuitive way (the archetypal approach). Looking at a work from any or all of these viewpoints will, most often, broaden our understanding of what it means to be human.

Unfortunately, however, we are sometimes unprepared for the experience the author wishes us to share. We may be too immature, too inexperienced, too insensitive, or too bored to consider or to understand the author's ideas. We should always keep in mind that what we get from a literary work is directly proportional to what we bring to it. If we bring open and perceptive minds, we will discover the pleasure and the insight that a well written work of literature can give.

❧ How to Read Literature[1]

Whatever your motivation may be, reading for pleasure, reading in preparation for an essay assignment or for class discussion, reading to help resolve another reader's questions, or reading for any combination of reasons, comprehension is pleasurable and lack of comprehension is frustrating. Two approaches, one general and one specific, will make reading literature a more pleasurable experience.

The general approach involves two steps:

1. Read the work quickly, concentrating on its literal level: who's who, what's happening, where is it happening, how is the action resolved?
2. Rethink the work. Is the author trying to make a point, to produce a reaction in me, to entertain? All three? How does the author want me to react? How do I know that? How do I react? Why? Why do I like, dislike, or have mixed feelings about the work? Is the outcome believable? Is it justified by what precedes it? Is the work conventional or unusual in terms of what I have read? What am I sure of? What is puzzling? Why?

Probably you will be able to answer some but not all of these questions. You are now ready for a more specific reading approach. This requires a second reading of the work, a reading focusing on six elements common to virtually all imaginative literature. As you slowly reread, using a dictionary whenever necessary, take your time in answering six questions, one on each of the six elements.

1. What is the significance of the title? The title may direct your attention to a crucial incident, may focus on and evaluate a key character, or may imply or state a theme embodied in the work. You may be sure the title is somehow significant; the author has chosen and phrased it purposefully. Is it literal or figurative, appropriate or ironic? If its significance is not apparent, try to understand it as you reread the work.
2. What does the author accomplish in his first and last sentences or lines? Their contents are inevitably significant as a function of their position. Do they unify the work? Do they emphasize an idea? Why does the work begin at this point and end at that point?
3. Are names of characters, settings, or objects chosen appropriately, ironically, or accidentally? Names can be helpful clues to an author's attitudes toward his material.
4. What instances of repetition can be detected? Repetition is a guarantee of significance. Why are particular incidents, images, or ideas repeated? Why are particular phrases repeated? What is the author trying to emphasize in each case?
5. What is the nature of the conflict(s) and what is its (their) resolution? Resolution of conflict frequently emphasizes a theme. How does the author want the reader to react to that resolution? How does the reader know what reaction is desired? If the conflict is unresolved, why has the author purposefully left it so?
6. How has the author foreshadowed the work's conclusion? In a well constructed work, every incident, every character, every detail has a function. What apparently insignificant details can now be seen as significant instances of foreshadowing? What patterns of character and incident are established to lead inevitably to a particular resolution?

In *How to Read a Book: The Classic Guide to Intelligent Reading*,[2] Mortimer J. Adler and Charles Van Doren emphasize the importance of reading "with total immersion" and of "letting an imaginative book work on you." They suggest that you "let the characters into your mind and heart; suspend your disbelief, if such it is, about the events. Do not disapprove of something a character does before you un-

---

[1] These reading approaches were formulated by Professor Allan Monroe of Moraine Valley College in Palos Hills, IL. Reprinted by permission.

[2] (New York: Simon, 1972).

derstand why he does it—if then. Try as hard as you can to live in his world, not in yours; there, the things he does may be quite understandable. And do not judge the world as a whole until you are sure that you have 'lived' in it to the extent of your ability" (218).

As you enter these imaginary worlds and become part of them, you will begin to understand the impact of the characters' experiences on their lives, and when you read and think about literature in this way, you will be engaged in critical thinking activities.

❧ Thinking Critically about Literature

"Thinking is any mental activity that helps formulate or solve a problem, make a decision, or fulfill a desire to understand. It is a searching for answers, a reaching for meaning. Numerous mental activities are included in the thinking process. Careful observation, remembering, wondering, imagining, inquiring, interpreting, evaluating, and judging are among the most important ones. Often several of these activities work in combination, as when we solve a problem or make a decision. We may, for example, identify an idea or dilemma, then deal with it—say, by questioning, interpreting, and analyzing—and finally reach a conclusion or decision."[3] Any composition or literature class (or any class for that matter) should help you develop your thinking skills—skills that you will use in every aspect of your education, your job, and your personal life.

In his *Taxonomy of Educational Objectives,* Benjamin Bloom and his colleagues identified mental operations that we engage in when we think and learn. They are application, analysis, synthesis, and evaluation.[4] Problem solving is also often added to this list.

Application involves using knowledge you have already acquired in a new or different situation. Analysis is the process of breaking down a whole by identifying and examining its parts, while synthesis involves a reverse mental operation of combining parts or ideas to form a new or expanded whole. Evaluation requires a judgment or decision about the whole and its effectiveness to determine if it has achieved its goals or objectives. And as its label suggests, problem solving attempts to identify a problem, determine its possible causes, and brainstorm for the best possible solutions.

Here are some ways that you can practice these skills while reading your assignments:

- **Keeping a Journal**—Writing is thinking because it forces you to formulate and shape your ideas in order to express them. That's why keeping a journal about your reading helps you develop your thinking skills. An easy way to begin is by writing your reaction to a work. Did you like it or dislike it? Why? Try to relate your response to specific characters or events in the story. What emotions did you experience while reading? Does the story remind you of others you have read? Writing out your responses to the questions you should ask while reading literature (see page 3) will help you formulate a response to questions that your instructor might ask during class discussion. Thinking critically before class is a great way to become an active learner—not just a spectator.

    A special type of journal is the *dialectical journal.* All you need to do is divide a page into two parts by drawing a vertical line down it. On one side, you can write your ideas as you read the work; on the other, you can record your thoughts and reactions after your instructor has covered the material. This double-entry approach can help you "to see relationships methodically, to discover and develop meanings."[5] By reviewing your initial response in light of what you have

---

[3] Vincent Ryan Ruggiero, *Teaching Thinking Across the Curriculum* (New York: Harper, 1988) 2.

[4] Benjamin A. Bloom, David R. Krathwohl, and Bertram A. Masia, *Taxonomy of Educational Objectives* (New York: McKay, 1956) 191–193.

[5] Ann Berthoff, *The Making of Meaning* (Upper Montclair: Boynton/Cook, 1981) 122.

❧

learned, you will be engaging in metacognition—thinking about your thinking and becoming more aware of your own thought processes. Synthesizing your ideas with those of your instructor and classmates will enable you to arrive at new insights into a work of literature. Plus, some of your entries could probably be turned into excellent themes.

Here is an example of a dialectical journal entry on Connie in Joyce Carol Oates' short story entitled "Where Are You Going, Where Have You Been?"

Before class	After class
I liked the story about Connie because she reminds me of some of my friends who are unhappy at home and who are anxious to grow up. She likes to flirt, and one day she flirts with a guy in a gold jalopy. When Arnold comes to her house to ask her out, she flirts with him again until she sees that he is older and that he is different. Connie wants what he has to offer—sex—but Arnold scares her (he scares me, too) to the point where she loses her will; she falls into his trap and follows him like a zombie. I don't know if she'll ever come back since she wants a different lifestyle.	Connie's unhappiness is due in part to her family's attitude toward her; her mother puts her down and her father ignores her. Maybe that's why she is looking for love from all the boys to make up for her lack of love at home. Arnold—who is older—may even represent a type of father-figure for Connie. Arnold may also represent perverse sexuality because of the way he talks about love-making. He may be scary because of his disguise which seems to be hiding his devil-like features—a wig to hide horns, makeup to hide his ugliness, and boots to hide his hooves. The devil is capable of mind control, so Connie may not come back at all; in fact, she may have been taken to a real hell!

In the first journal entry, the student responded on a personal level to the events in the story by comparing Connie to people she knows. Then she summarized the events in the plot, reacted emotionally to them, and predicted what Connie's eventual fate will be. In the journal entry written after class, the student probed more deeply into Connie's character by analyzing the reasons for her unhappiness and for her interest in Arnold. She then cited evidence to support her claim about Arnold's real identity, pointing out his similarities to the devil. These points, raised during class discussion by analyzing the details the narrator presented about the characters, helped the student see beneath the surface events of the story and move to the real heart of the characters—their motivation.

- **Making Lists**—As you read your assignments, you may not have the time to write a detailed journal entry, so making a list of words or short phrases that convey your insights is a good way to capture those ideas that can easily escape your memory. If you read with a pen or pencil (still great implements of communication) in hand, you can make a brief list of ideas or images that can stimulate your imagination and lead to future journal entries or even thesis statements. If you are used to making "Things-to-do" lists, it's an easy step to making "Things-to-think-about" lists as well.

- **Making Metaphors**—The metaphor, a way of seeing one thing in terms of another, is a favorite tool of writers. It is an implied comparison, an analogy that suggests the similarities that exist in often very dissimilar things. In that way, a metaphor combines the creativity of the imagination with the insights of the rational mind. In their classic lyric "I Am a Rock," Simon and Garfunkel use a metaphor to show how a person can become hardened and rock-like from broken relationships. Toni Cade Bambara in her short story "The Lesson" uses the setting of F. A. O. Schwarz as a metaphor for the world of the rich.

   As you read your assignments, you can create your own metaphors for the characters and settings you encounter by beginning with a statement of equality the way this student did when thinking about the central character in "The Secret Life of Walter Mitty" by James Thurber.

Walter Mitty is a _____ might become statements like Walter is a mouse, a tiger, a robot, a riddle, a magician, a VCR, a pawn, an old shoe, a copy machine. These metaphors for Walter suggest the multiple ways his character can be perceived, and, at the same time, they help develop the ability to think in terms of analogies. Why not give metaphor-making a try while you are doodling in the margins of your book or trying to capture the essence of a character for a thesis statement. It works!

- **Formulating Your Own Questions**—In most classes, students answer questions; they do not ask them. Unfortunately, this type of reactive behavior does not really prepare students to think on their own. As a student, you can reverse this passivity by becoming a questioner. As you read and find yourself wondering about any aspect of a work, write your question on a 3 x 5 card that you can use as a bookmark until the class meets. You can easily add questions that arise during class discussion on the same or additional cards. By asking your questions, you can turn any class into a discussion of the points that you find most interesting.

   Here are some questions students have raised in class about Oates' "Where Are You Going, Where Have You Been?": Why does Arnold have trouble standing in his boots? Can Arnold really see what's going on at Aunt Tillie's barbecue? Why does Arnold bring Ellie along if he plans on having sex with Connie? While these questions appear to be about the surface events of the story, they actually suggest the complexity beneath the narrative details; therefore, no question is "too simple" to raise as part of class discussion. If you are wondering about the meaning of something in the story, you owe it to yourself and to the class to ask about it. Questions stimulate the thinking process.

- **Solving Problems**—Narrative and dramatic works of literature revolve around a problem or conflict to be faced and solved by the protagonist. Although the author has resolved the conflict in some way by the end of the work, as an active reader and thinker, you could suggest other possible solutions to the conflict. What if the characters had made different choices? What if the circumstances were slightly different? What would you have done if you were the protagonist? What other possible solutions are there to the conflict? By asking questions that force you to think about and *beyond* the work, you are stretching your imagination and your problem-solving ability.

- **Concept Mapping**—You can visually outline a work by drawing a map or chart of its events, characters, relationships, or concepts, or by developing a time line of events or ideas. Doing this will help you analyze and then synthesize your ideas about the work as a whole. A concept map provides an overview that can quickly and easily be used for review purposes, like this visual analysis of the main plot and the subplot in *Ordinary People* by Judith Guest.

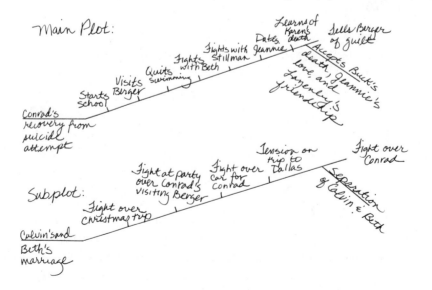

This type of "picture of the plot" can help you remember the chronology of events and help you see how they are causally connected to each other. A concept map for the various types of point of view appears on page 117. Putting events or ideas into charts or maps will help you see the connections between and among them.

- **Sketching a Character or a Scene**—The verbal and visual arts are closely related in that they both demand we enter into a work with our mind and with our imagination. There are times when an author supplies almost photographic detail about the characters and situations, and others when detail is vague and sketchy. By drawing—however roughly—our mind's picture of a protagonist or antagonist or scene, we can make it more concrete, more real. We are using our ability to synthesize, to put details together to create a whole. For example, Joyce Carol Oates supplies many concrete details about Arnold Friend in "Where Are You Going, Where Have You Been?" Could you put them all together in a sketch of Arnold? Does he look friendly or frightening? Little detail is supplied about Connie except that she thinks she is pretty. Can you discover a reason for the difference in the amount of descriptive detail Oates includes about these central characters? Does visualizing them help you understand their motives or their relationship? Go ahead—give sketching a try. Grab a pencil, and give your artistic side a chance to shine.

- **Collaborating with Your Classmates**—One of the best ways to prepare for class is to collaborate with others who have read the assignment. Collaborating can involve talking about your ideas and insights with another student or in a group, listening and responding to others' views, or reading/peer editing a student-written analysis of a work. Sharing your ideas with others will increase your understanding of any work of literature. In addition, collaborating will help you see how differently people perceive life and literature and how they express ideas in unique ways. An awareness of these differences can help you develop an open mind, an essential for working effectively with others.

You can practice your thinking skills whenever you engage in any of the above activities or whenever you **compare, contrast, classify, summarize, interpret, criticize, imagine, observe, look for assumptions, investigate, collect and organize data, form a hypothesis, make a decision, or apply principles in new situations.**[6] Performing these mental operations in relationship to composition and literature will strengthen your ability to think and to make judgments in a variety of educational, professional, and personal situations. After all, a primary goal of education is to help you become a critical thinker in all areas of life.

JUST ONE MORE THING

Literature is one of the humanities, so-called because its study makes one more fully human, more able to understand and appreciate the full range of human experiences and human emotion. Let the short stories, novels, poems, and plays teach you about life, about empathy, about "walking in another's mocassins."

---

[6] Louis Raths, Arthur Jonas, Arnold Rothstein, and Selma Wassermann, *Teaching for Thinking: Theory and Application* (Columbus, Ohio: Merrill, 1967) 5–17.

❧ The Elements of Literature ❧

> Complete the following worksheet by recording the definitions given in the preceding pages and in class discussions. These terms will be used frequently in any analysis of literature. Writing them in the space provided will help you learn the definitions and enable you to identify the concepts in the works you read.

Plot:

Plot pattern:
    Exposition:

    Complication:

    Climax:

    Resolution/Dénouement:

Conflict:

Sources of conflict:

Foreshadowing:

Characters:

Protagonist:

Antagonist:

Dynamic or round characters:

Static or flat characters:

Foil:

Epiphany:

Setting:

Point of View:

Theme:

Style:

Symbolism:

❦ **Plot Analysis Outline** ❦

> Completing an outline like this for each reading assignment will help you
> "get a picture" of the plot in a work of fiction. Keep in mind that this in-
> formation will not necessarily appear in this order in the work because of
> the choices the writer makes to produce the effect he or she wants.

I. Elements of exposition:

    A. Setting: Time _____ Place _____

    B. Characters:

        Protagonist: _____

        Antagonist(s):   _____

        Minor characters: _____

        _____

        _____

        _____

        _____

    C. Opening situation: _____

        _____

        _____

II. Source(s) of conflict:

_____

_____

_____

_____

III. Complicating incidents or rising action:

A. _____

_____

B. _____

_____

C. _____

_____

D. _____

_____

IV. Climax or turning point: _____

_____

_____

_____

V. Resolution or falling action: _____

_____

_____

_____

VI. Theme(s): _____

_____

_____

_____

Writing about Literature

Overview

An essay on literature or on any other published material is most successful when it is organized into introductory, body, and concluding paragraphs, and when the body paragraphs follow the pattern of generalization, introductory information for a supporting quotation, the quotation itself, and analysis. This literary analysis formula is based on the writer's need to supply proof or evidence to support the thesis statement.

Planning and Writing an Essay of Literary Analysis

Many students approach writing as something that only a few people can do—those few being the lucky ones born with writing ability. The fact is that writing well is a skill anyone can develop if he or she is willing to give it time, thought, and practice. Writing is a process that begins with thought, moves through planning, drafting, and revising, and ends with a logically organized and well supported essay.

Prewriting: Planning Your Essay

An important part of the process of writing about a piece of literature begins during the reading of the work. Analyzing a work accurately and completely usually requires more than one reading. A good way to begin your first general reading is to skim the work to get a sense of the characters and the beginning, middle, and end of the plot. Your second, more specific reading should be a more careful and methodical one during which you mark your text. The process of marking your book and making notes as you read to record your reactions and questions can be most helpful when you begin selecting quotes, details, and examples to use in your essay.

There are many ways to mark a text effectively. Many students like to use a highlighter to underline significant actions, dialogue, or narrated details. If words or images are repeated, noting that in the margin as well as underlining the examples will help you as you analyze and interpret the writer's intended meaning. Any ideas that occur to you as you study a work can be briefly noted in the margins or in the space at the top or bottom of the page. These thoughts can be important clues to the significance or meaning of the work. Other parts of a work that can be easily marked and noted are the names of the characters and details of their appearance, the main parts of the plot (exposition, complication, climax, and resolution), possible symbols, any uses of foreshadowing, and references to the theme, which is sometimes stated explicitly by the narrator or by a character in the work.

You can also use the prewriting techniques of brainstorming, freewriting, and clustering (sometimes called branching) to get your ideas about a literary work from your mind on to the page so that you can evaluate them concretely.

Brainstorming is based on the principles of free association and spontaneity of thought. In thinking about what you have read, you simply write down whatever comes to mind—a word, a term, a concept, a question, a complete sentence. Whether you are brainstorming alone or in a group, the objective is to generate as many ideas as possible by recording any and all possibilities that come to mind without judging their validity at this point. After all ideas—even those that seem improbable—are recorded, the evaluation phase begins to determine which ideas have potential as subjects for your essay. At this time, ideas can be clarified, combined, and expanded to help you formulate a thesis.

Here is a brainstorming list that was generated in five minutes by group of students who were discussing Flannery O'Connor's "A Good Man Is Hard to Find":

> Sneaky grandmother
> Crazy killer
> Dysfunctional family
> Bailey is a wimp.
> Kids are bratty.
> Power of religion
> Why did the Misfit kill his father?
> Misfit is the boss.
> Why does he have the baby killed?
> Bailey's wild shirt
>
> Mama's apron strings
> What does Red Sammy represent?
> Prison is brutal.
> June Star is mouthy.
> Why does the Misfit shoot the cat?
> Wife's silence
> Granny is selfish.
> Monkey—a symbol?
> Jesus freak
> Prison escape

When you have listed a good number of ideas, you can group similar concepts together to see if you have found a possible subject for an essay. This list contains several possibilities: the character of the grandmother, family relationships, the power of religion, violence and the prison experience, and the effects of a live-in grandmother on the family.

Another prewriting technique is *freewriting*. Freewriting means just that—you are free to write whatever comes into your mind without worrying about such elements as organization, development, grammar, or spelling. While thinking about a work as a possible subject for an essay, just record your thoughts without stopping to evaluate their relationship to the eventual focus of the essay. Try to write for at least ten minutes. If you draw a blank, write the name of the work or the author until an idea surfaces, or write, "My mind is blank."

When you finish the freewriting exercise, review your material, looking for ideas that you could develop by supporting them with details from the work. The judgments and inferences that you have recorded could become the basis for the thesis of your essay.

Here is a piece of freewriting done by a student who was thinking about doing an essay on the short story "A Good Man Is Hard to Find":

> The Misfit is a man without any feeling for human life. If he killed his father as the prison psychiatrist states, he is capable of killing others as he does so coldly when he comes upon Bailey and his family. The children are really innocent victims. What harm could they do to him? Maybe he has been brutalized to the point where nothing has meaning.
>
> The grandmother really wants to save her own life—she doesn't mention the others—but she is unable to reach The Misfit no matter how hard she tries. He rejects her claims that he is a good man and that he should pray. He knows he has done evil things but since he says he doesn't believe in Jesus, he's not worried about heaven or hell. The Misfit is just out for himself—he's heartless.
>
> Maybe his name is a clue to his personality. He doesn't fit in with society now and he didn't fit into his family either. He knows it, too, and that's why he has chosen his own name. Is it a name?—The Misfit—or is it a curse? Has he been ruined by his family or by prison? Is a man born evil or does he become evil as a result of the treatment he receives? Maybe he's a type of Frankenstein—a good man destroyed by his environment.
>
> Sean McQuillan

This response to the story—written in about ten minutes—contains several possible essay topics. The writer seems most interested in The Misfit and the reasons for his actions, so the essay could focus on the character of this criminal. Other focal points—like the references to The Misfit's family and his prison experiences—could lead to an essay on how environment shapes one's personality. And the reference to the grandmother's efforts to save only her own life could lead to an essay focusing on the family's relationships and the reasons for their lack of caring for each other.

Freewriting will help you discover your ideas by writing them down. It will also help you develop confidence in your ability to get in touch with the tremendous energy of your thoughts by escaping your judgmental self and stretching your mind and imagination.

Branching or clustering is another way to think on paper. To do this exercise, put the subject that you want to focus on in a circle in the center of a blank page. Then on branches growing outward from the center, record ideas that tend to cluster around related points. The branching exercise on the following page was done by the same student who did the freewriting after he decided to write his essay on The Misfit:

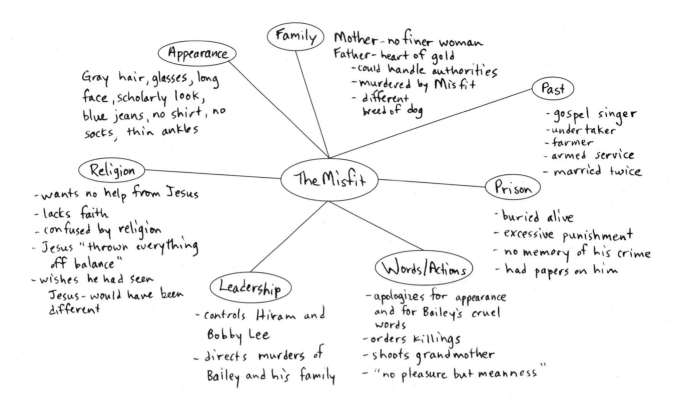

Thinking about possibilities and writing them down will help you find ideas that you could turn into possible thesis statements for your essay.

Formulating Your Thesis

After carefully reading and marking the text and doing a brainstorming, freewriting, or branching exercise, another part of the prewriting process involves formulating a thesis statement. The thesis summarizes what you intend to illustrate and prove in the body of the essay.

The thesis generalization is arrived at inductively as you note and add up the details in a work. For example, as The Misfit in O'Connor's "A Good Man Is Hard to Find" coldheartedly orders the murders of Bailey, his wife, and their three children and then personally kills the grandmother, the oldest member of the family, it is easy to see that he is a violent man with a psychotic personality. His words and actions are the specifics that lead to this generalization. He is truly a misfit, and this realization might lead you to look for the causes of his distorted human nature. A search of the text and a review of the points in the branching exercise suggest that his relationship with his father, his prison experience, and his religious confusion have shaped his personality, and this inference could function as the thesis for your essay. Keep in mind that your thesis is a starting point and that you may have to modify it or even scrap it if you cannot find convincing evidence in the text to prove it.

Outlining Your Essay

The thinking you have done to formulate your thesis should also guide you as you plan and make a preliminary outline of your essay. A paper on The Misfit could begin with the thesis that he is clearly a product of his environment, and the body of the essay would prove that statement by analyzing his family relationships, his experience in prison, and his confusion about Jesus. These last three points could be stated as part of the thesis to indicate how the body of the essay will be organized. The paper could then be outlined this way:

Introduction:

Complete thesis statement: The Misfit, a product of his environment, has been influenced by his father, by his prison experience, and by his religious confusion.

Body:

    I. The Misfit's personality has been shaped by his relationship with his father.
- A. Says father could handle authorities.
- B. States that father saw him as different.
- C. Murders his father and represses his crime.

  II. The Misfit's prison experience has also had a negative influence on his attitude toward life.
- A. Sees his punishment as excessive.
- B. Feels like he is buried alive.
- C. Finds pleasure only in meanness.

 III. Confusion over religion is the major cause of The Misfit's distorted personality.
- A. Lacks faith in Jesus.
- B. Wants no help and refuses to pray.
- C. Believes that Jesus is responsible for his twisted views.

Conclusion:

The Misfit, like all of us, is the sum total of his experiences, but unfortunately, most of his have been negative ones.

Understanding the Difference between Plot Summary and Analysis

To write an effective essay of literary analysis, you must understand the difference between plot summary and literary analysis. A plot summary of a work briefly recounts all of the major actions that constitute the plot and so describes the entire work in chronological order—the beginning, the middle, and the end. It tells "what happens next" and emphasizes the connections between these events. In contrast, literary analysis focuses on one small part of a work, perhaps its imagery or characterization or setting, and this narrowing of the subject permits you to delve more deeply into your topic. In proving your thesis, you may choose your evidence from any part of the work; you are not restricted by the chronological order of the events. In fact, you will probably not even mention most of the events in the work since you will be concentrating only on those that directly relate to your thesis. The fact that the family in "A Good Man Is Hard to Find" is on vacation, that the members are disengaged from each other, or that the grandmother finally sees the error of her ways would not be mentioned in the essay on the Misfit's personality. Analysis, then, breaks a work into its constituent parts and permits you to concentrate your attention on one limited area; it does not simply retell the story.

Finding Evidence

After you have chosen your area of concentration by formulating your thesis and developing your scratch outline, you are ready to begin choosing your evidence from the sections that you marked in your text. Look for statements that relate to your main points and mark them marginally with either key words—like family, prison, or religion for the paper on The Misfit—or with Point I, II, or III. That procedure will help as you begin to write your rough draft since you will need to quote from the text to prove your thesis. If you should choose to copy possible quotes onto note cards so that you can easily organize them, be sure to copy the page number and any marginal comments you may have made about the quotes when you were marking your text.

When selecting your final quotes from all of the possibilities that you have marked, look for material that contains important ideas that you will be able to expand upon, to delve into, to explore and explain when you comment on their significance. Like a good lawyer, you have to show the reader how the evidence you've chosen proves the claims in your thesis and topic sentences.

Considering Your Audience

Since all writing is intended to be read, it is essential that you keep your reader in mind as you compose your rough draft. The concept of audience is important in all the arts because they share the same general purpose: the communication of ideas. To assure communication, you should consider the reader's intelligence and experience.

When writing in a specific personal or business situation, it is easy to be specific about these points because you will probably have some personal knowledge about your reader. In a classroom situation, you will know your instructor, but you should not write with only him or her in mind. It is safer to broaden the concept of audience by assuming that your essay will have multiple readers who are as intelligent as you are, and while they may have had the experience of reading the work you are analyzing, they have not considered your particular thesis or the evidence needed to support it. Assuming that will help you include adequate detail and explanation; it will also help you avoid summarizing the plot which your readers already know.

Starting Your Draft: Choosing a Title

The essay actually begins with its title, but the title is often written after the rough draft has been completed. In choosing a title, remember that it should relate to your thesis, the main idea that the essay develops. A good title should tell the reader what your specific subject and its limitations are; therefore, using only the title of the work being discussed will not be effective because it does not indicate the specific area you are analyzing. You can, however, include the work's title in your own by adding your specific subject to it, as in Symbolism in "The Short Happy Life of Francis Macomber."

Titles should not—as a general rule—repeat or refer to the assignment. The title Walter Mitty: An Escapist is much better than the title A Character Analysis of Walter Mitty. Whether your title is straightforward—Sylvia's Point of View in "The Lesson"—or more creative—Sylvia's Piece of the Pie—it is important because it begins the impression your reader has as he or she starts to read your essay. A good title may take time to create, but it is worth the effort if it attracts your reader's attention.

Remember that the title of the essay is not put in quotation marks nor is it underlined, and only its major words are capitalized. Most often the title is not a complete sentence, but occasionally a question can be used effectively.

Writing Your Introduction

As you plan your introduction, keep in mind its functions: to interest your reader, to introduce the subject and its limitations, to state the thesis, and to suggest the organization of the essay itself. In a short essay, these points can be effectively conveyed in one paragraph, but a longer essay may require several paragraphs to provide all of the necessary background in a coherent and intelligible fashion.

Regardless of the length of your beginning, its first few sentences are critical if you wish to retain the interest created by your effective title. Whatever approach you choose to engage your reader, it should lead naturally to the ideas that follow and to the coming thesis statement. An essay that begins with an appropriate bang rather than an inaudible whimper will involve the reader in your ideas and make him want to read on.

These opening sentences are often referred to as the lead, and there are several techniques that may help you create effective "grabbers." You can begin with

- an appropriate rhetorical question that relates to the subject of your essay;
- a relevant quotation from the work itself or from another source;
- a brief passage of dialogue or description from the work;
- a description of your initial response to the work;
- a reference to a current issue or problem that relates to the work;
- a shocking, amusing, challenging, or clever generalization that will lead naturally to your thesis.

If handled effectively, the opening lines can lead smoothly to the necessary background information on the work being discussed. The background material should contain the full name of the author (who from then on in the essay is referred to by last name only) and the complete title of the work. Titles of short stories and poems are put in quotation marks, while titles of books and dramas are italicized or underlined in a typed text. This information can lead nicely to a very brief and general plot summary to refresh your reader's memory of the work or to acquaint him with it if he has not read it. Since your purpose is to analyze just one component part of the work, by building your summary around the intended subject of the essay, you can begin to limit your focus to the particular aspect of the work that you plan to discuss. This limitation will lead to your thesis—that sentence or those sentences that briefly state the main idea you intend to illustrate and prove in the body of the essay. The thesis is most often the last sentence or sentences in the introductory paragraph. This vitally important statement tells the reader what ideas will be discussed in the body of the essay and in what order they will be presented. The topic sentences for the body paragraphs can easily be written from a complete thesis statement.

Effective **introductions,** then, can generally be written by working these five points into a coherent, unified paragraph:

Opening lead:

Author's name:

Title of the work:

Brief plot summary of the work with a narrowing focus:

Thesis statement:

The following introduction contains these points and is based on the outline on page 19.

The Misfit's Twisted Personality

Lead

Title
Author
Plot summary

Thesis

What turns a man into a murderer? Does time in prison rehabilitate a man, or does it make him even more evil? Answers to these questions can be found in the short story "A Good Man Is Hard to Find"[1] by Flannery O'Connor. The Misfit, imprisoned for murdering his father, has escaped from prison and encounters a family of six after their accident on a lonely road in Georgia. He methodically orders the murder of Bailey, his wife, and their three children, and then he kills the oldest family member—the grandmother—by shooting her three times in the chest. *The forces that produced this evil, misshapen personality were The Misfit's relationship with his father, his experiences in prison, and his confusion over religion.*

Sean McQuillan

[1] Flannery O'Connor, "A Good Man Is Hard to Find" *The Complete Stories* (New York: Farrar, 1946). All parenthetical page numbers refer to the text in this edition.

Here are two additional student-written introductions that effectively illustrate the five-point pattern:

Connie's Journey from Her Dream World to the Real World

Lead

Author
Title
Plot summary

Thesis

In everyone's life, there comes a time when one must leave behind the innocence and naiveté of childhood and face the harsh realities of the adult world. Although most teenagers handle this period of their lives with relatively few problems, young Connie in Joyce Carol Oates' short story "Where Are You Going, Where Have You Been?"[2] faces her initiation into the "experienced" adult world with much hardship as a result of her traumatic visit from Arnold Friend on a quiet Sunday afternoon. Connie makes her mythic journey from innocence to experience as she goes off with Arnold to "the vast sunlit reaches of the land behind him" (54). *She has fantasized and dreamed about how she thinks love should be, but she finds her illusions shattered by Arnold's deceitfulness and perversity. Although she tries to deny this reality, she finally realizes she can't return to her innocent world, so she forges ahead to encounter the harshness of the adult world.*

Kathy Witczak

[2] Joyce Carol Oates, "Where Are You Going, Where Have You Been?" *The Wheel of Love and Other Stories* (New York: Vanguard, 1970). Used by permission of Vanguard, a Division of Random House, Inc. All parenthetical page numbers refer to the text in this edition.

Reality: There Is No Escape

Lead

Title
Author
Plot summary

Thesis

Do you have problems facing reality? If you do, you can learn a valuable lesson about life from *The Glass Menagerie* by Tennessee Williams. It is a touching drama about the joys and pains of the Wingfield family as they try to deal with the realities of their lives in the 1930's. Amanda Wingfield is a spirited woman who tries to keep a controlling hand on the lives of her children, Laura and Tom. In doing so, she causes many problems, particularly for Tom who has a love-hate relationship with her. *Through their conflict, Williams communicates the theme that even though it may seem easier to run away from an unpleasant reality, one must stand firm and face life for what it is. Tom tries to escape his trapped existence by escaping to the movies and then by running away, but he discovers that he has simply exchanged one problem for another.*

Tracy Rodriguez

As you can see, the introduction begins broadly and then narrows to focus clearly on the ideas that will be thoroughly discussed and illustrated in the body of the essay. Each of the above introductions has a complete thesis statement that organizes the essay around specific points, and once the order of those points has been established, it must be followed exactly in the body of the paper. That is why the order of the points in the thesis should be based on some logical organizing principle. You may choose to follow an idea as it develops throughout a work, thereby using a time or chronological order. When presenting causes, points of comparison or contrast, or examples, the order of climax—moving from the least important to the most important, from the weakest to the strongest—is always an effective organizing technique, one often used by lawyers as they present evidence to prove their case.

Writing Your Body Paragraphs

While the introduction is general and merely hints at what will come, the body of the essay is very specific and contains quotations and relevant concrete details from the work to prove the thesis statement. To help the reader follow your argument, each body paragraph should begin with a topic sentence that relates to a particular aspect of the thesis statement. This can be achieved by repeating key words from the thesis as the controlling idea in your topic sentence. Remember that a topic sentence is a limited generalization that will be proven with evidence from the work.

After the topic sentence, the writer usually supplies related generalizations and a brief introduction or context for the supporting quotations that will follow. A quotation is material that is copied word-for-word from the text; it may be taken from either the narrated portions of the work or from the dialogue sections. Introductory material prepares for the quote by briefly describing the situation it is taken from and by naming the speaker and listener if dialogue is quoted. This type of background material increases the coherence of the paragraph. One cannot simply jump from the topic sentence into a quotation; it must be properly introduced.

After the introductory information, the selected quotation is presented. It should be chosen carefully, for it must illustrate/clarify/prove your topic sentence. The quotation does not need to be lengthy, but it should contain significant details that you can enlarge upon and thoroughly explain to show *how* and *why* they prove your point. This analysis is the real content of the body paragraph, for it is here you get in your own ideas by commenting on the meaning, importance, relevance, and significance of the excerpt you have chosen to quote. Many students assume that the quotation alone is sufficient in proving their point, and they fail to recognize that, like a good lawyer, they must analyze and explain the importance of their evidence.

This explanation is not a simple restatement of the content of the quote in your own words; it is an analysis—a detailed accounting of *how* and *why* the evidence proves your claim. It goes behind the obvious meaning of the quote to focus on the implications and connotations of the quoted details. For this reason, one sentence of analysis following a quotation is never adequate. If you write just one sentence, you are probably generalizing, leaving the reader to infer what you mean. Keep in mind that good analysis should be three to four sentences in length and that this commentary is easier to write if you choose your evidence carefully. Some quotes will be loaded with ideas and significance, while others may be obvious facts or details that will lead nowhere. By picking your quotes intelligently, you will strengthen your paragraph and find yourself becoming an expert at writing analysis.

Since you want to present as much evidence as possible, after you have presented and analyzed the first supporting quote, you then transition to another relevant part of the work, introduce your second supporting quotation, quote your evidence, and then add more analysis to show how this new quote also supports and clarifies your main point.

The basic pattern of the **body paragraphs,** then, can be outlined this way:

- Topic sentence;
- Introductory information (background) for a supporting quotation;
- Quotation from the work that proves the topic sentence;
- Analysis showing how and why the quotation proves the topic sentence;
- Transitional words or sentences to prepare for a second supporting quotation;
- Introductory information for the quotation;
- Quotation that strongly and convincingly supports the topic sentence;
- Analysis—thoroughly developed—of the details in the quotation that prove the topic sentence.

Once you have become familiar with this basic pattern, you will not have to follow it rigidly in each paragraph of analysis that you write. You will probably find yourself combining parts of the pattern, quoting words or phrases from the work in your introductory sentences, including quotes in your analysis sections, and adding more than just two quotes per paragraph. These variations will occur naturally as you learn that the strength of your essay comes from your quoted details, so the more you include, the better your paper.

The following student-written paragraphs illustrate the basic pattern and its variations:

> The Misfit's early life was marked by ambivalent feelings about his father. When the grandmother suggests that he "'must come from nice people,'" The Misfit responds, "'My daddy's heart was pure gold'" (127), but then later he adds, "'He [his father] never got in trouble with the Authorities. . . . Just had the knack of handling them'" (129).[3] On the one hand, The Misfit suggests that his father was an upright man, a good man who lived a moral life, but his mention of the authorities implies that his father was an evil man who was clever enough to escape the punishment that his deeds deserved. This dual view suggests that The Misfit loved his father but that he also saw his father's flaws. This could lead to feelings of distrust that might have been fueled by his father's judgment of him. The Misfit tells the grandmother, "'My daddy said I was a different breed of dog from my brothers and sisters'" (128). This labeling could have affected The Misfit's self-esteem, and since his father said he was different, he decided to live out that role. He

was "'into everything'" (129), and that probably led to the conflict with his father which resulted in The Misfit's murdering him. Because The Misfit both loved and hated his father, his conscious mind cannot acknowledge this terrible act, and so he has repressed it. He denies his guilt when he tells the grandmother, "'It was a head-doctor at the penitentiary said what I had done was kill my daddy but I know that for a lie. My daddy died in nineteen ought nineteen of the epidemic flu and I never had a thing to do with it'" (130). The Misfit's confusion over his father's death parallels his confusion over his father's dual personality, and in fact, The Misfit exhibits the same type of behavior with Bailey and his family: he apologizes for his appearance and then violently murders them. Obviously, part of The Misfit's psychotic personality has been produced by his father's influence.

Sean McQuillan

[3] Excerpts from A GOOD MAN IS HARD TO FIND, copyright 1953 by Flannery O'Connor and renewed 1981 by Mrs. Regina O'Connor, reprinted by permission of Harcourt.

Arnold Friend destroys Connie's expectations of love by showing her how deceitful and perverse the real world is. After Connie realizes that Arnold and his friend Ellie aren't her age but are just pretending to be, she "felt a wave of dizziness rise in her . . . and she stared at him [Ellie] as if waiting for something to change the shock of the moment, make it all right again" (46).[4] Connie is shocked at the fact that Arnold and Ellie would pretend to be kids when, in reality, they are over thirty. This may be the first time someone has actually been dishonest and lied about something to Connie, and she just wants to wake up and learn it's all a nightmare, but she can't do that. Arnold shatters her dream world further when he explicitly describes what he's going to do with her once they're alone together. As he's describing the act of their lovemaking, Connie interrupts him, screaming, "'Shut up! You're crazy!' . . . She put her hands against her ears as if she heard something terrible, something not meant for her. 'People don't talk like that, you're crazy!'" (47–48). Connie can't believe that someone would actually use such profane language around her. She's frightened at the fact that love and sexuality, in reality, are not how they're "supposed to be," the way she thinks they should be in her dreams. Connie, through her traumatic meeting with Arnold and Ellie, is making her initiation into the adult world and reality in a way she had not expected.

Kathy Witczak

[4] Joyce Carol Oates, "Where Are You Going, Where Have You Been?" *The Wheel of Love and Other Stories* (New York: Vanguard, 1970). Used by permission of Vanguard Press, a Division of Random House, Inc. All parenthetical page numbers refer to the text in this edition.

Mrs. Mitty possesses a domineering trait that sometimes makes Walter question his own abilities. After he accidentally winds the chains around the car axles, she "always made him drive to a garage to have the chains taken off" (76).[5] She will not allow him to make the same mistake twice, so she takes control of the situation. Because she is constantly telling him what to do, he begins to feel inept. When he tries to remember what Mrs. Mitty has told him to buy at

[5] James Thurber, "The Secret Life of Walter Mitty" *My World and Welcome to It* (New York: Harcourt, 1970). All parenthetical page numbers refer to the text in this edition.

the store, he is concerned because "he was always getting something wrong" (76). Her need to dominate has made him reach a point where he cannot think for himself. Mrs. Mitty has convinced him that he cannot do anything correctly. When he takes her to get her hair done, "he drove around the streets aimlessly for a time . . ." (74). Because she makes all the decisions, Walter does not seem to function well without her. Her domineering nature also shows that she takes her husband for granted. Walter must be sure to get to the hotel before she does because ". . . she would want him to be there waiting for her as usual" (78). Her husband is forced to fit into her lifestyle. Mrs. Mitty expects everything to revolve around her schedule, and everything she does has priority over Walter's needs.

Linda Raftery

Note how quotations are used in the following student paragraph. Quoted words and phrases are even worked into the analysis sections:

In the novel *Ordinary People*,[6] Beth Jarrett is a perfectionist. When her sons were small, she spent her time and energy trying to maintain a "perfect" home. Calvin describes "her figure, tense with fury, as she scrubbed the fingermarks from the walls; she bursting suddenly into tears because of a toy left out of place . . ." (83). Beth resents the intrusion of the children into her world where "Everything had to be perfect" (83). Instead of relaxing and enjoying her children and recognizing their actions as merely stages in their development, Beth is driven by a senseless need for perfection even though it imposes an "impossible hardship . . . on them all" (83). Beth is afraid that a little untidiness will dispel the myth she has created of herself: a perfect house means a perfect Beth. Her fear of losing this image of perfection is also the reason for her refusal to accept that life is now irrevocably changed by the death of Jordan. When she finally expresses her emotions over his death, long after the funeral, all she can ask is "'How did this happen? How did it happen?'" (188). She cannot seem to accept the fact that life is imperfect and "that it is chance and not perfection that rules the world" (84). In order for the Jarrett family to pull through this ordeal, it requires an acceptance of the facts and a dedication to work together to find happiness. But Beth is a shallow person, unwilling to give of herself even to help her son, because "'she is not a sharer . . .'" (161). Such a person will not find happiness in life. Family means commitment, and commitment means giving, and it is only through true, unselfish giving—not by being perfect— that Beth will find real happiness.

Jeanette Bajcar

[6] From ORDINARY PEOPLE by Judith Guest. Copyright © 1976 by Judith Guest. Used by permission of Viking Penguin, a division of Penguin Books USA Inc. All parenthetical page numbers refer to the text in this edition.

Now that you have read through these sample body paragraphs, a good exercise for learning the literary analysis pattern is to read the examples again, this time labeling each part of the pattern in the margin. Remember that each part is important in achieving coherence and that the analysis sections are the most important of all because they reveal your understanding of the quoted excerpts and of the work as a whole.

Writing Effective Analysis: A Final Word

It is easy to slip into paraphrase when composing the analysis sections of the body paragraphs if you simply reword the content of the quotation that the analysis is supposed to support. Here is a student example from a paper on "A Good Man Is Hard to Find" by Flannery O'Connor that illustrates paraphrase rather than analysis following a supporting quotation:

> Bailey is a mama's boy. As he and his son are about to be taken off to the woods and shot by The Misfit's henchmen, Bailey says to his mother, "'I'll be back in a minute, Mamma, wait on me!'" (112) Bailey is going to die, but he tells his mother that he will come back from the woods. He wants his mother to wait for him because he refuses to face the fact that his life is over.

The two sentences following the quotation simply repeat the opening generalizations and the information in the quotation. This is paraphrase—not analysis of how and why the quotation proves Bailey is dependent on his mother.

Analysis of the same quotation might read something like this: Despite the fact that Bailey is married and the father of three children, he addresses his final words not to his wife but to his mother. He still seems to be tied to her apron strings; obviously, he has never gotten over his dependence on her. Because he is unable to function in his adult role, he needs his mother to make everything all right. As he faces his death, his dependent personality is fully revealed.

As you can see, paraphrase simply repeats the information in the quotation—it does not add any insight about why the writer chose the quotation to prove the topic sentence. Analysis, on the other hand, gets to the ideas behind the statement and explains how the details prove, illustrate, and clarify the topic sentence. Remember, the key is to choose meaningful quotations carefully and to explore and explain them completely.

Writing Your Conclusion

The conclusion of the essay lets the reader know that you have come to the end of your discussion. Its length will vary, depending on the length of your paper, but in a 500–750 word essay, one paragraph is usually adequate. Regardless of its length, it is very important because it is the last thing your reader perceives. Remember that your ending should logically follow from the introduction and the body of your essay and that it should leave the reader with a sense of completeness and closure.

You will be able to write effective conclusions if you keep in mind *the four S's: Signal, Summary, Significance,* and *Speed.* If you begin your final paragraph with a signal word or phrase like *thus, therefore,* or *and so,* or if you use the word *then* in the body of your sentence (Hemingway, then, used setting . . .), your reader will know that he is coming to the end of your discussion. That will prepare him for the summary of your thesis and its main points. Your summary should never be a word-for-word repetition of your thesis; it should be a creative rewording of your ideas, bringing them back for a final bow in the order they were presented in the body of the essay. Your repetition of the key words used in your discussion will help to unify your essay.

Your conclusion should always be more than a quickly written summary. It should emphasize—drive home forcefully—the significance or importance of the ideas you have been analyzing. Why were they important to you? Why did you choose this particular thesis to explore? What did you learn from your analysis? What should the reader learn from it? Explaining that will help the reader see your essay as more than just an assignment; it will be a creative, thought-provoking piece of writing.

Speed and style can help you reinforce the significance of your ideas as you write your final sentence. This sentence is sometimes called the *clincher sentence* because it holds your ideas together and drives them home in a decisive and conclusive manner. If you have been writing long sentences (most writers do when summarizing), change the speed or rhythm of your writing by ending with a short sentence. If you have been writing short sentences, try ending with a long, complex one. This change in the tempo of your style will help to give your essay a sense of finality that is so necessary to end impressively.

One last tip: it is often very effective to use the title of your essay or a close variant of it as your last line. That technique also gives a sense of unity and completeness to your work by bringing your reader back to your starting point, completing the circle of your journey.

Here are the conclusions that were written for the three essays introduced on pages 22–23. Read each introduction and then the conclusion to see how these two important parts of the essay complement each other.

Thus The Misfit had little chance in life to escape the influences that shaped his personality. He became like the man who raised him—a person capable of both good and evil—but the evil predominated, leading him to patricide. He viewed his punishment in prison as excessive and cruel because he was unaware of committing any crime, so to survive, he became excessive and cruel as well. His heart might have been softened by religion, but his need for physical proof of Jesus' deeds undercut his faith and left him without hope. For The Misfit, there truly is "'no real pleasure in life'" (133).[7]

Sean McQuillan

[7] Excerpts from A GOOD MAN IS HARD TO FIND, copyright 1953 by Flannery O'Connor and renewed 1981 by Mrs. Regina O'Connor, reprinted by permission of Harcourt.

Connie, then, was initiated into adulthood in a very frightening and unpleasant way. Through her experience with Arnold Friend, Connie's innocent dream world of love and sexuality is shattered. She sees the dishonesty and perversity of reality and tries to deny it as if it were a bad dream. However, once she realizes that is impossible, she accepts her fate and knows she must forge ahead and face the adult world. Connie's journey from innocence to experience is a journey everyone must make in order to grow up. Unfortunately, her journey is a traumatic one.

Kathy Witczak

And so, as the lid on Tom's box of entrapment is closed tighter and tighter, he tries to escape into the artificial world of the movies, and when that is not enough, he ultimately tries to escape by running away to find his own world of freedom and adventure. However, in reality, he only exchanges one box for another. Through Tom's trial and error, Williams is trying to show us that we cannot be freed from our own unpleasant reality by running away. What we find at the end of our flight might be harder to deal with than what we left. As in Tom's case, we may find that entrapment of the mind and heart is a lot harder to escape from than entrapment of the body. What we must do is stand firm, face our problems, and accept our lives for what they are. There is no escape.

Tracy Rodriguez

As you can see, each of these conclusions includes *the four S's—signal, summary, significance,* and *speed.* Together they can bring an essay to an effective and impressive end.

Revising Your Draft

A rough draft is just that—rough—so it needs some rewriting/revising to reflect your best efforts. If possible, you should allow some time to elapse before you begin this part of the writing process. That will help you analyze your work more objectively and more critically. You can start by focusing on higher order concerns such as the focus of your essay, organization, and development.

Since writers tend to discover new ideas and insights as they write, they sometimes drift away from their original thesis and actually develop a different **focus.** You can check your essay's **unity** by underlining the thesis and topic sentences and then reading each part of the essay again to make sure that each sentence and each paragraph relate directly to your main idea. If you find a shift in emphasis, you may have to revise your thesis or delete the irrelevant parts or rewrite them to make their relationship to the thesis a bit more obvious.

The **organization** of your ideas is another important concern in good writing. Have you presented your ideas in their most effective order? Did you consciously choose that order, or did it just "happen" as you put your ideas down on paper? Good writers make initial choices about the order of their thoughts, but they also recognize that the order sometimes needs to be revised to make it easier for the reader to understand and follow the points being discussed. Overall, the organizational pattern should clarify the progression of your ideas and should help the reader see how the ideas connect to each other.

To be effective, the body paragraphs must be **well developed.** Some writers are too general, failing to provide adequate supporting details or an in-depth discussion of their ideas. If you find that your paragraphs tend to be short, you can revise them by looking for areas that need to be expanded and explored. You may find that you need additional quotes from the work or that you need to add analysis so that your reader can understand your point.

When checking for **clarity,** keep in mind that wordiness can occasionally obscure your ideas, so try to eliminate any repetition or unnecessary words or phrases. Statements such as "in this quote," "this quote shows that," "in this story," "I think," "I believe that," or "in my opinion" should also be deleted. The reader knows when you are quoting or commenting on a quote, and it is understood that your comments reflect your thoughts, beliefs, and opinions.

As you reread your draft, be sure to check for **coherence,** the quality that makes your writing "hold together." The first sentence should obviously lead into the second, the second to the third, and so on throughout the paragraph. One device that helps to assure coherence is transitions, those words or phrases that show the reader how your ideas fit together. Addition words like *also, another, moreover, first, second;* effect words like *consequently* and *as a result;* contrast words like *on the other hand, in contrast, on the contrary;* comparison words like *in the same way, likewise, also, similarly;* and concluding words like *finally, therefore, and so,* and *thus* all help the reader see the relationships between and among your sentences and paragraphs as they blend into a coherent whole.

Consistency of verb tense is another important factor in achieving coherence. When writing about a literary work, use the present tense to describe the actions in the story and to explain your analysis of it. While you should try to stay with the present tense throughout your essay, there may be times when it will be necessary to use some form of the past tense to refer to events that obviously occurred before the theoretical beginning of the work. Now would be a good time to review the sample body paragraphs on pages 24–26 so that you can see how verb tense is handled in literary analysis.

If you check all these aspects of your draft and make any necessary changes, your essay should have all of the qualities of a solidly good piece of writing: **focus, unity, organization, development, clarity,** and **coherence.**

Editing Your Draft

Editing focuses on accuracy of expression, another important factor in writing since errors in sentence structure, spelling, punctuation, and mechanics interfere with the reader's concentration and understanding. Be sure to check for incomplete sentences (fragments), run-on or fused sentences (two sentences run together without punctuation to separate them or without a conjunction to join them), and comma splices (two sentences joined by just a comma because the conjunction has been omitted). If you are unsure of spelling, make a list of the words that you frequently misspell and consult it during this part of the writing process. Consulting a dictionary is even more beneficial because in addition to the spelling of the word, it often provides synonyms you can use in the future. If you are working on a word processor, be sure to take the time to use the spellchecker; it is a great time-saver.

Using punctuation accurately will improve the clarity of your sentences. Setting off introductory phrases or clauses, separating three or more items in a series, or separating the parts of a compound sentence with a comma helps the reader see how your ideas fit together. The semicolon and colon also help to separate your ideas since they are most often used like the period—to mark off a complete thought. And something as basic as mechanically indenting your paragraphs underlines the development of your thought and the organization of your essay.

If you know that you have weaknesses in any of these areas, now is the time to overcome them. Time and hard work will pay off in higher grades, and, more importantly, in higher self-esteem because of the sense of accomplishment that comes from mastering a subject. And, of course, these skills are necessary on any job.

After you have revised and edited your work, you are ready to prepare your final manuscript. Remember that even as you work at the computer, you may see areas where you can improve your essay, so keep on rewriting until you have put in the final period.

Proofreading Your Manuscript

After you have printed a copy of your manuscript, you owe it to yourself, your grade, and your reader to proofread it—to check it—for errors. Any number of things can go wrong when typing or word processing, such as typographical errors, omitted punctuation marks, omitted words or sentences, or even repeated words and sentences. You can find most or all of these errors by following some simple suggestions:

1. When working on a computer, read your essay on the monitor to spot any keyboarding errors, any omissions, or any repetition of words or sentences. Also, take the time to use the spellcheck feature of your word processing program. It will not, however, catch diction errors (*there* for *their* or *too* for *two*), and that is why the visual check is still necessary. Once you have printed your essay, check it again to insure that your ideas are accurately expressed.
2. Do another proofreading after time has elapsed so that you will be able to see your essay from a slightly different perspective. Read slowly (and aloud if your setting permits), forcing your eyes to focus on every word and every punctuation mark.
3. Always work with a pen in your hand so that you can immediately mark any corrections that you see. Remember that your goal is an accurate manuscript.

An essay that has been revised, edited, and proofread has a much better chance of earning a high grade than an essay that has not been rewritten and polished, checked for problems with expression, or reviewed for manuscript correctness.

Manuscript Form

A quick review of some of the basics of manuscript form will help you produce an attractive final copy of your essay. If you are given specific instructions by your instructor, be sure to follow them exactly.

1. Print your essay on good quality white paper. Double space the entire manuscript, and use an easy-to-read typeface.
2. Use a title page and center your title about four inches (24 lines) from the top of the page. Your word processing program may automatically move the cursor down one inch (six lines) from the top of the page, so be sure to consider that when typing the title. (Remember that your title is not quoted or underlined, and only the major words are capitalized.) Center your name, the course and section, your instructor's name, and the date 24 lines below the title.
3. Type your title again on the first page of your text one inch (6 lines) from the top of the page; then skip two lines and begin the text of your essay.
4. Leave one inch margins on all four sides, and number all pages consecutively (except the title page) in the upper right hand corner 3 lines from the top; then skip 3 more lines to begin the text. (If your word processing program automatically puts page numbers on another part of the page, be sure to ask your instructor if that number placement is acceptable.)
5. Make any necessary corrections as neatly as possible. Add missing words above the line by using a caret (∧) below the line at the appropriate place; delete by drawing a horizontal line through the material; substitute by deleting and writing the correct word or phrase above the line; and indicate transpositions in words or letters with this symbol: ∿.

Remember that the judging of your manuscript begins with an evaluation of its overall appearance, so take the time to produce an attractive copy. A good first impression goes a long way!

A Diagram of Essay Structure

The following diagram of the structure of an essay will give you an overview of the entire essay. All of the following chapters include a similar diagram, but its interior instructions vary with each specific assignment. If you review the diagram before beginning your paper, you will find it easier to organize your ideas.

By the way, this structural pattern is useful not only for works of literary analysis but also for any discussion of any published work in any field of study. It is also often employed in argumentative prose and in research papers.

Title

Your title should relate directly to the thesis and its development.

Introductory Paragraph:

Opening lead

Author's full name

Title of the work

Brief plot summary and narrowing of focus

Thesis statement—what you intend to prove in the essay, with some suggestion of the organization to be followed in the body of the essay.

Body Paragraphs:

Development of sequential parts of the thesis statement in separate paragraphs

Overall pattern for each body paragraph:
Topic Sentence
Introductory information for the quotations and supporting details which follow
Quotations and details from the work to prove the topic sentence
Analysis: explanation of the relevance, significance, and meaning of the quoted details
Transition to additional support
Introductory information to lead into a second supporting quotation
Quotation(s) to support the topic sentence
Analysis to show how and why the quotation proves the topic sentence

This basic literary analysis pattern can be adapted to include multiple quotations as the model essays in this chapter and in future chapters illustrate.

Concluding Paragraph:

Signal word

Summary of the thesis

Significance of the ideas that have been analyzed

"Speed" or tempo change to create a sense of finality

❦ The Real Thing: The Complete Essay

In this chapter, we have been talking about the major parts of an essay—the introduction, the body, and the conclusion—and we have examined the principles that make each part effective. But the whole is usually greater than the sum of its parts, so here is a complete essay for you to study since a real work of art can only be appreciated in its entirety. It was written by a student who was following the specific instructions and plan sheets presented in the chapter entitled Character Analysis.

An effective essay is the result of critical thinking, careful planning, and thoughtful writing and revising. To show you how these activities evolve in the writing process, a copy of the plan sheets the student writer completed is also included for you to study. The differences in the plan sheets and the essay represent changes the student made while writing and revising the second draft and printing the final copy.

Name _Tara Barth_   Section _01_   Date _9/30_

❧ Character Analysis Essay Plan Sheet ❧

Author: _Joyce Carol Oates_   Title: _"Where Are You Going, Where Have You Been?"_

Thesis: _Ignored by her father, resentful of her sister, and unloved by her mother, Connie sees no point in staying with her dysfunctional family._

Topic sentence: _Connie receives no attention from her father._

Supporting quote: page or line _p. 35_

Supporting quote: page or line _p. 35_

Topic sentence: _Connie resents her sister June and, at times, feels inferior to her because of constant praise June receives from their mother._

Supporting quote: page or line _p. 35_

Supporting quote: page or line _p. 38_

Topic sentence: _Unfortunately, Connie's life is void of the nurturing love and care of a mother._

Supporting quote: page or line _p. 34_

Supporting quote: page or line _p. 38_

Concluding points: _Within Connie lies a void crying out to be filled by an attentive father, an understanding sister, and a tender mother. Connie needs to feel cared for and loved by her family._

❧

Connie: A Teenager Crying Out for Love

The role of the family is very important, for most of a person's attitude toward life stems from the treatment she receives from her family. If an individual is raised in a stable and nurturing environment, it is likely that she will be happy and content with her life. However, if a person is brought up in a cold and uncaring home, it is probable that she will be unhappy and anxious to change her life. In the short story "Where Are You Going, Where Have You Been?"[1] written by Joyce Carol Oates, the fifteen-year-old protagonist, Connie, lives in a household that lacks caring and love. In the absence of parental care, she is unable to resist Arnold Friend's offer of physical love. *Ignored by her father, resentful of her sister, and unloved by her mother, Connie sees no point in staying with her dysfunctional family.*

Thesis Statement

Topic Sentence

Connie receives no attention from her father. He spends most of his time at work, and when he finally does come home, he does not interact with the family: "he wanted supper and he read the newspaper at supper and after supper he went to bed" (35). Connie's father is completely withdrawn and out of touch with his family. Instead of engaging in the usual dinnertime conversation, he closes himself off by reading the paper. Connie has to be hurt by his failure to acknowledge her. Like all children, she needs and yearns for his fatherly love and support. Unfortunately, Connie's father is so detached that he does not even defend her when her mother criticizes her: "He didn't bother talking to them much, but around his bent head Connie's mother kept picking at her . . ." (35). He is oblivious to the constant verbal abuse Connie receives from her mother. His failure to intervene in this situation clearly illustrates his lack of concern for her, and that causes her to feel unloved.

Topic Sentence

Connie resents her sister June and, at times, feels inferior to her because of the constant praise June receives from their mother. When Connie's mother talks to her sisters, she always puts June on a pedestal and complains about Connie: "'June did this, June did that, she saved money and helped clean the house and cooked and Connie couldn't do a thing . . .'" (35). Connie is hurt by all the complimentary attention June always gets. Connie is surely jealous of June because she wants to be seen in the same favorable light. As a result, Connie is unable to see June as a person; rather she sees her as an obstacle and a weapon: an obstacle standing in the way of Connie's receiving her mother's love and a weapon Connie's mother uses to justify her constant criticism of Connie. Connie's repugnance toward her sister is further increased by the way in which their mother speaks about her two daughters: "If June's name was mentioned her mother's tone was approving, and if Connie's name was mentioned it was disapproving" (38). Connie is made to feel inferior to June because, in their mother's eyes, June

---

[1] Joyce Carol Oates, "Where Are You Going, Where Have You Been?" *The Wheel of Love and Other Stories* (New York: Vanguard, 1970). Used by permission of Vanguard Press, a division of Random House, Inc.

can do no wrong. The continual praise of June has to bother Connie, and it creates a huge distance between them. Why should Connie want to stay in this no-win situation?

Topic Sentence

Unfortunately, Connie's life is void of the nurturing love and care of a mother. Her mother is always making derogatory comments about Connie's appearance: "'Stop gawking at yourself, who are you? You think you're so pretty'" (34). These remarks are incredibly cruel, especially since they are made by Connie's mother. As her beauty and youthfulness fade with age, Connie's mother grows insecure about her personal appearance. These feelings of uncertainty cause her to be envious of Connie's blossoming beauty. Rather than taking pride in and appreciating Connie's appearance, her mother is critical and judgmental of the way Connie looks. Connie's mother harbors ill feelings toward Connie, and these feelings surface continually. Connie and her mother are even incapable of engaging in the usual day-to-day conversation: "Sometimes over coffee they were almost friends, but something would come up—some vexation that was like a fly buzzing suddenly around their heads—and their faces went hard with contempt" (38). They are unable to communicate with each other, and this communication gap greatly affects Connie. As a young girl, she needs the guidance that only a mother can give. In the absence of this love and direction, she is forced to look elsewhere for acceptance.

Restatement of Thesis

Connie, then, desperately yearns to escape her family. *Within her lies a void crying out to be filled by an attentive father, an understanding sister, and a tender mother.* Connie, like any other teenager, needs to feel cared for and loved by her family. It is truly a great tragedy to see someone look for love in the wrong places.

Tara Barth

Tara's essay is effective because it has structure (a clearly defined introduction, body, and conclusion), and it follows a climactic organizational pattern that helps the reader understand the reasons for Connie's actions. Also, the body paragraphs are well developed; each contains several quotes from the story that are analyzed to show how they support and prove the thesis and the topic sentences. The essay as a whole is successful because it is a unified, coherent discussion of a protagonist's motivation in a work of fiction. By following the guidelines presented here and in future chapters, you, too, can write effective essays on literary topics.

JUST ONE MORE THING

Writing an essay is an exercise in structured creativity. While writing is a highly creative and thought-filled process, the writer can divide the work into parts, can follow formulas, and can still communicate ideas effectively. Shakespeare wrote 152 sonnets, all consisting of four parts (three quatrains and a couplet), all rhyming abab cdcd efef gg, and all containing universally applicable ideas. Working within a formula did not inhibit Shakespeare; similarly, following the patterns in this chapter should not inhibit your creativity or your thinking.

Using Quotations and Documentation in Your Essays

Overview

When you write about something you have read, it is easiest to illustrate/clarify/prove your thesis if you base your analysis on quotations from the work. When you use excerpts or ideas from primary or secondary sources, you must give credit to the original writer by using some form of documentation. Following a few simple guidelines will make this part of your writing easier to master.

Quoting and Documenting Your Sources

When you write about literature, you prove your thesis most effectively by quoting from the work you are analyzing. The short story, novel, poem, or play will be your primary source of quotations to explain and illustrate your ideas for the reader. Occasionally you will want to do—or will have to do—research to deepen your understanding of your topic; then you will be consulting secondary sources to gather your information. When you use either primary or secondary sources, you must use some form of documentation to tell your reader the source of your ideas and quotations. The recommended forms that follow are based on the 1999 edition of the *MLA Handbook for Writers of Research Papers,* a style sheet published by the Modern Language Association.

Incorporating Quotations

When you write essays of literary analysis, you will want to develop the body paragraphs with specific quotations from the text. When working with fiction, you may choose to quote from both narrative detail and dialogue, just as in drama you may quote from the text or from the stage directions. To incorporate this textual evidence into your essay, you should be aware of certain techniques that are generally followed by writers to achieve unity, coherence, and clarity. Reviewing the following guidelines now and then referring back to them when you are actually preparing your manuscript will help you make your essay more effective and more professional.

1. Words, phrases, or incomplete sentences that are quoted from the text should be worked coherently into your own sentences, as if they were your own words. Ellipsis is not necessary before or after the words or phrase unless you have omitted words within the phrase itself:

   ```
   The road Goodman Brown takes into the forest is "dreary" and
   "lonely," yet he feels that he is "passing through an un-
   seen multitude" (Hawthorne 90).¹
   ```

2. When quoting a complete sentence or more from a work, prepare for it with an introductory sentence followed by a colon or with a dependent clause or phrase followed by a comma. Double space this type of quotation into your text if it is under five typed lines.

   ```
   Goodman Brown is never the same after his fateful trip into
   the forest: "Often, awaking suddenly at midnight, he shrank
   from the bosom of Faith; and at morning or eventide, when
   the family knelt down at prayer, he scowled and muttered to
   himself, and gazed sternly at his wife, and turned away"
   (Hawthorne 106).
   ```

   or

   ```
   After Goodman Brown returns from his fateful trip into the
   forest, "Often, awaking suddenly at midnight, he shrank from
   the bosom of Faith; and at morning or eventide, when the
   family knelt down at prayer, he scowled and muttered to
   himself, and gazed sternly at his wife, and turned away"
   (Hawthorne 106).
   ```

3. If a quotation is more than four typed lines, it is set off from the text in block form by indenting ten spaces from the left margin. Lead into the quotation with a dependent clause or phrase followed by a comma or more typically with a complete sentence followed by a colon. Quotation marks are not used; if dialogue is being quoted, use only the single quotation mark. In long block quotations, put the textnote two spaces after the last punctuation mark.

   ```
   Not long after Goodman Brown enters the forest, he meets his
   companion:

             As nearly as could be discerned, the second trav-
             eller was about fifty years old, apparently in the
             same rank of life as Goodman Brown, and bearing a
             considerable resemblance to him, though perhaps
             more in expression than features. Still they might
             have been taken for father and son. (Hawthorne 91)
   ```

   Note: Long quotations are double spaced like the rest of the text.

4. When quoting dialogue, always indicate the speaker and listener before the quotation for purposes of clarity and coherence. Since dialogue is already quoted in the text, place double quotation marks at the beginning and end of the quote and change all the interior double quotation marks to single ones. When dialogue is being cited, follow the lead-in sentence with a comma.

   ```
   As he enters the forest, Goodman Brown says to himself,
   "'What if the devil himself should be at my very elbow?'"
   (Hawthorne 90).
   ```

---

¹ "Young Goodman Brown" *Mosses from an Old Manse* (New York: Books for Libraries, 1970).

5. When quoting three lines or fewer of poetry, work the quote into your double spaced text but separate the lines using a slash (/). Leave a space on either side of the slash and keep the capital letter at the start of the succeeding lines. When citing poetry, put the line or line numbers in parentheses after the quotation; use the word *line* or *lines* only in the first textnote to indicate that the number(s) refer to lines rather than pages. In succeeding notes, cite just the number(s).

```
When the speaker orders his sword, he wants it "A bit hard
to draw, / And of cardboard, preferably" (Olson lines 4-5).²
```

6. If you are quoting more than three consecutive lines from a poem, set them off from the text by leading into the quote with a complete sentence followed by a colon. Double space before and after the quote, double space the quote itself, and indent each line ten spaces from the left hand margin. If, however, the original lines follow an unusual spatial arrangement, try to reproduce that arrangement in your text. Do not use quotation marks around the excerpt if they are not used in the original text.

```
The speaker begins by ordering his sword:

        All right, armorer,
        Make me a sword—
        Not too sharp,
        A bit hard to draw,
        And of cardboard, preferably. (Olson 1-5)
```

Note: Identify the voice in a work properly. In lyric poetry, refer to "the speaker," but in narrative poetry or fiction, refer to the story teller as "the narrator."

7. In quoting an exchange of dialogue from a play, lead into the quotation with a complete sentence followed by a colon, and indent ten spaces from each margin. Put the speakers' names in all capital letters before their lines and follow the names with a period. Double space the quotation, and if a character's speech exceeds one line, indent subsequent lines three spaces from the start of the character's name. In block quotations, put the textnote two spaces after the last punctuation mark. In the textnote for a verse play, cite the act, scene, and line numbers in arabic numerals.

```
Hamlet is shocked by the Ghost's revelations:
        GHOST. I am thy father's spirit,

           Doom'd for a certain term to walk the night. . . .

        HAMLET. O God!

        GHOST. Revenge his foul and most unnatural murder.

        HAMLET. Murder! (1.5.9-10, 24-26)³
```

8. When quoting italicized stage direction or any italicized material, italicize or underline it in your text.
9. Any material copied from a text must be exact and enclosed in quotation marks. If any part has been omitted, the omission is indicated by an ellipsis consisting of three spaced periods placed within square brackets to differentiate your ellipsis from any the original writer may

---

² "Directions to the Armorer" by Elder Olson: Copyright © 1963 by Elder Olson. Reprinted by permission.
³ *Hamlet, William Shakespeare: The Complete Works* (London: Collins, 1970).

have used. There is no space after the bracket or before the first ellipsis point, but there is a space between the second and third points. An ellipsis can appear at the beginning, middle, or end of a quotation; other punctuation may be placed before or after the three periods. For example, if an ellipsis appears at the end of a sentence, use four periods (ellipsis plus a period), with no space before the first.

```
"Young Goodman Brown came forth at sunset into the street
at Salem village; but put his head back [. . .] to exchange
a parting kiss [. . .]" (Hawthorne 89).
```

Note: When quoting just a word or a phrase as part of your sentence as in Number 1 above, it is not necessary to use ellipses since it is clear that the quoted material is incomplete and that you are taking it from a larger source.

10. If you add any material to a quote or change it to fit grammatically into your sentence, you must put the new or changed material in square brackets:

```
"It was now deep in the forest, and deepest in that part
of it where these two [Goodman Brown and the devil] were
journeying" (Hawthorne 91).
```

```
The speaker tells his love that he wants her face to be "the
last face that [he'll] see" (McKuen line 15).⁴ (The line
originally read "the last face that I'll see.")
```

11. Capital letters in quoted material may be changed to lower case to fit into the body of your sentence.

12. Place commas and periods *inside* quotation marks, and put semicolons, colons, and dashes outside. If a question mark or an exclamation mark is part of the quotation, place it inside; if you have added it, place it outside the quotation marks.

13. If you are using parenthetical documentation (Modern Language Association forms) within your text, place the period after the parenthesis, the quotation mark before it.

```
"'With heaven above and Faith below, I will yet stand firm
against the devil!' cried Goodman Brown" (Hawthorne 98).
```

14. While using quotations in your essay is essential, remember that your thinking and your own words—as seen in your analysis of the quotations—should dominate the paper.

Using Textnotes/Parenthetical Documentation

"*Textnotes,* sometimes referred to as parenthetical documentation, are the . . . type of notes commonly used today in research writing; in fact, they are the preferred method of many instructors and students. Textnotes appear in the text (thus their name) within parentheses immediately following the citation. Textnotes are clear and simple, generally containing only the name [of the author or the title of the work if an author is not listed] and pagination. Textnotes refer the reader to the more complete bibliographic information which appears in the list of works cited (or bibliography) at the end of the paper. Because textnotes appear next to the citation they identify, they use no numbering system.

"The following example illustrates the use of textnotes:

. . . in fact, several American writers have seen this connection between the arts and the sciences. "Poe [equated] the poetic imagination with the scientific imagination. Already he has

---

⁴© 1969 by Rod McKuen and Stanyan Music Company. All Rights Reserved. Used by Permission.

stated that the imaginative mind worked by the perception of analogies; now he assumed that it also had the power of extrapolation" (Jacobs 416). Poe seems to be suggesting that the artist. . . .

In the Works Cited at the end of the paper, the complete citation would appear as follows:

```
Jacobs, Robert D. Poe: Journalist and Critic. Baton Rouge: Loui-
    siana UP, 1969.
```

"As you can see, textnotes are brief. They do not interrupt the flow of the prose. Also keep in mind that their purpose is to refer the reader to complete bibliographic information in the list of works cited at the end of the paper. Therefore, there is a connection between what appears in the text and what has to appear in the textnote. For example, if the text itself clearly identifies an author's name, there is no need for the name to appear in the textnote:

> . . . in fact, several American writers have seen this connection between the arts and the sciences. Commenting upon Edgar Allan Poe, Robert Jacobs observed that "Poe [equated] the poetic imagination with the scientific imagination. Already he had stated that the imaginative mind worked by the perception of analogies; now he assumed that it also had the power of extrapolation" (416). Poe seems to be suggesting that the artist. . . .

In the Works Cited at the end of the paper, the complete citation would appear as in the earlier example.

"If there is more than one citation per paragraph, insert the parenthetical acknowledgment after each citation (quote and/or paraphrase). The following is an example:

> . . . audience involvement in the horror movie was the next logical step for Hollywood. Even though many people think they are too good to look at horror, we all have within us what horror writer Stephen King calls the auto-accident syndrome. "Very few of us can forego an uneasy peek at the wreckage bracketed by police cars and road flares on the turnpike at night" (xv). This latent desire we have to view the horror was really brought into play in the horror movies of the early nineteen fifties with the advent of 3-d movies. "The very fact the three-dimensional films had concentrated on horror rather than on other less violent genres pointed the way to the next step: an increased audience participation was in order if the horror film was to survive. The producers organized a campaign of gimmicks that stopped short of nothing but actual frontal aggression on the public" (Clarens 138).

In the Works Cited, the following complete citation for each work used in the preceding paragraph would appear as follows:

```
Clarens, Carlos. An Illustrated History of the Horror Film. New
    York: Capricorn, 1967.

King, Stephen. Night Shift. New York: Doubleday, 1976.
```

Keep in mind that if [you] had used other sources, they too would be listed in the Works Cited.

"There are only a few more suggestions/guidelines to remember about working with textnotes. *One,* if the source is not written, there obviously will not be any pagination indicated in the note. *Two,* if the source you are citing is only one page, then there is no need to cite pagination in the note (the page number will be identified in the works cited list at the paper's end). *Three,* if you are citing authors who have the same last name, include a first initial to clarify which person is being cited in each instance. *Four,* if you are citing more than one work by the same author, include in the textnote the title (or an abbreviation of the title). A textnote to clarify which of Margaret Atwood's novels is cited would appear as

(Atwood, *Handmaid* 46–47). *Five*, if the work has more than one author but not more than three, list the last name of each person [and the page number]. If more than three authors are listed in the source, list the first author's last name followed by *et al.* [and the page number]."*

When you are quoting from only one primary source and you have identified it and the author in the introduction to your essay, it is acceptable to include just a page number or line number in the textnotes, omitting the author's name because it would be redundant. This is the approach used in the model essays in each chapter.

Overall, the simplicity and brevity of textnotes make them very easy to use, and as you can see, their use also makes it easier to type your manuscript since you no longer have to struggle with the placement of footnotes or the duplication of the same information in footnotes or endnotes and works cited/ bibliographic entries.

❧ Works Cited Entries for Nonelectronic Sources

The Works Cited page is a list of the works you used in writing your essay. It is ordered alphabetically by the author's last name or the first major word of the title if an author's name is not given, and the complete double-spaced list is placed at the end of your essay.

You can use the following models to prepare your Works Cited entries for nonelectronic sources by placing the information on your sources into the proper format.

Works Cited entry for a short story in a collection by one author:
> Bradbury, Ray. "August 2026: There Will Come Soft Rains." *The Martian Chronicles*. Garden City: Doubleday, 1958.

Works Cited entry for a short story in an anthology:
> Hemingway, Ernest. "Cat in the Rain." *An Introduction to Literature*. Ed. Sylvan Barnet, Morton Berman, and William Burto. 10th ed. New York: Harper, 1993. 20-22.

Works Cited entry for an additional work from the same anthology:
> Whitman, Walt. "A Noiseless Patient Spider." Barnet, Berman, and Burto 428.

Works Cited entry for a novel:
> Hemingway, Ernest. *A Farewell to Arms*. New York: Scribner's, 1929.

Works Cited entry for an introduction to a novel:
> Scribner, Charles, Jr. "Introduction: The Ripening of a Masterpiece." *The Old Man and the Sea*. By Ernest Hemingway. New York: Scribner's, 1980. 1-4.

Works Cited entry for a poem in a collection by the same author:
> Owen, Wilfred. "Dulce et Decorum Est." *The Collected Poems of Wilfred Owen*. Ed. C. Day-Lewis. London: Chatto, 1946. 95.

Works Cited entry for a poem in an anthology:
> Owen, Wilfred. "Dulce et Decorum Est." *Literature: An Introduction to Reading and Writing*. Ed. Edgar V. Roberts and Henry E. Jacobs. Englewood Cliffs: Prentice, 1986. 644.

---

* Randy DeVillez, *Step by Step: College Writing*, Fourth Edition. Copyright © 1989 by Kendall/Hunt. Used by permission.

Works Cited entry for a drama:
Miller, Arthur. *The Price*. New York: Viking, 1968.

Works Cited entry for a drama in an anthology:
Miller, Arthur. *Death of a Salesman. An Introduction to Literature.*
    Ed. Sylvan Barnet, Morton Berman, and William Burto. 9th ed.
    Glenview: Scott, 1989. 1025-1111.

Works Cited entry for a book of criticism:
Crompton, Louis. *Shaw the Dramatist*. Lincoln: U of Nebraska P, 1969.

Works Cited entry for a book by two authors:
Hardwick, Michael, and Mollie Hardwick, comp. *The Charles Dickens
    Encyclopedia*. New York: Scribner's, 1973.

Note: If the number of authors is three or more, you may choose to name just the first and add
et al. ("and others"), or you may choose to cite all the names in full in the order on the title page.

Works Cited entry for a multivolume work:
Daiches, David. *A Critical History of English Literature*. 2nd. ed.
    2 vols. New York: Ronald, 1970.

Works Cited entry for a collection of critical essays:
Muir, Kenneth, ed. *Shakespeare: The Comedies*. Englewood Cliffs:
    Prentice, 1965.

Works Cited entry for an essay in a collection of critical essays:
Welland, D. S. R. "Hemingway's English Reputation." *The Literary
    Reputation of Hemingway in Europe*. Ed. Roger Asselineau. New
    York: New York UP, 1965. 9-38.

Works Cited entry for a pamphlet:
Young, Philip. *Ernest Hemingway*. Minneapolis: U of Minnesota P, 1964.

Works Cited entry for an article in a magazine:
Poniewozik, James. "What's Entertainment NOW?" *Time* 1 October 2001:
    108-12.

Works Cited entry for a critical article in a journal:
Griffin, Peter. "A Foul Mood, a Dirty Joke: Hemingway's 'Cat in the
    Rain.'" *The Hemingway Review* 20.2 (Spring 2001): 99-102.

Works Cited entry for a book review in a journal:
Herrington, Anne J. "Cutting Across the Grain." Rev. of *Writing Per-
    mitted in Designated Areas Only,* by Linda Brodkey. *College En-
    glish* (Sept. 1997): 579-84.

Works Cited entry for an article in a literary reference work:
Gurko, Leo. "Ernest Hemingway and the Pursuit of Heroism." *Contem-
    porary Literary Criticism*. Eds. Carolyn Riley and Phyllis Carmel
    Mendelson. Vol. 6. Detroit: Gale, 1976. 226-229.

Works Cited entry for a published letter:
Whitman, Walt. "To Ralph Waldo Emerson." 2 December 1868. Letter 68
    of *Complete Poetry and Selected Prose and Letters*. Ed. Emory
    Holloway. London: Nonesuch, 1938. 981.

Works Cited entry for a lecture:
> Gates, Henry Louis, Jr. "Trickster-heroes." Harold Washington Library
>   Center, Chicago. 16 October 1997.

Works Cited entry for an interview:
> Brooks, Gwendolyn. Personal interview. 16 January 1998.

Works Cited entry for a film:
> *Hamlet*. Dir. Kenneth Branagh. Perf. Kenneth Branagh, Julie Christie,
>   Billy Crystal, Gerard Depardieu, and Charlton Heston. Castle Rock
>   Entertainment, 1996.

Works Cited entry for a recording:
> Hemingway, Ernest. *Ernest Hemingway Reading*. Caedmon, TC 1185, 1965.

Works Cited entry for an article in an encyclopedia:
> "Hemingway." *The New Encyclopedia Britannica*. 1988 ed.

Works Cited entries for multiple works by the same author:
If you are citing several works by the same author, list the author's name only in the first entry. In the following entries, replace the author's name with three hyphens and a period. After the period, skip two spaces and type the title and the publication information. Because all of the entries fall under the same author's name, alphabetize them by the first major word in the title.

Abbreviations for missing information:
If you are unable to supply the required publication information for any entry, you may use the following abbreviations for the missing parts:

No place
> N.p.: Wesleyan UP, 1994.

No publisher
> Middletown: n.p., 1994.

No date
> Middletown: Wesleyan UP, n.d.

No page numbers
> Middletown: Wesleyan UP, 1994. N. pag.

❧ Works Cited Entries for Electronic Sources

Since it is always necessary to document your use of information gained from outside sources, the latest advances in electronic research have made it necessary to develop new forms to cite ideas gained from this medium. The fifth edition of the *MLA Handbook for Writers of Research Papers* by Joseph Gibaldi includes twenty-four pages on how to cite electronic and online sources. In fact, an entire book by Xia Li and Nancy Crane entitled *Electronic Styles: An Expanded Guide to Citing Electronic Information* deals with the documentation of information from electronic sources. New ground is still being broken in these evolving electronic media, and as a result, standardization for formatting the various types of sources has not yet been achieved. The bottom line is that you want to let your reader know how to locate the source of your information.

Overall, works cited entries for electronic sources include the same information as entries for printed sources:

- author's or editor's name if listed,
- complete title in quotation marks,
- publication information, including, if relevant, the name of the periodical, journal or newspaper underlined, the volume and/or issue number, the date of publication, and the total number of pages or paragraphs (if numbered);
- the name of the vendor or computer service/network;
- the date you accessed the material;
- the URL (Uniform Resource Locator) or network address.

These entries would, of course, be interfiled alphabetically with your other sources.

The following examples illustrate the general format; if you are unable to locate all of the required information for the type of source you are using, accurately cite what information you do have in the appropriate order.

Works Cited entries for a CD-ROM database:

Hillel, Italie. "Author Updike Adding to Cyberworld with Own 'Electronic Wriggles.'" *Chicago Tribune* 14 August 1997, Evening Update ed.: 2. *Chicago Tribune*. CD-ROM. NewsBank, Inc. Oct. 1997.

Hope, Christopher. "Bloomsday Schoomsday." *New Statesman* 21 June 1996: 12. *ProQuest*. CD-ROM. UMI-Proquest. 1996.

Ingold, Barbara Seib. "Dickinson's 'A Narrow Fellow in the Grass.'" *Explicator* Summer 1996: 220-24. Public Library FullTEXT. CD-ROM. EBSCO. Aug. 1997.

"Poetry." *The Oxford English Dictionary*. 2nd ed. CD-ROM. Oxford: Oxford UP, 1992.

"Shakespeare, William." *Microsoft Encarta 97 Encyclopedia*. CD-ROM. Redmond: Microsoft, 1997.

Stirm, Jan. "'For solace a twinne-like sister': Teaching Themes of Sisterhood in *As You Like It* and Beyond." *Shakespeare Quarterly* Winter 1996: 374-86. *ProQuest*. CD-ROM. UMI-Proquest. 1996.

Wilson, Edmund. "Hemingway: Gauge of Morale." *The Wound and the Bow: Seven Studies in Literature*. 1941. Rpt. by Farrar, Straus, and Giroux, 1978. 174-97. *Discovering Authors*. Vers. 1.0. CD-ROM. Detroit: Gale, 1996.

Works Cited entries for online/Internet sources:

Arnesen, Eric. "Portrait of an Outsider: A Review of *Richard Wright: The Life and Times* by Hazel Rowely." *ChicagoTribuneOnline*. 2 September 2001. 5 September 2001 <http://chicagotribune.com/features/books/chi-0109010005sep02.story?coll=chi%2Dleisurebooks%2Dhed>.

Beatty, Jack. "The Bumbling Communicator." *Atlantic Unbound*. 6 September 2001. 12 September 2001 <http://the atlantic.com/unbound/polipro/pp2001-09-06.htm>.

Chatman, Seymour. "Soft Filters: Some Sunshine on 'Cat in the Rain.'" *Narrative* 9.2 (May 2001): 217. *Expanded Academic ASAP*. 20 August 2001 <http://infotrac.galegroup.com/itw/infomark/374/389/40172763w3/>.

Dupuis, Kelley. "Dubious Battles: Ernest Hemingway's Journeys to War." *EBSCOhost*. 26 August 2001 <http://www.ernest.hemingway.com/journeystowar.htm>.

Ebert, Roger. "If They Screen Them, Will you Come?" *ChicagoSunTimesOnline*. 5 September 2001. 10 September 2001 <http://suntimes.com/output/eb-feature/cst-ftr-ebert05.html>.

"Hemingway, Ernest." *Encyclopaedia Britannica Online*. 4 September 2001 <http://search.eb.com/b01/topic?eu=40801&sctn=1>.

Lane, Robert D. and Steven M. Lane. "Finding Patterns in Hemingway and Camus: Construction of Meaning and Truth." *NetFirst*. 20 August 2001 <http://www.websyntax.com/camus/analyses/patterns.asp>.

McKeague, Pat. "Revisions for *Writing about Literature: Step by Step*." E-mail to Kendall/Hunt. 31 Oct. 2001.

"Poetry." *OED Online*. 2nd ed. 1989. 15 August 2001 <http://dictionary.oed.com/cgi/entry/00182463>.

Schwarz, Jeffery A. "The Saloon Must Go, and I Will Take It with Me": American Prohibition, Nationalism, and Expatriation in *The Sun Also Rises*. *Studies in the Novel* 33.2 (Summer 2001): 180–201. *WilsonSelectPlus*. 20 August 2001 <http://firstsearch.oclc.org/webz>.

Straw, Deborah. "Key West: A Reader's and Writer's Haven." *Google*. 26 August 2001 <http://www.literarytraveler.com/hemingway/keywest.htm>.

"This Day in Literary History: September 7." *The History Channel Online*. 2001. History Channel. 7 September 2001 <http://www.historychannel.com/cgi-bin/frameit.cgi?p=http%3Awww.historychannel.com/tdih/html>.

Note: To cite an online source from your library that does not include a URL, complete the works cited entry by citing the name of the database (if known) which is underlined and followed by a period, the name of the service followed by a period, the name of the library followed by a comma, the city in which the library is located followed by a period, and the date of access followed by a period. If you can locate the URL of the service's home page, cite it in angle brackets followed by a period after the date of access.

Other Documentation Questions

If you encounter other types of sources or have questions about formatting your entries, consult your instructor and/or the fifth edition of the *MLA Handbook for Writers of Research Papers* available in libraries and bookstores. The Modern Language Association of America also has a web page that can be accessed by typing Modern Language Association or the URL www.mla.org/ in the search window on Yahoo, a web page directory.

JUST ONE MORE THING

Do you think of yourself as a scholar? You are, you know, when you follow the guidelines established by scholars within a particular discipline. By following the techniques recommended in this chapter, you will be joining the ranks of literary scholars who always use quotations and documentation when they work with sources. Intellectual honesty and accuracy are virtues all scholars share.

Character Analysis

Overview

One of the ongoing tasks of life is trying to understand ourselves, our reactions, our motives, our values. Literature can help us do that by showing human beings caught in conflict with themselves and/or some element of the world around them. By understanding their actions, we sometimes gain insight into our own.

Types of Characters

Using their medium of words, authors create characters who seem real to us. They are the people we meet in a story, poem, or play. The main character is called the **protagonist;** he or she is the person whose will moves the action of the plot. This character is usually trying to achieve a goal, and if the goal is an admirable one and the character exhibits admirable traits in the pursuit of it, he or she may also be called the **hero** or the **heroine.** If, however, the central character exhibits negative traits, such as being dishonest or inept, he or she may be labeled an **anti-hero.**

Since fiction is based on conflict, the protagonist struggles against an **antagonist,** another person, nature, society, technology, supernatural elements, or even himself. As the conflict increases and the protagonist struggles to achieve his goal, he reveals his personality through his words, actions, interactions, and choices. As the climax of the conflict approaches, the protagonist learns from the experience and by the end of the story has changed because of the insights that he has gained into life, himself, and others. Because of his change, the protagonist is said to be a **"round"** character, a term coined by E. M. Forster in *Aspects of the Novel.* Round characters truly seem real to us because of the way they are developed by the author. Like us, they have experiences that change the way they look at life; like us, they are **dynamic,** constantly evolving personalities.

In contrast, **"flat"** characters—another Forster term—usually do not change in the course of the story. They may serve as a catalyst for the protagonist's change, but most often they are **static,** unchanged by the action of the plot. Many flat characters serve minor roles in stories, so they are not fully developed as unique characters. When they exhibit traits that are usually associated with typical roles in literature, like the domineering mother or the corrupt politician, they may be labeled as **stereotypes** or **stock characters.** Occasionally a flat character may function as a **foil** who contrasts with the protagonist to emphasize character traits that are important to the plot.

The characters in Hemingway's "The Short Happy Life of Francis Macomber" illustrate the types of roles characters can play in fiction. The protagonist is Francis Macomber, a fact pointed out clearly by the title. He is a round character who undergoes a dramatic change from coward to brave man while on safari in Africa. One of Francis's antagonists in the story is his wife, Margaret. She is a flat character who does not change; she has always belittled Francis's manhood, and she does that in a final way by killing him just as he learns how to face life. Robert Wilson, the safari leader, is another flat character who serves as a foil for Francis. His bravery contrasts starkly with Francis's cowardliness, and his control over Margaret at the end of the story illustrates the control Francis would have had if he had lived. All of these characters are effective because of Hemingway's masterful use of characterization.

❧ Fictional Characters and Their Traits

Like people, fictional characters have personality traits that they exhibit in the course of the work. If authors want us to like or even love a character, they will give him or her likeable, lovable, admirable traits; if they wish us to dislike a character or to be indifferent to him or her, they will choose the character traits that will produce that effect.

Character traits are attitudes or behaviors that reflect one's personality, that combination of qualities that help to distinguish one person from another. For example, like people, characters may be brave or cowardly, supportive or sarcastic, domineering or submissive, cold or loving, passive or aggressive, open-minded or prejudiced, naive or sophisticated—the list goes on endlessly. To create these qualities, authors use a variety of methods of characterization, making their characters come alive on the page.

A Character's Physical Appearance and Name

As authors create their characters, one method they may use is to include some details of physical appearance. It is almost impossible to judge a person totally on his or her appearance in real life, but there are many stereotypes which authors may employ to evoke particular responses in their readers. There are, for example, particular aspects of appearance which the general public usually associates with manliness—thick hair (everywhere!), a ruddy complexion, broad shoulders, a muscular build, large, strong hands, and a deep voice. Weakness, on the other hand, may be suggested by thinning hair, a sallow complexion, rounded shoulders, a slight build, feminine hands, and a high-pitched voice. The femme fatale will probably have blonde hair, a fair complexion, a 38-24-36 figure, and long red fingernails. Chances are that the female heroine will have brown hair, a dark complexion, a motherly figure, and soft, gentle hands. Of course, the author could want to fool his readers and so reverse these stereotypes, as when the mild-mannered, soft-spoken little man turns out to be a brave soldier in a war story or a multiple murderer in detective fiction.

Most often, however, authors make a character's appearance fit the role he or she plays in a work. In Hemingway's "The Short Happy Life of Francis Macomber,"[1] Robert Wilson, the safari leader, is a man who has it all together. His appearance shows that he has adapted to the jungle setting and the dangers it holds: "He was about middle height with sandy hair, a stubby mustache, a very red face and extremely cold blue eyes with faint white wrinkles at the corners that grooved merrily when he smiled" (6). Hemingway also describes "his big brown hands, his old slacks, his very dirty boots . . ." (6). Wilson's description emphasizes his experience and his casual attitude toward his highly dangerous job.

Since authors are also naming their characters as well as describing them, it's a good idea to pay attention to the names characters have. In Hemingway's "The Short Happy Life of Francis Macomber," the

---

[1] Reprinted with permission of Charles Scribner's Sons, an imprint of Macmillan Publishing Company, from THE SHORT STORIES OF ERNEST HEMINGWAY. Copyright 1936 by Ernest Hemingway. Copyright renewed © 1964 by Mary Hemingway.

two male characters are named Robert and Francis. The first name obviously is strongly masculine, while the second is sexually ambivalent. This is another clue to the fact that Robert Wilson has mastered fear and faces life and death courageously, while Francis Macomber at the start of the story is a coward who runs from dangerous situations. Flannery O'Connor's Misfit in "A Good Man Is Hard to Find" and John Updike's Queenie in "A & P" are other characters whose names reflect their personalities. The Misfit is a violent criminal with a confused past, and Queenie walks, talks, and acts like a queen as she shops in a small-town A & P.

Be sure to watch, then, for details of appearance and for names when studying character; they can be good clues to a character's personality.

A Character's Actions

The actions of a character in a story are also clues to his or her personality. The old cliche "Actions speak louder than words" is particularly true in fiction, or as Aristotle put it, "Action is character." A character's behavior is usually motivated by his or her attitudes and values, so by examining behavior, readers can get to the heart and soul of a character. Like a psychiatrist, an informed reader seeks the reasons for actions to determine what they reveal about the inner person. For example, in "A & P" by John Updike, Sammy reveals that he believes in people when he confronts his boss, Lengel, about his treatment of three girls, while Lengel reveals that policy comes before people in his value system.

Authors will usually attempt to keep a character's actions consistent throughout a work once his or her personality and motives are understood. For example, June Star in "A Good Man Is Hard to Find" by Flannery O'Connor is consistently outspoken and insulting even though she moves from a familiar situation into a dangerous, threatening one. She says unkind things to her grandmother at home, and she even insults an escaped convict as he is about to murder her on a lonely back road in Georgia. Occasionally, however, authors might have a character "step out of character" to produce surprise or suspense in a work, but most often actions are reliable clues to a character's real self.

A Character's Choices

Since most narrative and dramatic works focus on characters involved in some type of conflict, they will probably need to make choices as they deal with their problems. As those choices are made, they reveal the character's values and self-concept and can serve as a basis for our judgments about him or her.

In "Gift of Grass" by Alice Adams, Cathy, the protagonist, is a sixteen-year-old who is seeing a psychiatrist—at her parents' insistence—because she does not want to return to school. On her way home from the doctor's office, she sees some kids she knows in the park, but rather than join them, she leaves the path and goes into the woods where she smokes marijuana. The choices Cathy makes here reveal that she feels uncomfortable with others, probably because of her lack of self-esteem. By choosing drugs and escape instead of friendship, she shows that she is unwilling or unable at this point to be open to others. This is emphasized when the psychiatrist asks her what she likes, and she chooses clouds and foghorns, both of which suggest obscurity and hiding from life. Cathy's choices, like ours in real life, reveal her conscious and unconscious personality.

A Character's Speech

Since there is no such thing as "small talk" in fiction, speech is also a clue to character. Every word spoken by a character is a clue to some part of his or her personality. Because authors must necessarily compress experience, they squeeze out all the conversational "fillers" and include only those statements which reveal character and advance the plot. You must realize, however, that a character's statements will not be like those of a writer in *True Confession*. The typical character will not tell you that he or she is unhappy, domineering, selfish, or psychotic. For example, in James Thurber's "The Secret Life of Walter Mitty," Mrs. Mitty will not say, "I'm domineering"; you will infer that she is when you hear her tell Walter, her husband, how to drive, to put on his gloves, and to buy overshoes. As a reader, you must take on the role of a psychiatrist who looks for the reasons behind a statement and for the personality traits a statement could reveal, making inferences and moving from the statement to the mind behind it.

It should be pointed out that isolated statements or statements taken out of context can sometimes be interpreted in various ways. For example, if a young man says "All girls adore me" to a girl he's just met and is trying to impress, it could mean that he's egotistical and suffering from a superiority complex or that he's shy and covering up for an inferiority complex. The point to remember is that statements by characters must be interpreted within the context of the story and in relation to the totality of the character revealed by all the methods of characterization employed by the author.

If you really listen to the conversation of people around you, you'll be amazed at what you'll learn and discover about them. Then apply that technique to fiction, and you'll be equally surprised.

A Character's Thoughts and Feelings

The statement "A penny for your thoughts" indicates a general desire to know what others are thinking. Although we ourselves can never get into the mind of another person, the omniscient narrator does when he records the thoughts and feelings of the characters. The purpose of reporting these details is to add depth to the characters in the story. They become more real to us as we see how their minds work and how they arrive at decisions that affect their lives and reveal their personalities.

In "The Short Happy Life of Francis Macomber,"[2] the omniscient narrator lets us into Margaret Macomber's thoughts as she contemplates the change in Francis from cowardice to courage: "she saw the change in Francis Macomber now. . . . 'You've gotten awfully brave, awfully suddenly,' his wife said contemptuously, but her contempt was not secure. She was very afraid of something" (26). These insights into her thoughts and fears show us that Margaret Macomber is very insecure—so insecure that she would even consider murder rather than lose her control over her husband. Learning a character's thoughts and emotions, then, teaches us a lot about the human personality and about the complexity of human motivation which can include such factors as love, hate, fear, revenge, status, power, fame, or fortune.

A Character's Past

A character's past often indicates some important things about his or her personality. Psychologists tell us that we are the products of our early environment and of our past experiences. Children growing up in the ghetto or in upper-class suburbs learn a lifestyle and a set of values much different from each other's. They usually imitate the adult patterns they see around them, not knowing that their basic personalities are being formed.

Authors are aware of the significance of a person's background, and they may choose to include biographical details to give the reader some insight into a character's makeup and motivation. As The Misfit relates details of his past in Flannery O'Connor's "A Good Man Is Hard to Find,"[3] it is easy to see that all of his experiences with death and brutality could have definitely made him the cold-hearted person

---

[2] Reprinted with permission of Charles Scribner's Sons, an imprint of Macmillan Publishing Company, from THE SHORT STORIES OF ERNEST HEMINGWAY. Copyright 1936 by Ernest Hemingway. Copyright renewed © 1964 by Mary Hemingway.

[3] Excerpts from A GOOD MAN IS HARD TO FIND, copyright 1953 by Flannery O'Connor and renewed 1981 by Mrs. Regina O'Connor, reprinted by permission of Harcourt Brace Jovanovich, Inc.

he has become: "'I been most everything. Been in the arm service, both land and sea, at home and abroad, been twice married, been an undertaker, been with the railroads, plowed Mother Earth, been in a tornado, seen a man burnt alive oncet,' . . . 'I even seen a woman flogged,' he said" (129–130). The Misfit's psychotic personality and his calloused attitudes toward life and death have been shaped by these experiences of his past. Since the past is always a good clue to the present and to the future, note the biographical details—family history, nationality, education, and significant life experiences—that an author includes and examine them as a psychiatrist or a detective would.

A Character's Comments about Other Characters

Do you ever talk about your friends or your family? Characters in fiction do, too, but their conversations are generally not just idle gossip. Their statements about each other are most often designed to reveal significant things about themselves and about the personalities and motives of the other characters. But just as you don't believe everything you hear about others in real life, it is also necessary in fiction to determine the reliability of the speaker. If the speaker is generally likeable because of the positive qualities he's been given by the author, his statements can generally be accepted and believed at face value. If, however, the speaker is generally disliked by most readers because of his negative qualities, his evaluations and judgments should probably be looked upon with skepticism. In Hemingway's "The Short Happy Life of Francis Macomber," for example, Robert Wilson is generally admired by most readers because of his courage and because of his cool efficiency as a safari leader. When he evaluates Margaret Macomber's motives and accuses her of murder at the end of the story, we are expected by Hemingway to agree with that judgment. On the other hand, James Thurber, in "The Secret Life of Walter Mitty," makes the reader dislike Mrs. Mitty because of her domineering super-mother attitude toward her husband. When she tells Walter that she thinks he's sick because he has talked back to her, the reader doubts her evaluation and generally believes that Walter is much healthier emotionally than she is. The intelligent reader of fiction always listens attentively to what characters say about each other, but he also evaluates the speakers before he accepts their judgments.

A Narrator's Comments about a Character

When a third-person narrator describes a character's motivation, it is usually a clue to his or her personality since one's inner qualities usually shape one's actions. In Hemingway's *The Old Man and The Sea*,[4] the narrator tells us about Santiago, the protagonist-hero: "Once there had been a tinted photograph of his wife on the wall but he had taken it down because it made him too lonely to see it and it was on the shelf in the corner under his clean shirt" (16). The loneliness the narrator ascribes to Santiago early in the novella alerts us to his sensitive and loving nature. Surely he loved his wife very much if the pain of seeing her picture is too much for him to bear. This quality is reinforced later when the narrator tells us Santiago "loved green turtles and hawk-bills with their elegance and speed" (36) and he "loved [the marlin] when he was alive and [he] loved him after" he had finally managed to kill him (105). Santiago's love for people and for nature is clearly portrayed by the narrator's choice of words, so when a narrator helps to define a character's qualities through narrated details, be sure to take note.

❧ Writing about Character: Step by Step

Writing about a character in any form of literature involves noting and analyzing the methods of characterization as the author employs them. They will enable you to characterize the people in a fictional work or a play or the speaker in a poem.

To write an essay analyzing character, simply follow these easy steps:

---

[4] (New York: Macmillan, 1952).

1. Choose a character who, for any reason, interests you, one whose personality you would like to explore in greater depth.
2. To formulate a thesis, choose one of the following organizational approaches or combine two or more:
   a. the traits that the character exhibits throughout the work;
   b. the causes of a character's actions, choices, or thoughts and feelings;
   c. the changes a character undergoes in the course of the work;
   d. the significant actions, speeches, choices, objects, or places that help to reveal a character's traits;
   e. the points of likeness or difference that exist between this character and another character in the work;
   f. the things that are said about a character by the other characters or by the narrator.
3. Locate specific pages and quotations in the short story/novel/drama/poem that prove the thesis points you have chosen. Look for the sections that directly relate to the subject character and to that character's actions and interactions with others.
4. In the thesis, determine a logical order for the presentation of your points. If a logical order cannot be determined, then employ a chronological or time order or an order of importance, saving the most significant point or the one with the strongest proof for the last position.
5. Organize each thesis point into separate body paragraphs by using the pattern of topic sentence, introduction to a quote, quotations/details, and analysis and by repeating this pattern as often as necessary within the paragraph to build your case. In developing the body paragraphs, remember that the analysis sections are the most important. Consider how the quotations/details illustrate, reinforce, or prove your point. If, for example, you say a character is submissive and then quote a section showing him following his wife's orders, you must explain *how* and *why* this behavior shows that he is submissive. Analysis always answers the questions of *how* and *why:* how and why does the example given in the quotation show/prove the topic sentence.
6. Conclude your essay by restating the points you've proven about the character and by emphasizing the importance or the significance of the character in the work as a whole.

The following diagram, model essays, and plan sheet will help you prepare to write a thoroughly developed and well supported essay.

Diagram of the Structure of a Character Analysis Essay

Title

Introductory Paragraph:

Open with interesting lead material.

Name the work and the author.

Give a brief summary of the plot and state the importance of the character you plan to analyze.

Begin to narrow your focus and work down to the thesis statement which embodies the key points from the organizational approach you have chosen.

Body Paragraphs:

In the first part of the body, discuss point one by beginning with a topic sentence which includes the key words from point one in the thesis. Lead into a quotation by giving it a brief background, quote from the work, and then analyze the quotation in relation to the generalization it supports. Repeat this pattern as often as necessary to thoroughly prove point one.

Analyze point two in the second part of the body. The topic sentence focuses on the second thesis point and is followed by introductory information for a supporting quotation, the quotation to support the topic sentence, and thorough analysis of the quoted excerpt. This literary analysis pattern should be used more than once within the paragraph to build solid content.

Discuss point three in the third part of the body. This paragraph should be developed in the same way as preceding body paragraphs, but it should be even stronger than those paragraphs since the last position is often considered a position of strength and importance.

Note: You may choose to divide the discussion of each thesis point into multiple paragraphs if the discussion becomes long and involved. If you use this approach for point one, try to be consistent and use it for all following points as well. Be sure to use transitions and to incorporate key words from the thesis into your topic sentences to indicate when you move to a new part of your discussion.

Concluding Paragraph:

Use a signal word somewhere in the conclusion to let the reader know that you are coming to the end of your discussion. Restate your thesis, summarize your main points, and emphasize the significance of the character's role in the work. Try to change the "speed" or tempo of the last few sentences to give your essay a sense of finality.

Four model essays are presented in this chapter to illustrate the point that each literary element can be found in all types of literature: short stories, novels, poems, and dramas.

The following student-written essay analyzes a character in a short story. The essay is effective because it is well organized and well developed through the use of the literary analysis pattern.

Miss Moore: A Special Role Model

Everyone needs someone special in life who is a good role model. In Toni Cade Bambara's short story "The Lesson,"[1] Miss Moore is that special person. The story focuses on several black children who live in the New York slums. Sylvia is the narrator and the group leader. One summer day, Miss Moore, a resident of their neighborhood, takes the children to an exclusive toy store on Fifth Avenue where she teaches them about life. *She accomplishes this through her intelligence, her caring, and her sense of justice.*

Miss Moore, an intelligent woman, knows how to handle the children's parents so that she can spend some time with the kids. Sylvia remembers that when Miss Moore "came calling with some sachet she'd sewed up or some gingerbread she'd made or some book, why then [the parents would] all be too embarrassed to turn her down and [the kids would] get handed over all spruced up" (88). Since Miss Moore wants to help the children, she always comes calling with gifts. Because she understands human motivation, she is able to get what she wants: the opportunity to influence the children's lives in a positive way. When Miss Moore and the children arrive at F. A. O. Schwarz, they look at a microscope, and Sylvia says, "Miss Moore ask what it cost. So we all jam into the window . . . and the price tag say $300. So then she ask how long'd take for Big Butt and Junebug to save up their allowances" (90). Miss Moore is cleverly leading the children to think for themselves. They can understand the price of toys compared to the size of their allowance, and that makes the lesson about money very realistic. By using her intelligence, she helps the children understand some important points about their economic position in society.

Despite the fact that the children's parents do not appreciate her efforts, Miss Moore really cares about the kids. Sylvia, remembering how their parents talked about Miss Moore "like a dog," says, "She'd been to college and said it was only right that she should take responsibility for the young ones' education, and she not even related by marriage or blood" (99–100). Miss Moore is different from most of the adults in Sylvia's neighborhood, and she knows that children need guidance and education if they are to change their lives for the better. Opportunities are limited in the slums of New York, but education can be the kids' ticket out; therefore, Miss Moore unselfishly gives up her time to show them the world outside their own. Sylvia comments on how much Miss Moore cares when she says, "It's purdee hot and [Miss Moore's] knockin herself out about arithmetic" (88). She puts all

Thesis Statement

Topic Sentence

Topic Sentence

[1] From *Gorilla, My Love* (New York: Random, 1972). Used by permission of Random House.

of her energy into her lesson, hoping that the children realize that there are big differences in the way people live because of their economic status. Her education has made her aware that to survive in the world, one must understand "real money" (88) and its power.

Topic Sentence   *Because she wants the children to be treated more justly, Miss Moore tries to show them the injustice that exists in society.* Miss Moore tells them "about what things cost and what [their] parents make and how much goes for rent and how money ain't divided up right in this country" (89). She is pointing out how unequal living standards can be in America. The children have only been exposed to their small world and do not realize how the economic system operates. However, Miss Moore knows that some hardworking people can barely afford to pay their rent and feed their children, while the privileged class can buy their children a toy with money that could feed an entire family. Sylvia finally realizes there is another way of life outside her own and remembers, "Where we are is who we are, Miss Moore always pointin out. But it don't necessarily have to be that way, she always adds then waits for somebody to say that poor people have to wake up and demand their share of the pie . . ." (94–95). Miss Moore recognizes that where a person lives determines what people think of him or her. And due to this perception, Sylvia and her friends who live in the slums have fewer opportunities in life, opportunities which could help them raise their standard of living. Miss Moore wants more for the children, so she tells them they have the right to demand their share of the wealth. By awakening their desire, she is offering them a better future.

Restatement of Thesis   *Because of her intelligence, her caring personality, and her desire for justice, then, Miss Moore exemplifies that special role model that children need while growing up.* In fact, as a result of her enlightened concern, the children are able to see beyond their isolated world, and Sylvia is inspired to strive for equality when she says, "ain't nobody gonna beat me at nuthing" (96). Her new determination is the result of Miss Moore's guidance. If there were more special people like her, perhaps many more children would escape poverty and get "their share of the pie" (95).

Deborah Wagner

Model Essay Two

This student-written essay focuses on a character in a novel. The essay embodies the structure and the literary analysis pattern that we have been talking about.

T. C. Berger: An Extra-Ordinary Man

Most people are ordinary, and Judith Guest's novel *Ordinary People*[1] is about an ordinary family of four named the Jarretts. It is the sad account of how, after losing one member of the family in a boating accident, the other members can no longer cope. Each person comes apart in his own way: Calvin, by doubting himself and his marriage; his wife Beth, by drawing into herself and refusing to communicate with her family; and their son Conrad, by trying to kill himself. Conrad starts to see a psychiatrist, Tyrone C. Berger, who is the key to his gradually putting his life back together. *Through Berger's understanding, sense of humor, and support, Conrad finds the self-confidence and the courage he needs to face whatever each day brings.*

Thesis Statement

Berger's efforts to understand Conrad help him to sense when his patient has something on his mind. One day, when Conrad is in his office, Berger says, "'Something is bugging you, something is making you nervous. Now what is it?'" (73). He prompts Conrad to voice his feelings, feelings which sometimes surprise even Conrad himself. Berger gives Conrad the opportunity to get things off his chest without being judged or condemned. He also helps Conrad to understand other people and teaches him not to expect too much from them when he says, "'Sometimes people say stupid things. They feel like they gotta say something, you know?'" (73). Berger helps Conrad realize that he isn't the only one who doesn't have his act together. Other people have faults, too, and Conrad slowly understands that he will have to lower his expectations. Through Berger's prompting, Conrad also comes to realize that it is okay to have feelings and to let them out once in a while. Berger tells him, "'Maybe you gotta feel lousy sometimes, in order to feel better. A little advice, kiddo, about feeling. Don't think too much about it. And don't expect it always to tickle'" (93). In Berger's office, Conrad has the opportunity to release those feelings, study them, and eventually understand that they aren't so bad after all.

Topic Sentence

Another key to Berger's success with Conrad is his quick wit and sense of humor. On Conrad's first visit to his office, Berger lightens the atmosphere after Conrad tells him he tried to kill himself by asking, "'What with? Pills? Gillette Super-Blue?'" This works with Conrad, and he quickly responds, "'It was a Platinum-Plus'" (39). Berger takes the seriousness out of a question by turning it into a joke. In doing this, he relieves a lot of tension and awkwardness surrounding it. Later, Berger tells Conrad that his schedule will be based on patient ratings: "'The higher I rate, the fewer times you gotta come. Example: You rate me ten, you only have to see me once a week.'" Conrad laughs and says, "'That's crazy,'" to which Berger responds, "'Hey, I'm the doctor. You're the patient'" (41). Berger's good humor rubs off a little on Conrad. He eventually begins to see that no matter how serious a problem is, there is always something about it to laugh at. And after laughing at it, it doesn't seem half so frightening.

Topic Sentence

Perhaps the most important reason behind Berger's success with his "'prize pupil'" (242) is the support he offers Conrad. He is able to let his

Topic Sentence

---

[1] From ORDINARY PEOPLE by Judith Guest. Copyright © 1976 by Judith Guest. Used by permission of Viking Penguin, a division of Penguin Books USA Inc.

guard down in Berger's office. During one session, he thinks that "it is relaxing to lie here with this placid man beside him, talking of anger and of change, without being irrevocably committed to it" (74). Berger doesn't tease him or criticize him or make him feel inferior. He simply listens, which is what Conrad needs the most. Conrad grows to depend on Berger, and Berger never lets him down. The day Conrad finds out his friend from the hospital has killed herself and his world starts crumbling around him again, Berger is there. Conrad wakes him by phone at 7:00 A.M., by saying, "'I need to see you.'" All Berger says is, "'Yes. Okay. Can you make it to the office in half an hour?'" (202). Berger is there when Conrad needs him most, and his panic subsides in Berger's reassuring presence. Without Berger, who knows what Conrad might have done? Berger becomes Conrad's closest friend because with him, Conrad can be himself. During one session, he confides to Berger, "'I feel like I've been in [a box] forever. Everybody looking in, to see how you're doing. Even when they're on your side, they're still looking in. . . . I never saw you out there, you know? You, I always saw inside the box. With me. . . . What I'm saying . . . I guess I think of you as a friend'" (127). Through Berger's support and care, he proves himself worthy of Conrad's trust, and in doing so, proves himself a worthy friend.

And so, even though the Jarretts look like an ordinary family from the outside, inside their lives are in a turmoil. Conrad is hit the hardest by his brother Buck's death. He loses control. This is disturbing to the reader because we see how fragile our lives can be. A tragedy such as a death in the family could happen to any of us at any time. Would we be able to cope? With someone like Berger to help us, we feel we probably could. *With someone like Berger to understand, humor, and support us, we could probably face anything.* It is comforting to know there are people like Berger in this world who don't mind putting themselves out to help others.

Bill Murphy

Restatement of Thesis

Model Essay Three

This student-written essay analyzes a character in a poem. The writer bases his interpretation on quoted lines from the poem which he explains and comments on in his analysis.

A Master of Life

Old age turns some people into couch potatoes who stop living and start merely existing. That will never happen to Ulysses, the great Greek hero who is characterized as a master of life in Alfred, Lord Tennyson's poem entitled "Ulysses."[1] *As he prepares to leave on his last adventure and*

Thesis Statement

[1] Alfred, Lord Tennyson, "Ulysses" *The Norton Anthology of English Literature,* ed. M. H. Abrams. 5th ed. (New York: Norton, 1987) 1950–1952.

addresses his son and his mariners, he reveals his adventurous spirit, his desire to pursue knowledge, and his determination to live life as fully as possible until he dies.

Topic Sentence *Ulysses' plan to leave Ithaca and give over the kingdom to his son Telemachus is prompted by his spirit of adventure.* He feels unproductive as the "idle king" (line 1) of a people who "hoard, and sleep, and feed" (5). These activities do not fit in with Ulysses' adventurous lifestyle. He does not want to spend his time gathering material wealth or focusing on his bodily needs. Ulysses is a man who "cannot rest from travel; [he] will drink / Life to the lees" (6–7). He does not want to stop going out to meet life; in fact, he wants to consume life, to drink in—with eagerness and pleasure—all the world has to offer. With a sense of pride, he describes his past adventures:

> Much have I seen and known,—cities of men
> And manners, climates, councils, governments,
> Myself not least, but honored of them all,—
> And drunk delight of battle with my peers,
> Far on the ringing plains of windy Troy. (13–17)

Ulysses' adventures have taken him from the cities to the battlefields and have given him insight into lifestyles and political systems, but most of all, they have taught him about himself. Interacting with others and reacting to new experiences have helped him to clarify his values and his beliefs; therefore, he wants to continue his adventures so that he can enjoy all that life has to offer.

Topic Sentence *It is his desire for knowledge that drives Ulysses' restless spirit.* In his eyes, "experience is an arch wherethro' / Gleams that untravelled world whose margin fades / For ever and for ever when [he] move[s]" (18–20). As he experiences new aspects of life, he realizes how much more there is still to be enjoyed and experienced. The more he knows, the more he realizes how much he still has to learn as new horizons present themselves. For Ulysses, it is "dull . . . to pause, to make an end, / To rust unburnished, not to shine in use!" (22–23) He must continue his pursuit of knowledge to escape boredom; he does not want to rust out but to continue to use and polish his intellect until he dies. His desire for knowledge makes "every hour" (26) exciting for it is a "bringer of new things" (28). With a positive attitude, he anticipates each hour of each day and the experiences it holds. His goal is "To follow knowledge like a sinking star, / Beyond the utmost bound of human thought" (31–32). To expand his mind, Ulysses wants to develop insight and understanding to depths never thought possible by the human mind. His thirst for knowledge has become a burning passion that drives him forward into life and new experiences.

Topic Sentence *Even while acknowledging approaching death, Ulysses is determined not to stop living.* He believes that "Old age hath yet his honor and his toil" (50). While he may not be able to do everything he did as a younger man, there are still deeds that he can accomplish before "Death closes all" (51). Ulysses is a realist about death and its finality, but he is not yet ready to die. He wants to perform "some work of noble note" (52) and "To sail beyond the sunset, and the baths / Of all the western stars, until [he] die[s]" (60–61).

With noble goals like these, he surely will lead a fulfilling life as he pursues his dreams "to seek a newer world" (57). This is not a man who waits for death; this is a man who sails into life with tremendous joy and anticipation. While he admits that he has been "made weak by time and fate," he is still "strong in will / To strive, to seek, to find, and not to yield" (69–70). His determination to keep on searching for adventure, for knowledge, for fulfillment is the mark of a man who has truly understood and enjoyed life and conquered death. What matters to Ulysses is not the destination but the trip itself. He enjoys all of life, and he is never going to give up his struggle to have it all.

Restatement of Thesis

Thus Ulysses' indomitable spirit is truly inspiring. *His desire for adventure, knowledge, and total fulfillment reveals that he wants to be fully alive—not just "a name" (11).* Through him, we can learn how to live life to the fullest now and in our old age. He scorns those who merely exist by saying, "As tho' to breathe were life" (24). In his view, life is an exciting adventure that ends only when "Death closes all" (51).

John Thompson

✎ Model Essay Four

Here is a student-written essay on the protagonist in the Greek tragedy *Oedipus Tyrannus.* The thesis focuses on the changes that Oedipus undergoes as he discovers his tragic fate.

A Hero for the Ages

Man is a fickle creature. What he cherishes today, he tosses away tomorrow. And yet, somehow, some things endure. One of these enduring treasures is *Oedipus Tyrannus*,[1] an ancient Greek tragedy by Sophocles. To save the city of Thebes, Oedipus vows to avenge the murder of Laius, the former king, but his search for the murderer is soon abandoned. Instead, it turns into a search for the truth of his parentage. This truth, once revealed, destroys him by proving that he unknowingly killed his father and married his mother as foretold by the oracle. But there is more to be said about Oe-

Thesis Statement

dipus. *He is a dynamic and powerful character who dominates the action of the play. A good and noble king, he cannot rise above his overwhelming arrogance; therefore, he seals his doom. In the end, he comes to know and understand his fate. These traits are what make him a true tragic hero.*

Topic Sentence

Oedipus is basically a good and noble man as are all tragic heroes. As the play opens, the city of Thebes is beset with plague. The people have gathered on the steps of the altar. Oedipus greets his "children" and asks the priest, "What brings you here? Some need? Some want? I'll help you all I

[1] *Sophocles, Oedipus the King.* © Oxford University Press, 1962. Reprinted from *Sophocles: Three Tragedies* translated by H. D. F. Kitto (1961) by permission of Oxford UP. All parenthetical page numbers refer to the text in this edition.

can" (1292). Oedipus questions his subjects about their needs and offers to help them overcome their difficulties. This shows that he is a benevolent ruler, truly interested in his subjects. Later, when Teiresias accuses him of being the "desecrator" (1298), the Chorus recalls his noble deed:

> For I saw how the king
> in the test with the Sphinx
> proved his wisdom and his worth
> when he saved this city from doom.
> No! I can *never* condemn the king! (1301)

Even though Oedipus has been accused of murder, the Chorus refuses to condemn him. Instead they choose to recall his heroic battle with the Sphinx. This reflects the great admiration and deep loyalty the people feel for their king. Similarly, Oedipus expresses love and concern for his daughters as he begs Creon to "take care of them" (1318). Creon replies, "I know how much you love them, how much you have always loved them" (1319). This reaffirms the love that Oedipus has always shown his family. Certainly, only a good and noble man could be both the donor and recipient of such deep-seated love and admiration.

Topic Sentence

Oedipus is more than proud—he reeks of arrogance. Many critics refer to this as his tragic flaw, another trait necessary for a tragic hero. This is first apparent when he greets his people at the altar: ". . . [I] came myself—I came, Oedipus, Oedipus, whose name is known to all" (1292). The imperious tone of his voice and the repetition of his name accentuate his feeling of self-importance. It is the condescending attitude of a proud man. Often, this pride is magnified by his anger, as when, fearful that the oracle will be fulfilled, he rages at the gods: "Hear me, you gods, you holy gods—I will never see that day! I will die before I ever see the stain of this abominable act!" (1306–07) In his rage and arrogance, he defies the gods and threatens to cheat them of their victory, even if he must kill himself to do so. His overwhelming arrogance, or hybris, spurs him to place himself above the gods and challenge them to battle, a battle he must lose. And lose he does, but, even then, his pride surfaces. Cursed by the gods, blinded by his own hand, he reminds us that he was certainly "the noblest of the sons of Thebes . . ." (1317). Even his fall from grace is not enough to squelch his pride, and he recalls his past glory. His flaw—his arrogance—though certainly lessened, has not been replaced with humility.

All tragic heroes must suffer a downfall, and Oedipus, too, falls from grace. The first mention of his impending doom occurs during the confrontation with Teiresias: "No—it is not I who will cause your fall. That is Apollo's office and he will discharge it" (1299). By naming Apollo, Teiresias emphasizes the certainty of Oedipus's downfall. No force on earth can sway the gods from their path. The Chorus reaffirms the certainty of his doom:

> Ambition must be used
> to benefit the state;
> else it is wrong, and God
> must strike it from this earth. (1307)

The Chorus interprets all that has gone before and comes to the conclusion that God has no choice; Oedipus must pay for his sins. This underscores the inevitability of his doom. All that remains to be decided is the degree to which he will suffer. This is revealed by the Chorus as Oedipus speaks with his people for the last time: "You have suffered equally for your fortune and your disaster" (1317). By referring to equal fortune and disaster, the Chorus implies that only a hero of epic proportion could fall to such depths of despair. Oedipus, like all tragic heroes, has fallen from grace.

Topic Sentence

At long last, Oedipus comes to know and understand his destiny; he is enlightened. Enlightenment is the last of the traits necessary to prove him a tragic hero. During the climax of the play, he bemoans his fate: "O God! O no! I see it all now! All clear! O Light! I will never look on you again! Sin! Sin in my birth! Sin in my marriage! Sin in my blood!" (1314) This is the first time that he openly admits the oracle has been fulfilled. He has, indeed, murdered his father and married his mother. This realization signals an awakening in him, an awareness of what he has done, a foreboding of what is to come. But this true insight is evident only after he has found the queen's body and blinded himself. Though first blaming Apollo for his pain and anguish, he admits his part: ". . . it was my own hand that struck the blow. Not his" (1317). With this admission, he shows his willingness to accept responsibility for his actions. The gods decreed and the oracle foretold, but he was the instrument of his own destruction. Conceding that he is "ready now" (1318) to live life on its own terms, the Chorus watches him leave and sings of poor Oedipus, "drowning in waves of dread and despair" (1320). He is a broken man who grasps for hope, just as a drowning man gasps for breath, but there is no relief except death. In the eternal darkness of his despair, Oedipus has been granted insight and, in gaining it, has shown himself worthy to be called a tragic hero.

Restatement of Thesis

Oepidus, then, possesses all the traits of a true tragic hero. He is good and noble, yet proud and arrogant; this paradox hastens his downfall and eventual enlightenment. But why has he survived through the ages? Perhaps the reason is that we choose to cling to those things which touch us most deeply and which are a reflection of ourselves. Oedipus touches us all. In him we see ourselves. We share a common bond; we share a common struggle. We share in his humanity.

Sandy Walshon

To review an essay that contrasts two characters, see the model essay entitled "They Would Have Been Good Women If . . ." on pages 246–248 in Chapter 13, Writing an Extended Literary Analysis Essay.

JUST ONE MORE THING

To make the characters seem more real to you, you might ask if they remind you of someone you know, for the traits characters in literature exhibit are probably similar to the personality traits your friends, family, and co-workers possess. Making these kinds of connections will make literature more enjoyable and more meaningful and will be of value on the job or in social situations where you often make judgments about others based on their appearance, their words, their actions, their choices, or their past.

❦ Character Analysis Essay Plan Sheet ❦

Author: _____ Title: _____

Thesis: _____

_____

_____

_____

_____

Topic sentence: _____

_____

_____

Supporting quote: page or line _____

Supporting quote: page or line _____

Supporting quote: page or line _____

Topic sentence: _____

_____

_____

Supporting quote: page or line _____

Supporting quote: page or line _____

Supporting quote: page or line _____

Topic sentence: _____

_____

_____

Supporting quote: page or line _____

Supporting quote: page or line _____

Supporting quote: page or line _____

Topic sentence: _____

_____

_____

Supporting quote: page or line _____

Supporting quote: page or line _____

Supporting quote: page or line _____

Topic sentence: _____

_____

_____

Supporting quote: page or line _____

Supporting quote: page or line _____

Supporting quote: page or line _____

Topic sentence: _____

_____

_____

Supporting quote: page or line _____

Supporting quote: page or line _____

Supporting quote: page or line _____

Concluding points: _____

_____

_____

_____

_____

_____

_____

❧ Peer/Self-Evaluation of a Character Analysis Essay ❧

> **Directions:** Make specific suggestions about each part of the essay, pointing out particular areas that the writer could improve. Keep in mind the qualities of good writing: unity, organization, development, clarity, and coherence.

I. Introduction

Is the lead relevant and interesting?

Are the author's full name and the title of the work correctly spelled and punctuated?

Does the brief plot summary focus on the events that lead coherently to the thesis?

Does the thesis name the subject character and list the points to be developed in the body paragraphs?

II. Body Paragraphs

Do the topic sentences contain key words from the thesis?

Are the supporting quotations properly introduced and relevant?

Are the analysis sections adequately developed?

Do the body paragraphs follow the order of the thesis points?

Are the body paragraphs unified and coherent?

III. Conclusion

Is a signal word included somewhere in the final paragraph?

Is the thesis effectively rephrased?

Is the significance of the thesis clear to the reader?

Is there a speed change between the last two sentences?

Is the final sentence an effective clincher?

IV. Expression

Are all the ideas expressed in complete sentences?

Are the sentences clear and correctly punctuated?

Are there any problems with subject-verb or pronoun-antecedent agreement?

Are all the words correctly spelled?

V. Overall Evaluation

Most effective part of the essay:

Least effective part of the essay:

List three specific actions which could be taken by the writer to improve this and future papers:

1.

2.

3.

Evaluator's name: _____ Date: _____

❧ Exercise on Analyzing Character ❧

> What inferences about her character can you make from this description of Amelia Evans in Carson McCullers' *The Ballad of the Sad Cafe*?[1] Consider such things as her name, her physical appearance, her actions, her choices, and her past.

"Miss Amelia was rich. In addition to the store she operated a still three miles back in the swamp, and ran out the best liquor in the county. She was a dark, tall woman with bones and muscles like a man. Her hair was cut short and brushed back from the forehead, and there was about her sunburned face a tense, haggard quality. She might have been a handsome woman if, even then, she was not slightly cross-eyed. There were those who would have courted her, but Miss Amelia cared nothing for the love of men and was a solitary person. Her marriage had been unlike any other marriage ever contracted in this county—it was a strange and dangerous marriage, lasting only for ten days, that left the whole town wondering and shocked. Except for this queer marriage, Miss Amelia had lived her life alone. Often she spent whole nights back in her shed in the swamp, dressed in overalls and gum boots, silently guarding the low fire of the still" (4–5).

Inferences based on Miss Amelia's name and appearance: _____

_____

_____

Inferences based on her actions: _____

_____

_____

Inferences based on her choices: _____

_____

_____

Inferences based on her past: _____

_____

_____

[1] (New York: Bantam, 1971).

Setting Analysis

Overview

Setting is the time and place that an author chooses for his work. These choices must be carefully made to make what happens in the work probable—and hence believable. Setting can also reveal much about the characters in a work, it can produce an appropriate background for the action of the plot, and it can help to communicate the theme of a work. The roles that setting can play are usually subtly employed, but once detected by the careful reader, they can add depth and effectiveness to a story's impact and message.

Setting and Its Functions

Once an author decides on a plot and creates characters to carry out those actions, he must also decide on a setting—a time and place—that will contribute to the work's impact and believability. The time of the action involves not only the general era—the past, present, or future—but also such specifics as the year, the season, the month, the day of the week, and the time of day. Place is the physical environment: the country, the state, the city, the town, the landscape, the climate, the weather conditions, the house, the furniture, and all of the possessions the characters own. The action may take place in a natural setting such as the sea, in a man-made setting such as a mental hospital, or in a combination of the two as the characters move from place to place. Whatever the setting, it must be carefully chosen by the author because it performs important functions in a literary work.

Setting and Probability

One function of setting is to increase the probability of certain events occurring in a work, for certain actions are more credible in some settings than in others. For example, if an author wanted to present the difficulties faced by a victim of a mugging, he or she would probably set the action in a large city where a mugging is more likely to occur rather than in a small town. Shark attacks and their effects on a nearby community would have to be set in a town near an ocean, as in Peter Benchley's novel *Jaws,* while a love story could take place anywhere since love is not restricted to any particular place or time. The action, then, must not only be possible but highly probable in the place and time chosen by the author to make the work realistic. Hemingway chose such a setting for his novella *The Old Man and the Sea.* When Santiago goes deep-sea fishing off the coast of Cuba in September, the month when the big fish come, it is probable that after 84 days without a catch, he will be successful. And catch the big one he does, an eighteen-foot marlin that weighs more than 1,500 pounds. It is also probable that Santiago will have problems bringing in his prize since he has gone far out to sea, his skiff is two feet smaller than the marlin, and the waters are shark-infested. The actions he takes as he tries to get back to shore are probable and credible in the setting chosen by Hemingway.

Setting and Atmosphere

A second function of setting is to produce an appropriate atmosphere or mood for the action of the plot. For instance, a perfect summer romance would be complemented by perfect summer weather—warm and full of sunlight. A troubled romance, on the other hand, might be set against cool weather and summer storms. The atmosphere of a work—bright, happy, humorous, blue, somber, tense, depressing (the list of adjectives goes on endlessly)—is produced by the combination of characters, their actions, and the setting in time and place. In "The Short Happy Life of Francis Macomber," for example, the atmosphere is tense, dangerous, and filled with hatred because of the personalities of Francis and Margaret Macomber and Robert Wilson, because of their dangerous hunting and their personal conflicts, and because of the African jungle environment. Each piece of fiction is permeated by a mood or atmosphere appropriate to the plot, the characters, and the setting.

Setting and Character

A third function of setting is to reveal a character's personality and values. Just as the places where you spend your time (your room, the lounge or the library at school, the hangout you choose) might reveal some interesting things about your personality, so, too, the places where fictional characters choose to spend their time are revealing. For example, when Sylvia, the narrator in Toni Cade Bambara's short story "The Lesson,"[1] states that she would rather "go to the Sunset and terrorize the West Indian kids and take their hair ribbons and their money too" (88) than go on a shopping trip with Miss Moore, she reveals that she is tough and hardened, just like the ghetto she lives in. She has to be in order to survive. Similarly, when we learn that Montresor, in Poe's "The Cask of Amontillado," has been spending time in the deep and dark catacombs of his family to prepare for his murder of Fortunato, we also learn of the deeper and darker side of Montresor's personality. He is truly an evil and cunning man.

Included in this area of revealing setting is a character's job or occupation. For example, Sammy's job as a checker in John Updike's short story "A & P" reveals his attitudes toward people. Sammy supports the idea that people are more important than policy, and so he quits his job over a clash in these values because he realizes that he must be an individual and act upon his beliefs. Robert Wilson's occupation as a safari leader in Hemingway's "The Short Happy Life of Francis Macomber" reveals his brave, courageous attitudes toward life and death. Only a man who understands life and who has made his peace with death could face danger so calmly each day. Authors usually place their characters in settings and in occupations that will reveal their personalities and the things that are important to them.

Setting, Character, and the Journey Motif

A fourth function of setting is to show changes in a character, so it is important to note when a character moves from one setting to another in a literary work. This physical movement, often in the form of a journey, usually signifies a psychological change in the character as well. For example, in "Araby" by James Joyce, the narrator, looking back on his past, describes his infatuation with his friend's sister. At the end of the story, he takes a train to Araby, a bazaar, to buy her a present, but while there, he realizes the vanity of his quest and becomes more realistic about relationships. The physical journey, then, parallels the narrator's mental journey from illusion to reality. In "The Short Happy Life of Francis Macomber," Hemingway takes Macomber on a journey to Africa where his fears become more concrete in the presence of the life-threatening lion and the wounded buffalo. When he can face them, he

---

[1] From *Gorilla, My Love* (New York: Random, 1972). Used by permission of Random House.

realizes that he can also face his fear of his wife and his fear of death, and he finally achieves maturity years after his twenty-first birthday. Whenever characters are on the move, consider the possibility that they could also be journeying from innocence to experience, from indecision to decision, from immaturity to maturity.

Setting and Theme

A fifth function of setting is to help communicate the theme or message in the work. The author of a work can communicate his ideas and attitudes about life by presenting the setting in particular ways. In the short story "A & P," John Updike presents his ideas about people who inhabit small conservative towns in the East. By describing the town, the A & P, and its shoppers (all a part of the setting) with details that reveal their conservative attitudes and their routine behavior patterns, he shows the power of tradition and its influence on thought and action. In "August 2026: There Will Come Soft Rains," Ray Bradbury uses setting to communicate his ideas about man's future and how—if he is not careful—his own technology will destroy him in a nuclear holocaust. When authors *repeat* details of setting, when they *emphasize* certain details, and when they note *unusual aspects* of setting, they are probably trying to convey an idea related to the theme in the work.

Setting and Symbolism

Setting can function on a symbolic level. A place can have two levels of meaning in a work—the literal and the symbolic—so that the author can emphasize or clarify certain ideas. In *The Old Man and the Sea*, the sea is a symbol for life—as water often is—so Hemingway can show that just as Santiago is undefeated in his struggle with the marlin, man is undefeated if he hangs on in life, if he never gives up the fight for whatever he prizes. D. H. Lawrence in "The Horse Dealer's Daughter" brings the characters of Mabel and Jack together in a pond (another water symbol) where Jack rescues her from suicide. Both characters go under the pond for a time, and when they rise from the water, they are changed people. They are reborn and discover passion they did not know existed before this life-changing baptismal experience. Where things happen, then, is as significant as what happens, so be sure to note these details of setting as you read and study a work.

Setting and Unity

Setting can also help to unify a work. The beginning and the ending of a literary work are places where authors express significant ideas they want us to consider. When a work opens with a focus on a particular aspect of setting and ends with the same emphasis, the author wants us to notice the unifying return to the beginning and to consider its significance. Tillie Olsen begins the short story "I Stand Here Ironing"[2] with those exact words and ends with the image of a dress "on the ironing board, helpless before the iron" (12). Between those opening and closing words, the first person narrator, an unnamed mother, describes her efforts to provide care for her first child, Emily. Now nineteen, Emily has survived very difficult life experiences and has developed her own defense—comedy—against the pain. By beginning and ending with the ironing setting, Olsen is suggesting that human beings are not helpless—like the dress—before the scorching power of life; they can choose to defy it, even to laugh at it. Her repetition of setting unifies the work and brings the reader full circle, back to the beginning, where the mother is engaged in an activity that shows the care and love she has for her family.

❧ Focusing on Setting

Try to observe the functions of setting and their implications as you read any work of literature. You will find that some writers rely heavily on setting to bring life to their work, while others include few

---

[2] In *Tell Me a Riddle* (New York: Dell, 1961) 1–12.

details of setting. The difference has to do with the writer's overall purpose, with what he or she is trying to achieve in the work. Note how Edgar Allan Poe uses setting to help achieve the effect of terror in his short story "The Fall of the House of Usher."[3]

> The room in which I found myself was very large and lofty. The windows were long, narrow, and pointed, and at so vast a distance from the black oaken floor as to be altogether inaccessible from within. Feeble gleams of encrimsoned light made their way through the trellised panes, and served to render sufficiently distinct the more prominent objects around; the eye, however, struggled in vain to reach the remoter angles of the chamber, or the recesses of the vaulted and fretted ceiling. Dark draperies hung upon the walls. The general furniture was profuse, comfortless, antique, and tattered. Many books and musical instruments lay scattered about, but failed to give any vitality to the scene. I felt that I breathed an atmosphere of sorrow. An air of stern, deep, and irredeemable gloom hung over and pervaded all (249).

From this detailed description of Roderick Usher's room—the "inaccessible" windows, "the black floor," the "feeble gleams of encrimsoned light," and "the dark draperies"—it is highly probable that unusual events could occur here. This room in an old decaying mansion stirs memories of Gothic horror and prepares us for the return of Roderick's twin, Madeline, from her cataleptic trance and then their falling dead together. The atmosphere, one of "sorrow" and "gloom," provides a fitting background for grief, despair, and death. It is obvious that Roderick has been deeply depressed; he is no longer involved with his "books and musical instruments," and he does not care about his "comfortless" surroundings. These details of setting and their relationship to Roderick's mental state convey the theme that a person's surroundings often reflect that person's attitudes and values. The confusion of furniture, books, and musical instruments suggests the confused and preoccupied mental state that Roderick is experiencing.

This brief excerpt from Poe's story is composed of what most readers refer to as description, and many skip such sections to get to the plot, the action. But when you stop to analyze the implications of this information, you can see how important setting really is. The great fictional detective Sherlock Holmes could look at a man's setting and deduce a great deal of information about him. You can do the same if, as you read, you try to detect the details that relate to time and place in a work: they can tell you about the likelihood of certain events occurring, about the emotional background, about the characters and their psychological state, and even about the author's theme.

❧ Writing about Setting: Step by Step

When preparing to write an essay which describes the functions of setting in a work of literature, simply follow these steps:

1. The best way to begin is to reread the work, carefully marking the details of setting that the narrator has described. Some works will contain only a few references to setting, while others will include many details, and certain works will be almost entirely setting. The best stories to choose for setting analysis, of course, would fall into the last two categories.
2. Once you have marked the details of setting, try to relate them to one or more of the functions of setting as you prepare to formulate your thesis:
    a. setting increases the probability of certain events occurring in the work;
    b. setting produces an appropriate mood or background for the action of the plot;
    c. setting reveals a character's personality and values;
    d. setting reveals a change in a character through the journey motif;

---

[3] Edgar Allan Poe, "The Fall of the House of Usher," *Edgar Allan Poe* (New York: Viking, 1945). All parenthetical page numbers refer to this text.

 e. setting helps to communicate the theme(s) in the work;

 f. setting brings out additional levels of meaning through the use of symbolism;

 g. setting helps to unify the work.

The function(s) that you choose to write about will form your thesis statement, and when ordering them in your thesis, always try to work from the least significant to the most significant to achieve climactic order.

3. In writing the body paragraphs, remember that the analysis of the quotes related to setting is the most important part of your essay. Try to show the reader *how* the quotes you've chosen illustrate, prove, clarify the function of setting you're writing about. If, for instance, you state that setting reveals personality and then after a brief context you quote a description of a character's home, you must explain *how* the house reveals the owner's personality, values, and interests. What would a person seeing the house infer about the owner? What character traits are revealed by the style of the house, its furnishings, or its lack of them? Remember that the depth of your analysis is important because it shows your understanding of the concepts involved in literary analysis. Thinking like a psychiatrist and a detective when you write your analysis should help. What things would they infer about a character from looking around his home?

4. In the conclusion, emphasizing the importance of setting and the significant functions of setting that you have analyzed will effectively and successfully restate your thesis, thereby unifying your essay and bringing your reader full circle.

The following diagram, model essays, and plan sheet will help you prepare to write a thoroughly developed and well supported essay on setting in a work of literature.

Title

Introductory Paragraph:

Open with interesting lead material.

Name the work and the author.

Give a brief summary of the work and a brief description of the setting in time and place.

Emphasize the importance of the setting and begin to narrow your focus to the thesis statement which is a list of the functions of setting which you plan to analyze in the body of the essay. (Remember that the functions of setting are to increase probability, to produce an appropriate atmosphere, to reveal personality, to communicate theme, to add symbolic meaning, and to unify the work).

Body Paragraphs:

In the first part of the body, discuss the first function of setting by beginning with a topic sentence which clearly states the function. Lead into a quotation by giving a brief introduction, quote details related to setting, and then analyze the quotation in relation to the function of setting you are proving. Repeat this pattern as often as necessary to thoroughly discuss the first function of setting.

Analyze the second function of setting in the second part of the body. The topic sentence names the function, and it is followed by introductory information for a quotation, the quotation itself to support the topic sentence, and thorough analysis of the quoted excerpt. This literary analysis pattern should be used frequently to build solid body paragraphs.

Discuss the third function of setting in the third part of the body. This part should be developed like the first two, but it should be even stronger since the last function of setting should be the most significant and the last body paragraph fills a position of strength and importance.

If you listed additional functions of setting in your thesis, discuss them by using the pattern outlined above, thoroughly developing your analysis sections.

Concluding Paragraph:

Use a signal word (i.e., and so, then, thus) in the first part of the conclusion to let the reader know that you are coming to the end of your discussion. Then summarize the functions of setting that you have analyzed and emphasize their significance in the work as a whole.

Model Essay One

The first student-written essay analyzes setting in a short story.

A Perfect Place for Murder

Committing the perfect crime requires a lot of planning. One must choose the perfect time and the perfect place—the perfect setting—if the crime is to go unsolved. This is what Montresor accomplishes in Edgar Allan Poe's "The Cask of Amontillado"[1] when he murders Fortunato, a man who had committed a "thousand injuries" (158) against him, for revenge. *Montresor's choice of setting—carnival time and the catacombs in his own home—heightens the probability of his getting away with his crime and provides the perfect atmosphere for his terrible deed.*

Thesis Statement

Topic Sentence

To increase the probability that he will not be caught, Montresor carefully picks the right time to carry out his murderous plan. That is why he chooses "dusk, one evening during the supreme madness of the carnival season" (159). The coming darkness makes it difficult to see others clearly, and the fact that the revelers are wearing costumes makes it even more difficult to identify those who are present. Fortunato has on "a tight-fitting parti-striped dress, and his head [is] surmounted by the conical cap and bells" (159). Fortunato's costume—dressed as he is as a clown or fool—is ironically appropriate for he is about to be fooled by Montresor's plan of tempting him with the opportunity to taste a rare but nonexistent Amontillado. This deception is made even easier to carry out because Fortunato "had been drinking much" (159). His ability to judge whether Montresor is telling the truth about the Amontillado is compromised by the alcohol he has consumed. He clearly states, "'I have my doubts,'" but he urges Montresor to take him to the place where Montresor plans to murder him. Montresor, who is dressed in a short cloak and is wearing "a mask of black silk" (160), goes off with his willing victim, and both are hard to identify as they approach Montresor's palazzo.

Topic Sentence

The setting for the murder—the catacombs under Montresor's palazzo—also increases the probability that Montresor's murderous actions will go undetected. To make sure that he and Fortunato will not be seen together in his home, Montresor eliminates all possible witnesses by telling his servants not to leave the house, and then he brags about his cleverness: "These orders were sufficient, I well knew, to insure their immediate disappearance, one and all, as soon as my back was turned" (160). Montresor now has the place to himself. No one has seen him arrive with his victim, so no one would ever suspect that the missing Fortunato could be in Montresor's palazzo. When they enter, they go down "a long and winding staircase" which leads to "the damp ground of the catacombs of the Montresors" (160). The burial place of past generations of Montresor's family is lined with "walls of piled bones, with casks and puncheons intermingling" (161). The two men are now in an area where few visitors are taken

[1] In *An Introduction to Literature*, ed. Slyvan Barnet, Morton Berman, and William Burto, 10th ed. (New York: Harper, 1993) 158–164.

and where a few more bones will not be suspect. The presence of the casks reassures Fortunato that the object of their search—the Amontillado—is growing near. The victim is totally unsuspecting, falling nicely into Montresor's trap.

Topic Sentence

The catacombs provide the perfect atmosphere for Montresor's diabolical plan. Below ground, the "cavern walls" are covered with "white webwork" (16) created by the foul air at that depth. Montresor and Fortunato are "below the river's bed" where the nitre "hangs like moss upon the vaults" (161). The eerie scene is a perfect place for a murder; there is little air and so little light that it is hard to see: "It was in vain that Fortunato, uplifting his dull torch, endeavored to pry into the depths of the recess. Its termination the feeble light did not enable [him] to see" (162). Fortunato does not realize that he is walking into his tomb, a grave-sized recess surrounded by "walls of solid granite" to which Montresor chains him (162). It is not long before Fortunato is entombed alive, and when Montresor throws "a torch through the remaining aperture" and then forces "the last stone into its position," (164), Fortunato's death by suffocation is assured. Montresor has chosen the perfect place for carrying out his revenge since "for the half of a century no mortal has disturbed" (160) Fortunato's bones.

Restatement of Thesis

Montresor, then, has chosen an appropriate setting for a perfect crime. The timing of the murder with the carnival makes it easy for him to hide his identity and to remove any possible witnesses from his home, and the death-filled atmosphere of the catacombs is an appropriate backdrop for his vengeful murder of Fortunato. Montresor understands that the time and place of any action seriously affect the quality of the outcome. The setting is the secret.

Robert Ditta

Model Essay Two

The following student-written essay contrasts two different settings in Ernest Hemingway's novel *A Farewell to Arms*.

Life and Death

Ernest Hemingway uses setting very effectively in his novel *A Farewell to Arms*.[1] In a contrast of Books One and Five, it is easy to see how setting is a powerful tool in literature for conveying ideas. In Book One, the central character, Frederic Henry, is introduced as an ambulance driver at the Italian-Austrian front during World War I. There he lives the life of a sol-

[1] Reprinted with permission of Charles Scribner's Sons, an imprint of Macmillan Publishing Company from A FAREWELL TO ARMS by Ernest Hemingway. Copyright 1929 by Charles Scribner's Sons, renewed 1957 by Ernest Hemingway. All parenthetical page numbers refer to the text in this edition.

dier, not really caring about morality or anything other than himself. He meets a nurse named Catherine Barkley who, at first, is just another conquest for him. And, as in all wars, there are death and destruction; Frederic himself is seriously wounded in the leg. However, in Book Five, Frederic and Catherine, in love and awaiting the birth of their child, live on a mountain side in Switzerland, where the war is far away and all they have to do is love each other. But even in Switzerland there is death. *Hemingway clearly creates two different atmospheres and reveals different aspects of Frederic's personality with the use of setting; however, both situations emphasize the same theme: no matter how one lives his life, death is inevitable, and it can happen at any time; what matters is not the duration of life, but rather the quality of life.*

Thesis Statement

Topic Sentence

In Book One, the setting creates a wartime atmosphere filled with destruction and turmoil. The town of Gorizia, Italy, after a summer of fighting, is changed by the war: "The forest had been green in the summer when we had come into the town but now there were stumps and broken trunks and the ground torn up . . ." (6). War is destructive to nature; it turns something that is beautiful into something that is dead and gloomy. It will probably be many years before the Gorizian forest in all its beauty comes alive again. The turbulence of war can also be felt in the way Frederic is awakened while at the front: "The battery in the next garden woke me in the morning. . . . I could not see the guns but they were evidently firing directly over us" (15). To be awakened by guns going off outside a window must be a very stressful situation. During war, soldiers live, sleep, and get up to its sounds. Frederic is experiencing first hand the chaotic, destructive, and depressing atmosphere of war.

Topic Sentence

In contrast, the setting in Book Five creates an atmosphere that is calm and romantic. In Montreux, Switzerland, where the war is far away, nature still thrives: "Out on the lake there were flocks of grebes, small and dark, leaving trails in the water when they swam" (292). This is how life should be—peaceful and beautiful; in this setting, the joy of life can be seen and felt. Also in contrast to Book One, the way in which Frederic is awakened in the morning shows a totally different atmosphere. In Book Five, the only thing that wakes him is the peaceful silence of falling snow: "We [Frederic and Catherine] stayed in bed with the fire roaring in the stove and watched the snow" (296). This is romance at its best. Is there a better place to wake up in the morning than in a cabin on the side of a Swiss mountain during a winter storm? The beautiful and loving atmosphere of Book Five and the ugly and hateful atmosphere of Book One are both achieved through the use of setting.

Topic Sentence

As Frederic's setting changes, so does his character. The changes in Frederic, from a proud and self-centered soldier in Book One to a peaceful and loving civilian in Book Five, are obvious with the changes in his surroundings. In Book One, from the furnishings in Frederic's room, it is clear that he is a soldier: "my things hung on the wall, the gas mask . . . the steel helmet. . . . My Austrian sniper's rifle with . . . the lovely dark walnut, cheek-fitted, *schutzen* stock . . ." (11). What is more proper in the room of a soldier than instruments of war? Frederic's guns and his equipment are probably the most important possessions he has, and the fact that he displays them indicates that he possesses them with pride, a true virtue of a soldier. Soldiers, however, also have another quality: with the threat of death forever hanging over their heads, they are often very selfish. Frederic displays this trait when he first begins a relationship with Catherine: "This was better than going every evening to the house for officers where the girls climbed all over you. . . . I knew I did not love Catherine Barkley nor had any idea of loving her. This was a game . . ." (30). He gives no second thought to Catherine as a human being—he sees her only as an object that can keep him satisfied. Frederic sees sex and love as a game that he plans to win. In an atmosphere of war, he is a typical soldier.

Topic Sentence   *In Book Five, however, in the tranquility of Switzerland, Frederic is a different person.* Here he is peaceful and loving. Even the furnishings in Frederic and Catherine's room are much more homey: "The small room with the stove was our living room. There were two comfortable chairs and a table for books and magazines" (290). Gone now is the need for guns; all Frederic needs is to be with Catherine to feel secure. Without the danger of war threatening him at every corner, he can enjoy peaceful civilian life. Again, Frederic's attitude toward Catherine changes significantly with the setting. His words to her make it clear he is now in love with her: "'I'm no good when you're not there. I haven't any life at all any more'" (300). Frederic loves Catherine so much that he has become one with her. If he were to be without her, he would not be whole. This is a drastic change from when he was independently selfish. It is not unusual for a person to change when his environment changes, and Frederic certainly has changed with his.

Topic Sentence   *Hemingway also uses setting to communicate his theme that since life will inevitably end in death, the length of life is not of the utmost importance because it cannot be controlled; therefore, efforts should be made to improve the quality of life.* In the wartime setting of Book One, there is always death. Soldiers die in battle as Passini, an ambulance driver, did. Frederic knew that "there was no need to try and make a tourniquet because he was dead already" (55). Scenes like this are all too common in war, yet death from a less violent cause is also suffered abundantly because disease is prevalent, too. In the late fall one year during this war, cholera struck, "but it was checked and in the end only seven thousand died of it in the army" (4). How can there be anything but misery in war when suffering is so common? It is expected that with war comes death, but in war, there is no glory. The people are not happy; Passini sums it up when he says, "'It could not be worse'" (50). If death comes when there is no happiness in life, then life is useless.

Topic Sentence   *However, every situation of life will end in death, even in the romantic setting of Book Five.* Catherine has a difficult time giving birth, and the baby, a boy, is born dead. The doctors "'couldn't start him breathing. The cord was caught around his neck . . .'" (327). The baby never has the chance to experience the joy of life the way Catherine has, but she still suffers the same fate as the baby when she hemorrhages. Frederic "went into the room and stayed with Catherine until she died" (331). Life that is cut off at its peak is better than life that never reaches its peak. At least Catherine's life had some meaning; she and Frederic were happy for a time, and they both believed they "had a fine life" (306). It seems so much more positive to die while experiencing happiness than to die in misery, and that is exactly what Hemingway is trying to say. By showing Frederic's closeness to death in two different settings, Hemingway is showing that even though the death of Catherine and the baby has a much more personal impact on Frederic, the short happy time he spent with her is much more meaningful than all the time he spent without her.

Restatement of Thesis

And so, by contrasting the setting of Books One and Five, we can see how significant setting can be in a literary work. The atmosphere, the personalities of the characters, and the theme are emphasized by Hemingway's effective use of setting. He put Frederic Henry into two different life-and-death situations to give us the opportunity to see how someone reacts to these situations. Even though Frederic escaped death in war, he could not escape death altogether. But did it not make more sense for him to choose the life that made him the happiest? How many of us can honestly say that if we were to die tomorrow, our lives have been as we have wanted? Are we miserable like the people in Book One, or are we happy like Frederic and Catherine in Book Five? Hemingway tells us that we had better choose happiness and make the most of our lives because we do not know if we will be here tomorrow.

Tracy Rodriguez

Model Essay Three

This student-written essay analyzes three functions of setting in the following poem by James Dickey.

Cherrylog Road[1]

Off Highway 106
At Cherrylog Road I entered
The '34 Ford without wheels,
Smothered in kudzu,
With a seat pulled out to run   5
Corn whiskey down from the hills,

And then from the other side
Crept into an Essex
With a rumble seat of red leather
And then out again, aboard   10
A blue Chevrolet, releasing
The rust from its other color,

---

[1] James Dickey "Cherrylog Road" from *James Dickey Poems* 1957–1967, Wesleyan UP by permission of UP of New England.

Reared up on three building blocks.
None had the same body heat;
I changed with them inward, toward   15
The weedy heart of the junkyard,
For I knew that Doris Holbrook
Would escape from her father at noon

And would come from the farm
To seek parts owned by the sun   20
Among the abandoned chassis
Sitting in each in turn
As I did, leaning forward
As in a wild stock-car race

In the parking lot of the dead.   25
Time after time, I climbed in
And out the other side, like
An envoy or movie star
Met at the station by crickets.
A radiator cap raised its head,   30

Become a real toad or a kingsnake
As I neared the hub of the yard,
Passing through many states,
Many lives, to reach
Some grandmother's long Pierce-Arrow   35
Sending platters of blindness forth

From its nickel hubcaps
And spilling its tender upholstery
On sleepy roaches,
The glass panel in between   40
Lady and colored driver
Not all the way broken out,

The back-seat phone
Still on its hook.
I got in as though to exclaim,   45
"Let us go to the orphan asylum,
John; I have some old toys
For children who say their prayers."

I popped with sweat as I thought
I heard Doris Holbrook scrape   50
Like a mouse in the southern-state sun
That was eating the paint in blisters
From a hundred car tops and hoods.
She was tapping like code,

Loosening the screws,
Carrying off headlights,
Sparkplugs, bumpers,
Cracked mirrors and gear-knobs,
Getting ready, already,
To go back with something to show   60

Other than her lips' new trembling
I would hold to me soon, soon,
Where I sat in the ripped back seat
Talking over the interphone,
Praying for Doris Holbrook   65
To come from her father's farm

And to get back there
With no trace of me on her face
To be seen by her red-haired father
Who would change, in the squalling barn,   70
Her back's pale skin with a strop,
Then lay for me

In a bootlegger's roasting car
With a string-triggered 12-gauge shotgun
To blast the breath from the air.   75
Not cut by the jagged windshields,
Through the acres of wrecks she came
With a wrench in her hand,

Through dust where the blacksnake dies
Of boredom, and the beetle knows   80
The compost has no more life.
Someone outside would have seen
The oldest car's door inexplicably
Close from within:

I held her and held her and held her,   85
Convoyed at terrific speed
By the stalled, dreaming traffic around us,
So the blacksnake, stiff
With inaction, curved back
Into life, and hunted the mouse   90

With deadly overexcitement,
The beetles reclaimed their field
As we clung, glued together,
With the hooks of the seat springs
Working through to catch us red-handed   95
Amidst the gray breathless batting

That burst from the seat at our backs.
We left by separate doors
Into the changed, other bodies
Of cars, she down Cherrylog Road   100
And I to my motorcycle
Parked like the soul of the junkyard

Restored, a bicycle fleshed
With power, and tore off
Up Highway 106, continually   105
Drunk on the wind in my mouth,
Wringing the handlebar for speed,
Wild to the wreckage forever.

                                         1963

Digging for Gold

Setting is a word that is used to describe when and where a specific event takes place. It looks like a verb but functions as a noun. It looks like it would be a simple thing to describe, but its function is so amazingly complex that a myriad of tomes could not do it justice. Nowhere is this mixture of simplicity and complexity more evident than in the poem "Cherrylog Road" by James Dickey. Simply put, the action is a forbidden rendezvous between young lovers; the setting is an abandoned junkyard, sometime in the speaker's past. However, both the action and the setting are much more complex. The action includes the speaker's rite of passage, and the setting is crucial to how he perceives himself and the world around him. He sees himself as an adventurer, tempting fate as he crosses the threshold to maturity. He sees the junkyard as alive, crawling. It crawls with memories and ghosts, fear and anticipation, reptiles and vermin, rot and decay. Each detail of the lush, jungle-like setting has been burned into the speaker's brain, as if by the blazing North Georgia sun. *The setting works on both the*

Thesis Statement *simple and complex levels. It functions at the simplest level by providing an appropriate spot for the secret rendezvous. Its complexity becomes evident as it helps to reveal the speaker's love of danger and to communicate Dickey's theme that an active imagination intensifies experience.*

Topic Sentence *At the simplest level, the setting provides an appropriate place for the action of the plot, a forbidden rendezvous.* It is "Off Highway 106 / At Cherrylog Road" (lines 1–2), suggesting that the junkyard is in an out-of-the-way spot. Most state routes or highways are called by a street name as they go through a town. It is only as they pass through open country that they are referred to by number. Surely, lovers would like such an out-of-the-way spot to meet. Once inside, the speaker moves "toward / The weedy heart of the junkyard" (15–16). By moving to the center of the yard, the chances of the lovers' being seen by anyone from the road are greatly reduced, and the overgrown nature of the junkyard implies that it is not regularly visited by either customer or scavenger. As Doris crosses the junkyard to join the speaker, she removes parts from the wrecks, "Getting ready, already, / To go back with something to show" (59–60). By meeting in the junkyard, Doris is supplied with a perfect alibi should her father become suspicious. She need only show him the bits and pieces that she has collected to explain her absence from home. Dickey has found the perfect place for the lovers to meet. It is out of the way, deserted, and provides an alibi for Doris.

Topic Sentence   *In a more complex way, the setting helps reveal the speaker's love of danger.* Crossing to the center of the junkyard to wait for Doris, he slowly moves from car to car, "Sitting in each in turn / . . . leaning forward / As in a wild stock-car race" (22–24). Not content to imagine the power and speed of the cars, he compounds the risk by imagining himself in a wild competition with others. By pretending to be in a stock-car race, he uses the setting to show his love of danger. His love of danger next surfaces as he describes Doris's father. Portrayed as a hard man, short of temper and prone to physical violence, the father poses a threat to both Doris and the speaker. Should they be found out, he would take a strop to Doris:

> Then lay for [the speaker]
> In a bootlegger's roasting car
> With a string-triggered 12-gauge shotgun
> To blast the breath from the air. (72–75)

Since there is no reason to doubt the threat that Doris's father poses, one must wonder why the speaker would take such a risk. He professes no love for Doris, and there must be other girls to choose from; therefore, one can logically assume that some measure of his fascination with her is due to the threat that her father poses. This threat, coupled with the presence of the father that he deliberately conjures up as he listens for Doris, adds to his sense of excitement. The longer he dwells on the frightening image of the father, the more excited he becomes. He is young, vibrant, staring danger straight in the face. The wrecks have lost their battle with life, but he will win his. And should he lose, he would rather be blasted from this earth by the gun-wielding father than to merely sit and rot, like the wrecks in the junkyard. The surrounding death and decay act as a perfect foil to the speaker and emphasize his love of danger. Later, after completion of the sexual act, he leaves the junkyard on his motorcycle: "Drunk on the wind in my mouth / Wringing the handlebar for speed / Wild to be wreckage forever" (106–108). Riding a motorcycle in itself gives hint to the adventurous spirit of the speaker. But he purposely adds more risk to the situation. Whether he is intoxicated by the sex, his sense of power, or life itself is unclear. What is clear is that he is deliberately adding danger to the situation by tearing off at breakneck speed while fully aware of the possible consequences. In fact, he seems to be tempting fate by inviting it to make him a permanent part of the junkyard, to unite him with the setting.

Topic Sentence   *Finally, Dickey has combined the simplicity of the setting and the complexity of the human mind to communicate the theme that any experience can be enriched by an active imagination.* Crossing the abandoned junkyard becomes a memorable experience for the speaker. He proceeds slowly; he pauses often. Entering car after car, he changes "with them inward" (15). Just as surely as the cars are changing, are rusting and rotting from the ravages of time and the elements, he is changing. He compares the inevitability of his change, his growth, his maturation, to the changes he sees in the cars. Through imagination, the setting has helped him to better understand that the changes within him are unavoidable, just as the changes in the cars are unavoidable. Nearing the heart of the junkyard, he does not see himself climbing in and out of rusting cars that crawl with insects. Instead, he sees himself as "An envoy or movie star / Met at the station by crickets" (28–29). He enhances his experience by imagining himself to be a celebrity and the insects to be his entourage. An active imagination has allowed him to use his environment to form a positive mental image of himself. But nowhere is his imagination used to enrich an experience more obvious than in the sexual encounter. Here, again, he uses the wildlife to his advantage:

> So the blacksnake, stiff
> With inaction, curved back
> Into life, and hunted the mouse
> With deadly overexcitement. (88–91)

The speaker fantasizes during the climactic sexual act. He is the hunter; Doris is the prey. He is the victor; Doris is the victim. By giving free rein to his imagination, he has used the setting to intensify his enjoyment of the sexual act. By identifying with the setting, he is able to go beyond physical gratification and satisfy his deeper emotional needs as well.

Restatement of Thesis

And so it is obvious that Dickey has found the perfect setting for "Cherrylog Road." It works on all levels. *Its simplest function is to provide an out-of-the-way spot that insures secrecy for the lovers. Its more complex function is to allow the reader a glimpse into the speaker's personality and his love of danger. But its most important contribution is to communicate the theme that any experience can be enhanced by an active imagination.* Through skillful choice and masterful use of setting, Dickey has created a poem that masquerades as a simple narrative. But, in reality, it is a complex poem that offers the insightful reader much more. Reading "Cherrylog Road" is like digging for gold. The more you scratch the surface, the more you find.

Sandy Walshon

JUST ONE MORE THING

Just as setting can add levels of meaning to a short story, novel, poem, or play, setting also adds to the visual effectiveness of films as the success of movies like *Titanic* and *Saving Private Ryan* so powerfully illustrate. The time and place provide powerful backdrops for moving and memorable action.

❧❧ **Setting Analysis Essay Plan Sheet** ❧❧

Author: _____ Title: _____

Thesis:_____

_____

_____

_____

_____

Topic sentence: _____

_____

_____

           Supporting quote: page or line _____

           Supporting quote: page or line _____

           Supporting quote: page or line _____

Topic sentence: _____

_____

_____

           Supporting quote: page or line _____

           Supporting quote: page or line _____

           Supporting quote: page or line _____

Topic sentence: _____

_____

_____

           Supporting quote: page or line _____

           Supporting quote: page or line _____

           Supporting quote: page or line _____

Topic sentence: _____

_____

_____

Supporting quote: page or line _____

Supporting quote: page or line _____

Supporting quote: page or line _____

Topic sentence: _____

_____

_____

Supporting quote: page or line _____

Supporting quote: page or line _____

Supporting quote: page or line _____

Topic sentence: _____

_____

_____

Supporting quote: page or line _____

Supporting quote: page or line _____

Supporting quote: page or line _____

Concluding points: _____

_____

_____

_____

_____

_____

_____

❧ Peer/Self-Evaluation of a Setting Analysis Essay ❧

> **Directions:** Make specific suggestions about each part of the essay, pointing out particular areas that the writer could improve. Keep in mind the qualities of good writing: unity, organization, development, clarity, and coherence.

I. Introduction

Is the lead relevant and interesting?

Are the author's full name and the title of the work correctly spelled and punctuated?

Does the brief plot summary include a description of the setting in time and place?

Does the thesis state the functions of setting that will be discussed in the body paragraphs?

II. Body Paragraphs

Do the topic sentences contain the functions of setting listed in the thesis?

Are the supporting quotations properly introduced?

Are the supporting quotations relevant to the setting?

Are the analysis sections adequately developed?

Do the body paragraphs follow the order of the thesis?

Are the body paragraphs unified and coherent?

III. Conclusion

Is a signal word included somewhere in the paragraph?

Does the summary rephrase the functions of setting listed in the thesis?

Is the significance of the setting stated and explained?

Is the final sentence an effective clincher?

IV. Expression

Are all the ideas expressed in complete sentences?

Are the sentences clear and correctly punctuated?

Are there any problems with subject-verb or pronoun-antecedent agreement?

Are all the words correctly spelled?

V. Overall Evaluation

Most effective part of the essay:

Least effective part of the essay:

List three specific actions which could be taken by the writer to improve this and future papers:
1.

2.

3.

Evaluator's name: _____ Date: _____

❧ Exercise on Setting ❧

Complete the following chart by describing the probable personality traits and personal values of characters in the following settings or occupations.

Setting/Occupation	Personality Traits	Personal Values
A plastic-covered living room		
A cluttered, messy living room		
A dark bedroom cluttered by scattered books and musical instruments		
A bar or lounge		
A college classroom		
A job as a bank clerk		
A career as a doctor		
A career as a rock star		

In what place and time and with what characters would the following incidents be likely to occur? What would be an appropriate atmosphere or background? Be as specific as you can.

Incident	Setting	Characters	Atmosphere
A brief but passionate love affair			
A clash between liberal and conservative values			
A family crisis			
A violent murder			
A moral struggle about religious beliefs			
A transition from adolescence to maturity			

Theme Analysis

Overview

Literature is a record of the joys and sorrows of being human. It embodies ideas about the human condition, and these ideas are identified by the term "theme." When we grasp the meaning of a work (the author's insights into life, the themes), we have enlarged our own sensibilities; we have grown from a shared literary experience.

An Explanation of Theme

Literature has two major purposes: to entertain and to instruct. We are entertained as we become involved with the characters and their situations. We want to know what happens next, and when we think about the plot outcome, we forget about our own problems and temporarily escape our own reality. Instruction emerges as we watch the people in the work solve their conflicts and as we learn from their experiences. An effective work makes us think about life, for the author wants us to consider his insights into our common experiences. These insights or ideas are the *themes* in the work. They are not morals designed to teach us how to conduct our lives; they are ideas that make us think about life and about our values, and any time we evaluate our own philosophy of life, we become more aware of who we are and of what life means.

Theme can also be explained as the central idea or the unifying idea in a work, and in that sense, it is directly connected to the general subject of the work. If the work is a love story, the theme probably relates to love in some way. If the author is writing a war story, he or she obviously wants us to think about war and its relationship to human life. But theme is more than just a summary of what the story, poem, or play is about. The theme is a statement about life in general that we infer from the particular events in the work as a whole. If the work is long, complex, and rich in ideas, it probably contains multiple themes that make us think about many different aspects of the human condition.

For example, Hemingway's "The Short Happy Life of Francis Macomber" is not just a story about a rich American killed while on safari in Africa. When we understand that Hemingway is saying something about everyone's life in his story, then we can universalize his characters and their situations. He is writing about Francis and his efforts to deal with his doubts and fears, but he is also writing about all of us who haven't learned how to face our fears, how to face life. He is writing about Francis' coming of age, but he is also writing about all of us who can master fear through courage. When he defines the "short" (courageous) "life" of Francis as happy, he is communicating his theme through his definition of a happy life—one in which fear is mastered through courage, one in which death is accepted and therefore overcome. When Milton Kaplan compares a love relationship to a dandelion in the poem "Roots," he is telling us that not all loves are good or beautiful or fulfilling, but regardless of their quality, they send their roots deep into our hearts, minds, and memories. And when Tennessee Williams writes about the Wingfield family in his drama *The Glass Menagerie,* he is really writing about all family relationships and how those involved are affected by them.

The theme, then, is a statement about life based on the characters and the events in the work. Discovering the ideas the author wants you to examine can be challenging, but the process is easier if you read the work thoughtfully and carefully. A quick review of How to Read Literature on pages 3–4 will remind you about the key steps in the reading process. Then as you study the work and pay close attention to the details the author includes, your understanding of it will grow, and you will be more likely to find the underlying ideas that relate to the theme(s).

How Themes Emerge in a Work

Theme is a very important part of any work of literature, and as such, it has a shaping influence on many of its parts. Because theme is meaning, it helps to form the underlying structure of a work, so references to theme can often be found in the work's title and subject matter, the setting, the dialogue of the characters, the symbolism, the imagery, and the plot outcomes.

Title and Subject Matter

Often the title of a work and the subject matter it deals with provide good clues to the author's theme. The title of a work is chosen carefully because it is the first thing the reader perceives. We have seen how Hemingway's title "The Short Happy Life of Francis Macomber" focuses our attention on the general subject matter of one man's life which was short but happy. As we read on to discover what Macomber's life was like and why it was short but happy, we are really searching for the main idea or theme in the work. When we learn that Macomber has not always been happy because of his fear of his wife and of life in general, we can see the change that occurs in him as he courageously faces his castrating wife and the double reality of life and death in the charge of a wounded buffalo. We have now arrived at the heart of the story, and we understand the title and the theme almost simultaneously. One is happy, according to Hemingway, when one faces life and all it entails with courage. Even though life is a game that man cannot win, what matters is how he conducts himself while he is being destroyed.

The title of Toni Cade Bambara's short story "The Lesson" also provides a clue to the theme of the story. After reading the title, one wonders what the lesson is about and what is to be learned from it. When we understand that the students are a group of black children from the ghetto who are taken to an exclusive toy store on New York's Fifth Avenue and when we watch them compare their economic position to that of upper-class whites, we learn with them about the tremendous gap between the upper and lower classes in America, and we understand the sense of injustice the children feel. These are some of the ideas or themes that Bambara hints at through the title. It is always a good idea, then, to pay close attention to the title and the overall subject matter of the work when attempting to formulate an expression of the theme.

Setting

One of the functions of setting—the time and place of the story—is to help communicate the author's ideas and attitudes about life. If the setting is carefully and thoroughly described or if details from the description are repeated or given unusual emphasis of any kind, the author could be using setting to help convey his theme in the work. In "Gift of Grass," Alice Adams creates a character named Barbara who works as an interior decorator. The house that she shares with her daughter and second husband has been tastefully decorated in cool blues and greens, and everything is always in order, bringing out Barbara's reserve and her need for perfection. Unfortunately, these personality traits keep her from truly communicating with her daughter who is so confused about her goals in life that she has turned to drugs as an escape. The author's emphasis on this perfect setting helps to bring out the theme that a beautifully decorated house is not a guarantee that it will be a home where "messy" human problems can be dealt with openly and lovingly.

Dialogue

Occasionally an author will have one of the characters in a story make a statement that embodies the main ideas in a work. For example, in John Updike's "A & P,"[1] Sammy, the first person narrator, describes his reactions to his decision to quit his job over the manager's treatment of three girls in the store in their bathing suits by saying, "My stomach kind of fell as I felt how hard the world was going to be to me hereafter" (196). Sammy's realization drives home the theme that standing up for the rights of others demands a willingness to sacrifice and that life is often hard for people who act on their beliefs.

These statements of theme frequently occur at the climax or shortly after that in a work, especially if a character has experienced an epiphany, an insight into life and experience. At the end of "A Good Man Is Hard to Find,"[2] The Misfit says of the grandmother whom he has just shot, "'She would of been a good woman . . . if it had been somebody there to shoot her every minute of her life'" (133). This statement suggests the theme that many people become "good" only when they know they are about to die. If people lived each day as if it were their last, the world would be a more loving place, and a good man would be much easier to find. Theme, then, can be directly expressed by the characters, so pay close attention to what they say, particularly during the climax and resolution of the work. The climax is that moment when the action is most intense, a time when the characters face major decisions or crises or moments of self-discovery. What they do and say in those moments can bring you to the heart of the work, to the central ideas that form the life force of the work. And as the tension resolves and the plot ends, the last lines will in some way focus on a key point that usually unifies the work and emphasizes an idea, a theme.

Symbolism

To make complex or abstract ideas more concrete, some authors use symbolism to communicate their themes. In "The Horse Dealer's Daughter," for example, D. H. Lawrence has Mabel Pervin symbolize an extremely moody and emotional person. At this point in her life, she is irrational and has decided on suicide. The person who saves her from drowning in the pond is Dr. Jack Fergusson, symbolizing the rational man who lacks an emotional life; he, too, is unhappy. By bringing them together at the pond for a symbolic baptism/rebirth and then by having them marry, Lawrence is suggesting through the symbols that we need to have a balance of emotion and reason in our lives and that we need to be whole people to be happy. And so through Mabel and Jack who represent two sides of human nature, Lawrence conveys his theme.

Imagery

Images are words and phrases that appeal to one of our five senses. Authors use them primarily to help us visualize the scene, the characters, or the action so that we can participate in the work more fully.

---

[1] John Updike, "A & P," *Pigeon Feathers and Other Stories*, First ed. (New York: Knopf, 1962). Used by permission of Alfred A. Knopf, Inc. All parenthetical page numbers refer to the text in this edition.

[2] Excerpts from A GOOD MAN IS HARD TO FIND, Copyright © 1953 by Flannery O'Connor and renewed 1981 by Mrs. Regina O'Connor, reprinted by permission of Harcourt, Brace Jovanovich, Inc.

By appealing to our imaginations, images can also help us understand the theme or message in the work. For example, in his poem entitled "Dulce Et Decorum Est," Wilfred Owen uses a cluster of images to depict battle-worn soldiers who are victims of a gas attack. His vivid description of a young soldier's death helps to convey his theme that dying for one's country is not good or sweet but horrifying and tragic. In her work "What's That Smell in the Kitchen," poet Marge Piercy uses images of burnt food, warfare, and leftovers to convey her theme that the housewives of America are beginning to fight back against the neglect and oppression of their husbands and society. By adding up the images, then, you can "sense" what the author is saying about the subject of the work.

Plot Outcomes

Themes also relate to the incidents in the plot, to the plot outcome (a happy or sad resolution of the conflict), to the characters, and to their words and actions. In the drama *The Glass Menagerie*, for example, when Tennessee Williams presents a family problem of what to do with a shy, introverted family member, we know that he is saying something about parents who try to run their children's lives and about personal freedom to choose one's own life style. When Amanda's plan to marry off her daughter fails, we learn that interfering parents can sometimes cause pain and suffering for their children. As we watch Amanda, Laura, and Tom struggle with their problems, we learn about them through their words and actions. We realize that they all find reality painful, and they use escapes to help them cope. Through them we learn that reality can't be changed until it is faced, and so the play ends unhappily, without a real resolution. These themes, in addition to others, permeate the drama as a whole and represent Williams' view of family life as a complex web of personal goals and ambitions entangled with family ties and responsibilities.

Our Response to Themes

As readers, we infer the author's themes and examine his or her views on life, and then we evaluate them in relation to our own lives. If we accept them, they enlarge our own feelings and sensibilities; even if we reject them, they have still helped us clarify our personal views. Through literature, then, we have learned about life and about ourselves. We have been exposed to ideas that we may not have considered before, and while they may not relate to our lives at this point in time, they may help us to understand life better at some point in the future.

❧ Writing about Theme: Step by Step

When preparing to write an essay which analyzes the theme in a work of literature, simply follow these steps:

1. Choose a work that conveys a theme you can agree with, one that perhaps you have experienced in your own life. This will enable you to think more clearly about all possible aspects and ramifications of the theme.
2. Express your ideas about the theme in a sentence or two. This statement is the main part of the thesis; it tells the reader the major insights into life that you plan to explore in your essay.
3. Consider the possible ways that themes emerge in a work and choose the one or ones that best suit the theme you plan to discuss:
   a. the title and subject matter of the work;
   b. the setting in time and place;
   c. the dialogue of the characters at key points in the work;
   d. the symbols that stand for ideas;
   e. the imagery that helps make the ideas more vivid and concrete;
   f. the work as a whole through the plot outcomes.

Your choice is important because it is stated as the second part of your thesis and it determines how the body of your essay will be organized.

4. The body paragraphs relate both to the theme and to the way it emerges in the work. The topic sentence states the aspect of the theme to be developed and generally indicates how it will be illustrated by leading into some introductory information for the supporting quotation to follow. The quotation directly relates to theme development, and the analysis explores the idea about life that is illustrated by the quotation. This pattern of generalization/introductory information for the quotation/the quotation/analysis is used again after a brief transition which carries the reader from one part of the work to another; in fact, the more the pattern is used, the better the body paragraph. Always keep in mind that the last body paragraph is an important one because of its climactic position; as a result, it should be developed in even more detail than the other body paragraphs.

5. The concluding paragraph is a thorough discussion of the theme as it applies to the literary work itself and then to real people who might be in similar circumstances. This focusing on the particular and on the universal aspects of the theme brings home the fact that literature can teach all of us about the joys and sorrows of life. Not only do the characters learn through their experiences—we learn also by sharing them.

The following diagram, model essays, and plan sheet will help you write a well developed essay on theme in a work of literature.

Diagram of the Structure of a Theme Analysis Essay

Title

Introductory Paragraph:

Open with interesting lead material.

Name the work and the author.

Give a brief summary of the work and state the theme to be analyzed.

Indicate how the theme will be traced through the work, i.e., through the thematic significance of the title and subject matter, through the setting, through a specific character or characters and their words and actions in the work, through symbolism or imagery, through a series of related incidents in the plot, usually ordered chronologically, or through any other logical means.

Body Paragraphs:

In the first part of the body, discuss the first aspect of the theme by beginning with a topic sentence which generalizes about the theme. The next few sentences provide background information for the supporting quotation which follows. The analysis should focus on how the theme is revealed and developed through the quotation. Be sure to explore the *ideas about life* that the quotation illustrates. This pattern of generalization/ introductory information for the quotation/the quotation/analysis should be used as much as possible in each paragraph to thoroughly illustrate the theme and its development.

The second part of the body illustrates the next aspect of the theme as stated in the thesis. The topic sentence introduces the theme, and the remainder of the paragraph is developed through introductory statements that lead into direct quotations which are followed by in-depth analysis.

Discuss the remaining parts of the theme's development in the last part of the body. The topic sentences relate to the theme, and then the literary analysis pattern is used. The last paragraph, because of its important position, should be thoroughly developed.

Concluding Paragraph:

Discuss and explain—in detail—the theme which was stated in the introductory paragraph. The topic sentence clearly restates the theme, and the rest of the paragraph summarizes how the theme is revealed in the work and then explores the theme's universal significance. Show how the theme relates to everyone's life because of the universal human condition.

Model Essay One

This student-written essay analyzes theme in a short story.

The Power of Pride

Pride is known as man's greatest sin since it was pride that led to Adam and Eve's fall in the Garden of Eden. It is also the sin of Montresor and Fortunato in Edgar Allan Poe's short story "The Cask of Amontillado."[1] Montresor has been insulted by Fortunato, and his pride leads him to seek revenge. He cleverly plays upon Fortunato's pride and leads him to his death with the promise of tasting a nonexistent cask of Amontillado. *Through these characters and their actions, Poe communicates his theme that pride leads to a man's downfall.*

Thesis Statement

Topic Sentence

The power of pride is clearly seen in the character of Montresor. His pride in his family name is so great that "when [Fortunato] ventured upon insult, [Montresor] vowed revenge" (309). He cannot let himself be put down because he would appear to be weak and inferior, so he plans his revenge carefully. His desire to punish Fortunato is related to his family motto, "*Nemo me impune lacessit,*'" which means "No one dare attack me with impunity" (312). Obviously his ancestors felt that they were above reproach, and their pride made them feel that any attack should be met with even greater force. That's why Montresor cannot turn the other cheek; he feels it is his duty to crush any "'serpent'" (312) who would dare to attack his honorable name. This belief leads him to his moral downfall as he plans and executes the murder of Fortunato.

Topic Sentence

Fortunato's pride leads him into the trap that Montresor so cleverly lays for him. Montresor knows that Fortunato has "a weak point.... He prided himself on his connoisseurship in wine" (309). Interestingly, Montresor sees Fortunato's pride as a weakness (he sees his own as a strength), and like the clever man he is, Montresor preys upon this point, creating a nonexistent cask of Amontillado that he knows Fortunato will do anything to taste. To insure that, Montresor goes even one step further and teases Fortunato's pride by saying that he plans to have Luchesi taste the wine because "'if anyone has a critical turn, it is he'" (310). Fortunato's pride cannot accept that anyone is better at wine tasting than he is, so he insults both Montresor and Luchesi by saying, "'You have been imposed upon; and as for Luchesi, he cannot distinguish Sherry from Amontillado'" (311). So great is Fortunato's pride that he does not see the effect his insults have upon Montresor; he believes that he can say and do anything because of his superior skills. Little does he know that his pride is leading him into Montresor's trap.

Topic Sentence

Montresor continues to play with Fortunato's intense pride as he leads him to his death. Several times Montresor offers to turn back with Fortunato because of his cough and the dampness of the catacombs, but Fortunato insists, "'Let us go on'" (313). He cannot admit to any physical

[1] In *Edgar Allan Poe* (New York: Viking, 1945). All parenthetical page numbers refer to the text in this edition.

weakness that would interfere with his ability to taste-test the Amontillado. He must also prove that Montresor was taken advantage of; that would make him feel even more superior. Knowing that Fortunato will not turn back because of his pride, Montresor leads him to the crypt where he plans to bury him alive, saying, "'Proceed,' . . . 'herein is the Amontillado'" (314). Fortunato steps blindly in, and in a moment, Montresor has "fettered him to the granite" (314). The pride of both men leads them to his terrible moment. Montresor's pride causes him to commit murder without thinking for a moment about its immorality, and Fortunato's pride blinds him to the effects of his insults and to his murderer's intentions. His pride leads him like a lamb to the slaughter.

Restatement of Thesis

And so, Poe's theme that pride leads to the downfall of man can be clearly seen through the actions of Montresor and Fortunato. Both men are flawed by their intense pride and so are led to ruin by it. In fact, Montresor's pride is still so great that after fifty years he is bragging about his perfect crime. He cannot see how pride led him to an evil and immoral act. Through both Montresor and Fortunato, Poe is suggesting that man can easily be led astray by pride, and that can lead to spiritual and physical ruin. Obviously pride is a weakness that man has had to contend with since the time of the Garden of Eden, and since we are all prey to its sting, we must always be on guard against this deadliest of sins.

Marikay Kane

Model Essay Two

Here is a student essay on the theme in the following poem by Edmund Waller. The speaker's words to the rose bring out the poet's message.

Go, Lovely Rose

Go, lovely rose,
Tell her that wastes her time and me
That now she knows,
When I resemble her to thee,
How sweet and fair she seems to be.

Tell her that's young,
And shuns to have her graces spied,
That hadst thou sprung
In deserts, where no men abide,
Thou must have uncommended died.

Small is the worth
Of beauty from the light retired;
Bid her come forth,
Suffer herself to be desired,
And not blush so to be admired.

Then die, that she
The common fate of all things rare
    May read in thee:
How small a part of time they share
That are so wondrous sweet and fair.

Live in the Now

Many people would agree that the most beautiful flower is the rose. Its velvet petals, its sweet fragrance, its vibrant colors, and even its thorns have been described by writers through the centuries. In "Go, Lovely Rose,"[1] written more than two hundred years ago by Edmund Waller, the speaker personifies the rose and makes it his emissary, asking it to describe its life and its death to his beloved. *Through the speaker's words to the rose, Waller communicates the theme that life, like beauty, passes too quickly and must be seized to be enjoyed.*

One of the most beautiful parts of life is the experience of loving and being loved. Unfortunately, the speaker is suffering from unrequited love and decides that the rose may be able to communicate with his beloved where he has failed. In the first stanza, he begins his instructions to his emissary:

> Go, lovely rose,
> Tell her that wastes her time and me
>   That now she knows
> When I resemble[2] her to thee,
> How sweet and fair she seems to be. (lines 1–5)

The speaker is frustrated by the fact that his beloved is resisting his advances by wasting time they could spend making love. Obviously he has tried using compliments to win her over by comparing her beauty to that of the rose. By sending her the rose, he hopes that his compliments will take on new meaning as she enjoys its sweetness and its beauty, two attributes of life and love at their best. The speaker realizes that "time" (2) must be used, not wasted, if life is to be lived to the fullest.

To emphasize the fact that youth and beauty are meant to be enjoyed, the speaker continues his instructions to the rose:

> Tell her that's young,
> And shuns to have her graces spied,
>   That hadst thou sprung
> In deserts, where no men abide,
> Thou must have uncommended died. (6–10)

Since the speaker's beloved is young, she feels that there will always be time for love and its compliments. However, just as a rose in the desert is not admired but destroyed by the heat, so, too, will the young woman's beauty go unapplauded if she continues to hide it from others. Time will cause it

Thesis
Statement

Topic Sentence

Topic Sentence

---

[1] Edmund Waller, "Go, Lovely Rose," *The World's Best Poems*, ed. Mark Van Doren and Garibaldi M. Lapolla (Cleveland: World, 1921) 465.

[2] compare

to fade, and those who would have admired "her graces" (7) will also be victims of time and die.

Topic Sentence   *Through time and experience, the speaker has learned that "Small is the worth / Of beauty from the light retired"* (11–12). Beauty only has value if it is enjoyed and appreciated by others. That's why the speaker tells the rose to "Bid her [his shy beloved] come forth, / Suffer herself to be desired, / And not blush so to be admired" (13–15). By hiding from the speaker's offers of love and his expressions of desire and admiration, the young woman is really hiding from life. Perhaps because she is young, she does not realize, the way the speaker does, that time waits for no one and lost opportunities can never be regained. Life should not be put off—it should be put on and enjoyed.

Topic Sentence   *Realizing that life and beauty must sometime die, the speaker wants his beloved to share that realization, so he tells the rose to ". . . die, that she [his beloved] / The common fate of all things rare / May read in [the rose]* (16–18). Death is the "fate" (17) that all living things share—even "rare" (17) things like a beautiful rose and a beautiful woman. The speaker wants his beloved to see her own death in the death of the rose to learn "How small a part of time they share / That are so wondrous sweet and fair" (19–20). Her knowledge of life's brevity should make her aware that the precious present should not be wasted; it should be spent in the company of others whose love and admiration will make all of life seem "sweet and fair" (20).

Restatement of Thesis   *And so, through the speaker's directions to the rose, Waller brings out his theme: life is short and should not be wasted.* The speaker is aware of the nature of time, life, and beauty; they all fade and die, and if they are not enjoyed, they will be lost forever. If he can convince his beloved of that fact through the life and death of the rose, then she will share her time and beauty with him before they fade and die. Like the young woman, we, too, need to learn to "seize the day." Many people put off life and love until they earn enough money or get a better job or graduate from college, and sometimes they find that life or love is lost. They have given up precious time that could have brought them happiness and pleasure. They learn too late to live in the now.

Bryan Dypkowski

≫ Model Essay Three

The following student essay illustrates how theme emerges through the characters' words and actions in a play.

A Decisive Awakening

"The only question left to be settled now is—are women persons?"

Susan B. Anthony

This simple yet meaningful question is one that women and men have struggled to answer through history. Do society and males view women with equal rights and the legal claim to achieve these rights? In the drama *Slam the Door Softly*,[1] Clare Boothe Luce suggests that this question has not been resolved for many men or women. In this challenging play, Nora Wald comes to terms with this issue through her powerful and moving decision to leave her husband and children for an uncertain future. Nora is an educated woman who has often tried to share her insights on life with her husband, Thaw, but she is constantly tuned out and left to feel inferior. Finally she sees that her only hope to find her self-esteem lies outside of her family. *Through Nora and Thaw, Luce effectively communicates her theme that inequality in the sexes still prevails in society and in the male's perception of a woman's ascribed role. And, in the end, a woman must come to terms with this inequality and be responsible for her own life.*

Inequality towards women has been and continues to be prevalent in our society. Thaw works for Stove Mountain Life Insurance Company, and he enthusiastically describes to Nora an ad the insurance company has in *Life:* "It's the kind of ad that grabs you. This sad-faced, nice-looking woman of 50, sitting on a bench with a lot of discouraged old biddies, in an employment agency. Great caption . . . Could this happen to your wife?" (1122). The advertising industry is perpetuating the idea that even in death, a good husband cares for his wife. The ad portrays a group of unhappy, weary, worn-out women who have been unable to find jobs. This picture is worth a thousand words. To women, it extends the idea that attempting to secure a job is difficult and discouraging. And the subliminal suggestion is that a caring man will save them from ever being a part of such a group. Later, Nora tells Thaw she feels the advertising industry pictures women as failures, and she also reminds him of how women have been treated through history:

> Do you know what brutal things men have done to women? Bought and sold them like cattle. Bound their feet at birth to deform them—so they couldn't run away. . . . Freud was the foremost exponent of the theory of the natural inferiority of women. You know, 'Anatomy is destiny'? (1128, 1130)

Nora reminds Thaw that power is held in high esteem in society, yet powerful men have perpetrated deplorable things on women. Nora is a college graduate who is aware of society's injustices to women, and now she finds herself bound like these women to a disagreeable life. She regrets that she was an admirer of Freud when she was a student, and now she has come to see his ideas in a new light. His theory that one's sex determines one's success in life should read that it is not important to develop your talents and share them with the world unless you are a man.

Thaw reveals his attitude about women as subordinates in his words and actions. When he cannot imagine why Nora wants to leave, she reminds him that for the last year she has tried to talk to him about her working, and

[1] Clare Boothe Luce, *Slam the Door Softly.* Reprinted by permission of Richards Rosen Press, Inc. Copyright © 1971 by Clare Boothe Luce.

his response was frustrating to her: "You always laughed at me. You said I was too old to be a Playboy Bunny, and that the only job an inexperienced woman my age could get would be as a saleswoman" (1132). Thaw's laughing at Nora's ideas is a sure way to bring a conversation to a standstill and to convey the message that her life is not worth talking about. His sexual remark that Nora is too old to be a Playboy Bunny reinforces his belief that women should be appealing sex objects, since this is a role he sees women capable of filling. Finally, his remark that Nora is inexperienced shows her he does not value the experience she gained by managing a home and the daily demanding decisions of seeing to his and the children's needs. When Thaw realizes Nora intends to leave him, he angrily tells her he wants to know the reason even if he has to sock her. However, he now is aware physical violence no longer threatens Nora, and so he tries another approach: "Nora, sweetheart! You know I couldn't really hurt you. *(kisses, kisses)* Baaaby, what do you say we call it a night? *(Scoops her up in his arms)*. You can tell me all about in bed" (1127). Thaw has revealed his adherence to Nora's earlier remark that the traditional way for men to handle women is to "sock 'em and screw 'em" (1127). He believes he has a right to physically abuse a woman if she has offended him, and he continues to believe he has the right to physically use Nora for his own sexual gratification. Thaw is playing a power game, and either way, he wants to believe he is the winner by some physical evidence. Men solve their problems with words and through them come to terms with their differences, but Thaw does not believe this principle applies to Nora since he believes women are incapable of meaningful conversation. His actions show Nora she is unworthy of the respect he has for other men.

Topic Sentence

Nora finally faces the inequality in her life and searches for her identity and her worth in her own fashion. She loves her children, and Thaw acknowledges that she is a wonderful "little" mother. Nora is a caring mother who does not shun her responsibility to her children easily, but she realizes her responsibility to find herself must be a priority in order to achieve a wholeness and balance in her family life. Nora has begun to internalize Thaw's perspective of her as "little," and she discloses to Thaw what would happen if she stayed with him: "If I don't stop shrinking I'll end up secretly hating you, and trying to cut *you*—and *your* son—down to my size" (1134). Nora is beginning to see her self-esteem dwindle and her creativity dry up, and she is becoming that "little woman" Thaw envisions. She remembers the old adage, "Misery loves company," and she knows if she stays, she will resent and bear malice toward Thaw. In addition, she will transfer her bitter anger onto her son, who represents future male domination. She wants to enlarge her life and hold no male responsible for its outcome. Thaw urges Nora to think of what she is giving up. He believes only a man can offer a woman the type of life she seeks and that marriage is the most successful deal a woman can make:

> THAW. When you're 50, Nora, if you don't leave me, you'll be the wife of the president of Stove Mountain Insurance Company. Sharing my wealth, sharing whatever status I have in the community.

NORA. Just now I feel that the best deal I, Nora Wald, can hope to get out of life is to learn to esteem myself as a person . . . to stop feeling that every day a little bit more of my mind—and heart—is being washed down the drain with the soapsuds. (1134)

Nora does not want to seek her self-esteem through Thaw's achievements. Certainly she has her own sense of identity and worth. She can no longer ignore her strong feelings of doom if she allows her intelligence and love for life to dissipate. Nora needs to believe in herself again, and so she rejects Thaw's philosophy of marriage's being the only place a woman can find fulfillment.

Restatement of Thesis

And so, through society's and Thaw's prejudice, Luce shows how females have been discriminated against in both blatant and subtle ways. Nora represents a woman who is aware of the havoc this inequality brings into her life and of the decisive but painful decisions an individual must make to rectify it and seek uniformity and fair treatment for herself. Obviously inequality is a fact of life, and most of us can recall instances of being oppressed as well as being the oppressor. But it is always wrong, for one person is hurt because of it while the other person becomes less for being its instrument. We need to be on guard against our unjust treatment of others as well as our being unjustly treated. We must stand up for and at times fight for our right to become fully human, with a sense of connectedness to others seeking this same goal. Perhaps then Susan B. Anthony's question will have an answer.

Kathy Hynes

JUST ONE MORE THING

Try to be one on whom, as Henry James put it, "nothing is lost." Open up to life and to literature to discover the richness of human experience. "The unexamined life is not worth living" according to the Greek philosopher Plato. Literature can give you the chance to examine life from just about every possible human perspective and to learn from the ideas those perspectives convey. If you read widely, you will be able to say with the Roman playwright Terence, "Nothing human is alien to me."

❧ Theme Analysis Essay Plan Sheet ❧

Author:_____ Title:_____

Thesis:_____

_____

_____

_____

_____

Topic sentence:_____

_____

_____

Supporting quote: page or line _____

Supporting quote: page or line _____

Supporting quote: page or line _____

Topic sentence:_____

_____

_____

Supporting quote: page or line _____

Supporting quote: page or line _____

Supporting quote: page or line _____

Topic sentence:_____

_____

_____

Supporting quote: page or line _____

Supporting quote: page or line _____

Supporting quote: page or line _____

Topic sentence: _____

_____

_____

Supporting quote: page or line _____

Supporting quote: page or line _____

Supporting quote: page or line _____

Topic sentence: _____

_____

_____

Supporting quote: page or line _____

Supporting quote: page or line _____

Supporting quote: page or line _____

Topic sentence: _____

_____

_____

Supporting quote: page or line _____

Supporting quote: page or line _____

Supporting quote: page or line _____

Concluding points: _____

_____

_____

_____

_____

_____

_____

_____

❧ Peer/Self-Evaluation of a Theme Analysis Essay ❧

> **Directions:** Make specific suggestions about each part of the essay, pointing out particular areas that the writer could improve. Keep in mind the qualities of good writing: unity, organization, development, clarity, and coherence.

I. Introduction

Is the lead relevant and interesting?

Are the author's full name and the title of the work correctly spelled and punctuated?

Does the brief plot summary focus on the events that lead coherently to the thesis?

Does the thesis state the theme and state how it will be developed in the body paragraphs?

II. Body Paragraphs

Do the topic sentences contain key words/ideas from the thesis?

Are the supporting quotations properly introduced and relevant?

Are the analysis sections adequately developed?

Do the body paragraphs follow a logical order?

Are the body paragraphs unified and coherent?

III. Conclusion

Is a signal word included somewhere in the final paragraph?

Does the topic sentence restate/rephrase the theme?

Do the following sentences show how the theme relates to the work?

Is the universal application of the theme explained?

Is the final sentence an effective clincher?

IV. Expression

Are all the ideas expressed in complete sentences?

Are the sentences clear and correctly punctuated?

Are there any problems with subject-verb or pronoun-antecedent agreement?

Are all the words correctly spelled?

V. Overall Evaluation

Most effective part of the essay:

Least effective part of the essay:

List three specific actions which could be taken by the writer to improve this and future papers:

1.

2.

3.

Evaluator's name: _____ Date: _____

❦ Exercise on Theme ❦

> Assume that you are an author and that you want to share the following insights into life with your readers. Write a brief summary of a plot that would illustrate these themes.

Love is often blind:_____
_____
_____
_____
_____

Man can be a violent creature:_____
_____
_____
_____
_____

Parenting is difficult:_____
_____
_____
_____
_____

The transition from adolescence to maturity isn't always easy:_____
_____
_____
_____
_____

Money doesn't necessarily bring happiness:_____
_____
_____
_____
_____

The crime and the punishment are not always equal:_____
_____
_____
_____
_____

You can't solve your problems until you face them: _____

_____

_____

_____

_____

_____

_____

_____

Love can hurt: _____

_____

_____

_____

_____

_____

_____

_____

Life isn't always fair or just: _____

_____

_____

_____

_____

_____

_____

_____

Drugs can be deadly: _____

_____

_____

_____

_____

_____

_____

_____

Point of View Analysis

Overview

An important element of fiction is the point of view or the view point from which the story is told. It is essential to note who's telling the story, what his or her role is in it (if he or she appears as a character), and what the narrator's or story teller's personality is, for the teller of the tale controls the emotional effect of the story upon the reader and determines the story's theme or message.

Analysis of Point of View

You are a natural story teller, and you naturally use one of two different points of view when you tell a story to others. If you are describing an experience in which you were directly involved, you will most likely use the first-person point of view to tell about your actions and feelings. For example, you might describe your activities on a Saturday night by saying, "*I* went to a movie that was great, and then *I* went to *my* favorite pizza place with *my* friends." You automatically tell about yourself by using the first-person pronouns, *I*, *my*, *mine*, and *me*.

If, however, you were not involved but were just reporting on your friend's activities, you would automatically use the third-person point of view: "*Bob* went to a movie with *Crystal*, and then *he* took *her* out for pizza." Here you naturally use the third-person pronouns—*he, she, him, her, his, hers, they, them, their*—to talk about others. This distinction between first-person stories and third-person stories creates two different points of view that authors can choose from when writing prose fiction or poetry:

1. First-person participant point of view
2. Third-person nonparticipant point of view.

First-Person Participant Point of View

When an author chooses to use the first-person participant point of view, he will have *one of the characters in the story* narrate the events. The story teller will then use the first-person pronoun "*I*" to describe himself and his actions and to identify his statements. For example, we know we are into a first-person story when Edgar Allan Poe begins "The Cask of Amontillado" with Montresor's statement: "The thousand injuries of Fortunato I had borne as I best could, but when he ventured upon insult, I vowed revenge."[1] The *I* clearly stands out and indicates that Montresor, a character in the story, will be the story teller.

Types of First-Person Point of View

In a first-person story, the narrator may be a **major character** in the action, perhaps the protagonist or the antagonist. In Poe's story, Montresor is the protagonist who plots and carries out the murder of his "friend" Fortunato. He is directly involved in the action; in fact, his will moves the action of the entire plot. Sometimes, however, an author may choose to have the first-person narrator function as a **minor character,** acting mainly as a witness to the events he describes for the reader. This is the technique used by F. Scott Fitzgerald in *The Great Gatsby;* he created Nick Carraway, a neighbor and friend of Gatsby's, to describe Gatsby's relationship with Daisy and Tom Buchanan.

Another variation of the first-person narrator is the use of a naive story teller, one who is unaware of the true significance of the events he or she is describing. This type of narrator, sometimes called the **innocent eye,** usually creates an ironic effect in a story, for the informed reader can see the meaning of the events more clearly than the naive story teller. Often the events are the reverse of what the narrator perceives them to be, hence the ironic effect. This can be seen in Ring Lardner's story "Haircut" when he has a naive barber tell a customer about the accidental death of Jim Kendall, the town bully. From the details Whitey narrates, it is easy for the reader to infer that Jim was actually murdered, an inference that Whitey was never perceptive enough to make.

Character of the First-Person Narrator

All of these types of first-person point of view draw us into the action of the work because they give us a sense of closeness to the story teller; it is as if we were listening to an eyewitness, perhaps to one of our friends telling us about something that happened to him or her. And just as some of our friends are honest and others like to exaggerate, so, too, first-person narrators can have different personalities and different degrees of trustworthiness. Therefore, as critical readers, we must analyze the narrator's personality and reliability, for as the teller of the story, his character shapes our view of the action; we see things through his eyes and learn about his judgments, attitudes, and values.

If the narrator appears to be sensitive and perceptive, he is probably reliable, and his judgments of the other characters are usually accurate and meant to be accepted by the reader. This can be seen in the story "Guests of the Nation" by Frank O'Connor where Bonaparte, a young, sensitive soldier, is the narrator whose assessments of Donovan, Belcher, Hawkins, and the war they are involved in are meant to be shared by the sensitive and perceptive reader. If, on the other hand, the narrator is insensitive and imperceptive, as in Ring Lardner's short story "Haircut," his judgments should be carefully evaluated. We are obviously meant to see the narrator's limitations and to make our own assessment of the events in the work.

The Effects of First-Person Point of View

It is essential in a first-person point of view story to analyze the narrator's character (through his or her thoughts, words, and actions) because he or she controls our **emotional response** to the events and shapes our understanding of **the theme** they convey. A perfect example of this occurs when a couple that we know quite well breaks off a relationship. When the fellow tells his side of the story, the chances are good that the emotional response he will produce in us is sympathy for him and anger at his girl. The theme of his narration will probably be "I am a good guy and totally innocent, and she is all

---

[1] Edgar Allan Poe, "The Cask of Amontillado" *Poe's Tales of Mystery and Imagination* (New York: Weathervane, 1935) 36.

wrong." However, when his girl gets a chance to narrate the same events from her point of view, we will probably feel sympathy for her and anger at her boyfriend. This time the theme will be "I am a good girl and totally innocent, and he is all wrong." We all know that when we tell our "side" of a story (our point of view), we can tell it in such a way as to produce a particular emotional effect in the hearer, and we can control the message we want our listener to pick up. The same thing is true in fiction. The narrator's character determines the overall emotional effect the story will have on the reader, and it also determines the theme in the work.

It is also important to note the time frame within which the first person narrator is recounting his experiences. If he is describing events as they happen or shortly thereafter, his understanding of them and their significance may be limited. If, however, considerable time has passed between the events and his narration of them, he will have had a chance to analyze them and weigh their importance. This distancing can be seen in James Joyce's short story "Araby" where the narrator, an older man, describes his teenage infatuation with a friend's sister. From the vantage point of maturity, he now sees his relationship as a type of religious quest for a romanticized ideal, an illusion that is shattered by the harsh realities of the bazaar.

❦ Third-Person Nonparticipant Point of View

When an author decides to use the third-person nonparticipant point of view, he will create a narrator or story teller who will use third-person pronouns to refer to all of the characters in the story. This type of point of view is usually easy to identify from the first few sentences of a work when characters are referred to by name or by third-person pronouns as in the first sentence of "Young Goodman Brown"[2] by Nathaniel Hawthorne: "Young Goodman Brown came forth at sunset into the street at Salem village; but put his head back, after crossing the threshold, to exchange a parting kiss with his young wife" (89). You can see the third-person pronouns here, but they are even easier to see in sections of dialogue from a story, as in this exchange between Goodman Brown and his wife, Faith:

> 'Dearest heart,' whispered she, softly and rather sadly, when her lips were close to his ear, 'prithee put off your journey until sunrise and sleep in your own bed to-night. . . .'
> 'My love and my Faith,' replied young Goodman Brown, 'of all nights in the year, this one night must I tarry away from thee . . .' (89).

Notice that while the characters refer to themselves with the first person pronoun *I*, it is the tag lines ("whispered she" and "replied Goodman Brown") that clearly indicate the use of third person point of view.

Types of Third-Person Nonparticipant Point of View

The broad category of third-person nonparticipant point of view can be divided into at least four different types: **objective, omniscient, limited omniscient,** and **stream-of-consciousness.**

The **third-person objective point of view,** sometimes called *camera-eye, fly-on-the-wall,* or *dramatic,* is characterized by a narrator who uses third-person pronouns to describe only the characters' words and actions. Only those things that a camera (audio and video) could record or that a fly on the wall could observe are presented in the story. The following example is from "The Lottery"[3] by Shirley Jackson:

---

[2] Nathaniel Hawthorne, "Young Goodman Brown" *Mosses from an Old Manse* (New York: Books for Libraries, 1970). Parenthetical page numbers refer to the text in this edition.

[3] Shirley Jackson, "The Lottery" *The Magic of Shirley Jackson,* Stanley Edgar Hyman, ed. (New York: Farrar, 1966). All parenthetical page numbers refer to the text in this edition.

'Nancy next,' Mr. Summers said. Nancy was twelve, and her school friends breathed heavily as she went forward, switching her skirt, and took a slip daintily from the box. 'Bill, Jr.,' Mr. Summers said, and Billy, his face red and his feet overlarge, nearly knocked the box over as he got a paper out. 'Tessie,' Mr. Summers said. She hesitated for a minute, looking around defiantly, and then set her lips and went up to the box. She snatched a paper out and held it behind her. (144)

The details that Jackson includes in the narration, such as Nancy "breathed heavily," Bill Jr. "nearly knocked the box over," and Tessie "snatched a paper out," are things that could be noted by a careful observer of the action. By using the third person objective point of view, Jackson is able to sustain suspense about the nature and the purpose of the lottery. The reader feels that he is watching a drama unfold through the characters' words and actions.

When an author uses the **third-person omniscient** point of view, he or she creates a narrator who describes the characters' thoughts as well as their words and actions. Here the story teller is an omniscient (all-knowing) god who sees all and tells all as he enters the mind of some or all the characters. Some examples of verbs that indicate the author is recording the characters' thoughts are *knew, thought, realized, understood, experienced, saw, heard, felt, feared, hoped*—or even *lied*. An example of this type of narration is Hemingway's "The Short Happy Life of Francis Macomber."[4] The omniscient narrator tells us the thoughts of Francis, Margaret, Robert Wilson, and even those of the wounded lion. Here the narrator describes Wilson's thoughts about Margaret and Francis:

So, Robert Wilson thought to himself, she *is* giving him a ride, isn't she? Or do you suppose that's her idea of putting up a good show? How should a woman act when she discovers her husband is a bloody coward? She's damn cruel but they're all cruel. They govern, of course, and to govern one has to be cruel sometimes. Still, I've seen enough of their damn terrorism (10).

Authors frequently choose the third-person omniscient point of view because it permits the narrator to delve into the minds of the characters, examining their thoughts, feelings, and emotions. When the narrator presents this information in a neutral way without making judgments about it, he is using **objective omniscience;** if he evaluates and passes judgment on the characters' thoughts and actions, he is using **editorial omniscience.** Both approaches enable us to get inside the characters so we can see how complex and involved human nature and human motivation really are.

The narrator must always be honest about the characters' thoughts (he must be reliable) so that the reader will know when he is in a character's mind and when he is in the real world. Occasionally, however, a narrator may violate these principles of honesty and obvious shifts from the real to the mental world of a character to produce a different effect on the reader or an unusual twist in the plot outcome. This occurs in Ambrose Bierce's "An Occurrence at Owl Creek Bridge" when the reader believes that Peyton Farquhar is actually escaping rather than just fantasizing his escape moments before his death. The narrator shifted from objective reality to subjective reality without signaling that shift to the reader.

Another type of third-person narration is the **limited omniscient point of view.** Here the narrator limits his omniscient powers and enters the mind of only one of the characters in a work. Only this character's thoughts and emotions are revealed so he or she becomes, in Henry James's words, "the center of consciousness" in the story. All of the other characters are seen from the outside as they relate to the point-of-view character. Thurber uses this point of view in "The Secret Life of Walter Mitty." Walter is the

---

[4]Reprinted with permission of Charles Scribner's Sons, an imprint of Macmillan Publishing Company, from THE SHORT STORIES OF ERNEST HEMINGWAY. Copyright © 1936 by Ernest Hemingway. Copyright renewed © 1964 by Mary Hemingway.

only character whose mind is entered, and we learn about his fantasies and his real-life inadequacies. Because we see these parts of Walter, we can empathize with him. His wife, however, seems to earn our contempt because we witness only her cold words and actions; we never learn what she really thinks about Walter and their life together. The limited omniscient point of view, then, often creates different reader responses to the characters. We tend to understand the character whose thoughts and feelings we can share and to be less accepting of those whose motives we do not know.

Stream-of-consciousness may be considered a fourth type of third person point of view. Here the author intermingles the mental world and the "real" world of the character in the way the human mind actually perceives reality—as a mixture of the objective world and its private, subjective consciousness. In its purest form, this narrative technique, originated by James Joyce in *Ulysses*, is an unpunctuated stream of thought that records both the conscious and the unconscious activity of the mind. This brief excerpt is from Molly Bloom's forty-six-page interior monologue that ends the work:

> . . . that thunder woke me up as if the world was coming to an end God be merciful to us I thought the heavens were coming down about us to punish when I blessed myself and said a Hail Mary like those awful thunderbolts in Gibraltar and they come and tell you theres no God what could you do if it was running and rushing about nothing only make an act of contrition . . .[5]

Occasionally authors who choose to use the stream-of-consciousness point of view will modify it by using some punctuation to make the text easier to follow.

As you can see, then, point of view is complex. The following concept map provides an overview of the different types:

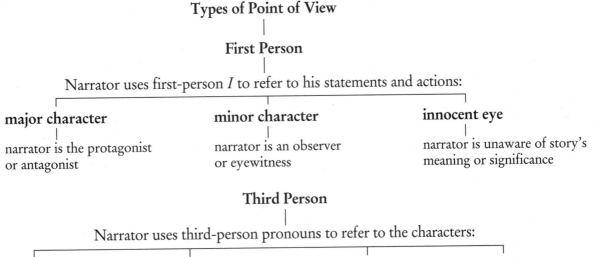

Types of Point of View

First Person

Narrator uses first-person *I* to refer to his statements and actions:

major character	**minor character**	**innocent eye**
narrator is the protagonist or antagonist	narrator is an observer or eyewitness	narrator is unaware of story's meaning or significance

Third Person

Narrator uses third-person pronouns to refer to the characters:

objective	**omniscient**	**limited omniscient**	**stream-of-consciousness**
narrator describes *only* the words and actions of the characters	narrator describes the *thoughts,* words, and actions of all or most of the characters	narrator enters the mind of *only one* major character who becomes the *"center of consciousness"* in the story	narrator describes the mental and the real world of the character(s) in an unpunctuated stream of thought

---

[5] James Joyce, *Ulysses* (New York: Vintage, 1961) 725.

Obviously there are many different types of point of view an author may choose from, and while each has its advantages and its limitations, one thing is sure: the point of view makes the work unique. Another point of view would have produced a totally different story.

✤ Writing about Point of View: Step by Step

When preparing to write an essay that analyzes the use of point of view in a work of literature, simply follow these steps:

1. Practically speaking, it's best to choose a work that uses the first-person or third-person limited omniscient point of view because in this type of narration, the author presents the story as perceived by a single character. It is also possible, of course, to analyze the third-person omniscient point of view by focusing on one of the main characters in the work, or to analyze the effects/advantages of using the third-person objective or dramatic point of view.

2. The essay's thesis should include the following points:
   a. a list of three of the most significant character traits of the first-person narrator or of the limited omniscient point-of-view character;
   b. a description of the emotions you feel toward the first-person narrator or the limited omniscient point-of-view character and/or the other character(s) in the work;
   c. a statement of the theme(s) that emerge from the way the first-person narrator or the limited omniscient narrator tells the story.

3. A brief character analysis forms the first part of the body of the essay. Use one supporting quotation to prove each of the character traits you listed as the first part of the thesis. This "mini" character sketch of the narrator is important because the narrator's personality produces the emotions we feel toward him or her and toward the other characters in the work, and it determines the theme(s) in the work as well.

4. In the second part of the body, examine the emotions you feel toward the characters in the work. Do you like them? Do you dislike them? Do you feel happy for them, or do they stir your emotions of pity and fear? Relate these emotions to certain sections of the work so that you can support your views with quotations and details from it, proving that your emotional response is the result of the narrator's description of the characters and their words and actions.

5. The last part of your essay should explore the themes which emerge because of the way the narrator tells the story or because of the insights the readers receive by being in the mind of one of the characters. Themes are the ideas about life that the work illustrates. They usually relate to the subject matter of the work and to life in general. Sometimes a work contains a direct statement of the theme, while in other works, the theme emerges from the interaction of the characters and from the general plot outcome.

6. In the conclusion, explain why the author's choice of point of view is a good one and what is gained by telling the story through the consciousness of this particular narrator.

The following diagram, model essays, and plan sheet will help you organize and write a well developed essay on point of view in a work of literature.

Diagram of the Structure of a Point of View Analysis Essay

Title

Introductory Paragraph:

Open with interesting lead material.

Name the work and the author.

Identify the point of view in the work and give a *brief* plot summary.

Name *the point-of-view character* and list three of his or her character traits.

State that the *emotions* experienced by the reader and the *theme* in the work are the effects of the point of view.

} Thesis

Body Paragraphs:

In the first part of the body, establish the character of the narrator. Begin with a topic sentence that lists the three traits from the thesis and then briefly prove/illustrate each one by using the literary analysis pattern: background information which leads into a quotation from the work, the quotation itself, and then analysis which explains how the quotation proves/clarifies the character trait.

In the second part of the body, describe the emotions the typical reader feels toward the narrator and the other characters because of the way the narrator talks about himself and others. The topic sentence should relate these emotions to the point of view, stressing that they are an effect of the way the story is told. Explain each emotion by using the literary analysis pattern: generalization, introduction to a quotation, the quotation, and analysis.

The third part of the body explains the themes which emerge in the work as a result of the way the narrator tells the story. The topic sentence relates theme to point of view, and then the theme or themes are illustrated through the use of the literary analysis pattern.

Concluding Paragraph:

Use a signal word (i.e., and so, then, thus) in the first part of the conclusion to let the reader know that you are coming to the end of your discussion and then explain why the author's choice of point of view is a good one and what he gains by telling his story through the consciousness of this particular narrator.

Model Essay One

The following student-written essays illustrate the overall structure used in point-of-view analysis. The first essay focuses on a first-person major-character narrator and the effects produced by the way he tells his story.

A Matter of Pride

Have you ever longed to get revenge against someone who injured you or your good name? "The Cask of Amontillado"[1] by Edgar Allan Poe is a story of such vengeance. It is told in the first person by Montresor, the main character. The story begins with Montresor's declaring that he has been the victim of Fortunato's insufferable actions and insults long enough. Montresor then goes on to tell how he lured Fortunato into the catacombs beneath his house in order to achieve his revenge by murdering Fortunato. *From the details he recounts, it is obvious that Montresor is an extremely vengeful, cunning, and cold-hearted person who wants us to dislike his victim and to admire him for committing the perfect crime. Through Montresor, Poe conveys the theme that pride can lead to one's destruction.*

Montresor's vengeful, cunning, and cold-hearted personality is obvious from the way he plans and carries out the murder of Fortunato. He openly expresses his desire for revenge by immediately stating, "The thousand injuries of Fortunato I had borne as I best could, but when he ventured upon insult, I vowed revenge" (309). He is not a person to turn the other cheek; in fact, he is so intent on getting revenge that he makes a solemn promise to go through with his plan. He is incapable of forgiveness; it is a quality not found in his evil personality. On the night of the murder, he cunningly eliminates the possibility of witnesses:

> There were no attendants at home; they had absconded to make merry in honor of the time. I had told them that I should not return until the morning, and had given them explicit orders not to stir from the house. These orders were sufficient, I well knew, to insure their immediate disappearance, one and all, as soon as my back was turned. (310)

Montresor uses reverse psychology on his servants. He tells them to stay, knowing full well that as soon as he leaves, they, too, will leave. Now Montresor has Fortunato all to himself, and after he has him chained to the wall, Montresor's cold-heartedness surfaces as Fortunato attempts to free himself: "The noise lasted for several minutes, during which, that I might hearken to it with the more satisfaction, I ceased my labors and sat down upon the bones" (314). Montresor is sadistic in his enjoyment of Fortunato's suffering. He coldheartedly relishes every moment of Fortunato's vain efforts to escape death, for now that his plan for revenge is a reality, he wants to savor all of the details of his victim's pain.

[1] Edgar Allan Poe, "The Cask of Amontillado" *Edgar Allan Poe* (New York: Viking, 1945). All parenthetical page numbers refer to this edition.

Thesis Statement

Topic Sentence

Montresor paints a negative picture of Fortunato to create feelings of dislike toward him and to put himself in a positive light for his actions. Fortunato's tremendous ego is evident in his attitude toward the ability of others to judge wine as well as he can. He tells Montresor, "'You have been imposed upon; and as for Luchesi, he cannot distinguish Sherry from Amontillado'" (310). In one sentence, Fortunato insults Montresor's ability to buy wine and Luchesi's ability to judge its quality. Fortunato has no qualms about putting others down to make himself feel superior. In Montresor's eyes, Fortunato is an insulting boor who deserves to be silenced. On the other hand, Montresor's claim that he has suffered a "thousand injuries" (309) at the hands of Fortunato shows that he wants to be seen as a patient and long-suffering man who can take a lot before he decides that enough is enough. When Fortunato finally crosses the line by insulting him, Montresor plans the perfect crime, and he wants us to admire him for it when he brags, "For the half of a century no mortal has disturbed [Fortunato's bones]" (314). Montresor cleverly planned every detail of Fortunato's murder and carried it out perfectly. Without a body, there is no way to prove that a crime has been committed, and so Montresor has achieved perfect revenge, an admirable accomplishment in his eyes.

Topic Sentence   *Through the use of Montresor as his narrator, Poe communicates the theme that pride can lead to a man's downfall.* Fortunato's flaw is easily spotted by Montresor: "He had a weak point—this Fortunato. . . . He prided himself on his connoisseurship in wine" (309). Because of Fortunato's pride in his wine-tasting ability, Montresor knows that he can trick him into going to the Montresor wine cellar to taste a nonexistent cask of Amontillado. Fortunato cannot see that he is being led to the slaughter; he is blinded by his egotistical pride. Montresor, too, is led to his downfall by his pride. He cannot allow a man like Fortunato to humiliate him, so he kills him, believing that he is above the moral order because of his family motto: "No one dare attack me with impunity" (312). Montresor sees Fortunato as "a serpent" (312) that he has the right to crush because he has been insulted. Unfortunately, Montresor fails to realize that he is as flawed as Fortunato, for his pride leads to his moral downfall—the crime of murder.

Concluding Topic Sentence   *And so Poe's use of Montresor as the narrator is effective because as the protagonist, his will moves the action of the plot.* No one else could possibly know what his true feelings are toward Fortunato, and no one else could give as vivid a description of the actual events leading up to the murder itself. Finally, since no one knows of the murder because Montresor has committed the perfect crime, he is the only possible person who could tell the story.

Brian Smith

Model Essay Two

This essay analyzes the use of third-person point of view in a short story by Katherine Mansfield.

The Old and the Lonely

Thesis Statement

The Beatles sang about all the lonely people when they introduced the world to "Eleanor Rigby." Katherine Mansfield introduces us to another lonely person in her short story entitled "Miss Brill."[1] The protagonist is an older woman whose life consists of teaching her English students, reading the newspaper to an old man four days a week, and going to the park concert on Sundays. While in the park, she fantasizes about being part of a stage production and is feeling needed and wanted until a young couple insult her and her fur piece and destroy her illusions. *By using the third-person limited omniscient point of view, Mansfield reveals Miss Brill's sensitivity, loneliness, and fantasies. Then through a shift to third person objective point of view, Mansfield creates a feeling of disappointment over the insensitivity of the young couple, produces sympathy for Miss Brill, and communicates her theme about the lonely lives of the elderly.*

Topic Sentence

By sharing Miss Brill's thoughts and emotions, it is easy to see that she is sensitive, lonely, and living in a world of fantasy. As she walks to the park for her usual Sunday concert, she is tuned in to her inner feelings: "And when she breathed, something light and sad—no, not sad, exactly—something gentle seemed to move in her bosom" (549). Miss Brill is keenly aware of her own emotions, carefully evaluating what she feels. She does not want to acknowledge that sadness is part of her life even though she is isolated and lonely, for when she sits on her usual park bench, she does not speak to others: "She had become really quite expert, she thought, at listening as though she didn't listen, at sitting in other people's lives just for a minute while they talked around her" (550). Being a part of others' lives eases Miss Brill's loneliness. Since she has no real life of her own and doesn't interact with others, her eavesdropping helps her find some way out of her isolation. To really feel connected to others, she begins to fantasize about how she is part of a theatre production: "They were all on stage. . . . Even she had a part and came every Sunday. No doubt somebody would have noticed if she hadn't been there; she was part of the performance after all" (552). This fantasy puts Miss Brill into something bigger than her lonely existence. Her image of herself as unimportant is overturned because even she is involved; her isolation is lessened because she is not left out after all. Her fantasy world gives her an importance she does not have in the real world.

Topic Sentence

The shift in point of view which takes us from Miss Brill's inner world to the world of objective reality reinforces the emotions the reader feels toward the young couple who destroy her fantasy world and toward Miss Brill herself. Just as she begins to feel involved and accepted, she listens in on a world-shattering conversation as a young couple complain about her pres-

[1] In *The Short Stories of Katherine Mansfield* (New York: Knopf, 1967) 549–554.

ence: "'Why doesn't she keep her silly old mug at home?' 'It's her fu-fur which is so funny,' giggled the girl" (553). The couple are totally insensitive to Miss Brill. They are aware that she can hear every word, and yet they shamelessly criticize her appearance and her precious fur piece. Their cruelty evokes a sense of disappointment for their lack of respect for the older Miss Brill. She, of course, is devasted, which strengthens the reader's sympathy for her. She is unable to carry out her usual Sunday routine—stopping to pick up "her Sunday treat . . . a slice of honeycake at the baker's" (553)—which gives some joy and flair to her lonely existence. "But today she passed the baker's by, climbed the stairs, [and] went into the little dark room—her room like a cupboard." (553). She is saddened and shattered by the harshness of the real world, and for now—at least—will take refuge in her little room and return to her isolation where she is safe from the cruelty of others. Her plight stirs the reader's deepest feelings of sympathy and empathy.

Topic Sentence

Mansfield's shift between omniscient and objective point of view helps to bring out the theme that many older people lead very lonely lives. Miss Brill does not want to accept the fact that she is old and alone, so she mentally sets herself apart from the people in the park: "Other people sat on the benches and green chairs, but they were nearly always the same, Sunday after Sunday, and—Miss Brill had often noticed—there was something funny about nearly all of them. They were odd, silent, and nearly all old . . ." (551). Like Miss Brill, the old people fill their lives with the same routine each Sunday. Their silence emphasizes their isolation from each other which contributes to their loneliness. They escape their "dark little rooms" (551) by coming to the park, but they do not escape the pain of their lonely lives. Miss Brill, too, lives alone in a "room like a cupboard," and when she realizes that the young couple do not want her company, she returns there to put away her fantasies and her fur, and as she does so, she thinks "she heard something crying" (554). Whether she imagines her fur is crying or she herself is crying over being insulted really does not matter. The pain of feeling alone and rejected is real, and that pain is felt by many older people who do not have contact with friends or family and are often forgotten by the young who have little respect for the elderly.

Restatement of Thesis

And so Mansfield does a sensitive job of using point of view to reveal Miss Brill's character, to emotionally involve the reader, and to convey her theme about the loneliness of many elderly people who live alone. This poignant portrait of Miss Brill brings out the fact that there are many Miss Brills in our world who feel left out of life. If one looks at these lives from the outside, however, this would not be evident, for the elderly—like Miss Brill—have become quite expert at hiding their loneliness. That's why the use of both points of view is effective in presenting a complete picture of Miss Brill's lonely life.

J. C.

❧ **Model Essay Three**

Here is an essay on the point of view in the following poem by Robert Browning.

My Last Duchess

FERRARA

That's my last Duchess painted on the wall,
Looking as if she were alive. I call
That a piece of wonder, now; Frà Pandolf's hands
Worked busily a day, and there she stands.
Will't please you sit and look at her? I said   5
"Frà Pandolf" by design, for never read
Strangers like you that pictured countenance,
The depth and passion of its earnest glance,
But to myself they turned (since none puts by
The curtain I have drawn for you, but I)   10
And seemed as they would ask me, if they durst,
How such a glance came there; so, not the first
Are you to turn and ask thus. Sir, 'twas not
Her husband's presence only, called that spot
Of joy into the Duchess's check; perhaps   15
Frà Pandolf chanced to say "Her mantle laps
Over my Lady's wrist too much," or, "Paint
Must never hope to reproduce the faint
Half-flush that dies along her throat." Such stuff
Was courtesy, she thought, and cause enough   20
For calling up that spot of joy. She had
A heart—how shall I say—too soon made glad,
Too easily impressed; she liked whate'er
She looked on, and her looks went everywhere.
Sir, 'twas all one! My favor at her breast,   25
The dropping of the daylight in the west,
The bough of cherries some officious fool
Broke in the orchard for her, the white mule
She rode with round the terrace—all and each
Would draw from her alike the approving speech,   30
Or blush, at least. She thanked men—good! but thanked
Somehow—I know not how—as if she ranked
My gift of a nine-hundred-years-old name
With anybody's gift. Who'd stoop to blame
This sort of trifling? Even had you skill   35
In speech—(which I have not)—to make your will
Quite clear to such an one, and say, "Just this
Or that in you disgusts me: here you miss,
Or there exceed the mark"—and if she let
Herself be lessoned so, nor plainly set   40
Her wits to yours, forsooth, and made excuse,
—E'en then would be some stooping; and I choose
Never to stoop. Oh, Sir, she smiled, no doubt,
Whene'er I passed her; but who passed without

Much the same smile? This grew; I gave commands;   45
Then all smiles stopped together. There she stands
As if alive. Will't please you rise? We'll meet
The company below, then. I repeat,
The Count your master's known munificence
Is ample warrant that no just pretense   50
Of mine for dowry will be disallowed;
Though his fair daughter's self, as I avowed
At starting, is my object. Nay, we'll go
Together down, Sir. Notice Neptune, though,
Taming a sea-horse, thought a rarity,   55
Which Claus of Innsbruck cast in bronze for me!

The Deadly Duke

Do you realize that every time you talk about others you reveal significant things about yourself? That is one of the messages that emerge from Robert Browning's famous dramatic monologue entitled "My Last Duchess."[1] In the poem, the Duke of Ferrara, a town in Italy, is describing a painting of his "last Duchess" to an emissary of a Count whose daughter the Duke is hoping to marry. *In this first person narrative, the Duke talks about his last wife's character, and as he does so, he reveals his jealousy, his vanity, and his overwhelming pride. Instead of creating negative emotions toward the Duchess by his comments, he ironically produces admiration toward her and dislike toward himself. Through his use of the Duke as a narrator, Browning brings out the theme that pride can lead to moral corruption.*

Thesis Statement

Topic Sentence

By the way the Duke describes his wife's actions and his feelings about them to the Count's representative, he reveals that he is a jealous, vain, and proud individual. As the two men look at the painting of the Duchess done by "Frà Pandolf" (line 6), "the depth and passion of [her] earnest glance" (8) impress the emissary, and he asks about the cause of them. The Duke's reply reveals his jealousy: "Sir, 'twas not / Her husband's presence only, called that spot / Of joy into the Duchess's cheek" (13–15). Obviously, the Duke feels that only he should be the object of her attention. He is jealous of her undiscriminating looks that he says "went everywhere" (24). His anger about her graciousness to others is caused by his vanity. His feelings of superiority are evident when he complains about the Duchess's attitude toward the kindness of others:

> . . . She thanked men—good! but thanked
> . . . as if she ranked
> My gift of a nine-hundred-years-old name
> With anybody's gift. (31–34)

The Duke believes that his heritage places him far above everyone, and the Duchess wounds his vanity by not acknowledging that superiority. Because

---

[1] Robert Browning, "My Last Duchess" *Robert Browning's Poetry*, ed. James F. Loucks (New York: Norton, 1979) 58–59.

of his pride, he refuses to explain his feelings about her behavior to her, saying that "would [require] some stooping; and I choose / Never to stoop" (42–43). He is too proud to even acknowledge his jealousy, for that could be considered a human flaw. To admit to any weakness would be degrading to the great Duke of Ferrara.

Topic Sentence *The Duke's criticism of the Duchess's graciousness makes the reader admire her and dislike him.* He says that "She had / a heart . . . too soon made glad / Too easily impressed" (21–23), but this suggests that the Duchess had a genuine and sensitive nature that made her appreciate all of life. She was not vain or haughty like the Duke. She could enjoy the simple things of life like "the dropping of the daylight in the west" (26), a "bough of cherries," or a "white mule" (26–27) as much as she enjoyed the Duke's "favor at her breast" (25). Rather than an indictment, this behavior shows her sincere and honest nature, so different from the Duke who comes off as a deceptive manipulator. In his discussion with the emissary, he claims that the Count's "fair daughter's self, . . . / . . . is [his] object" (52–53) in the same breath that he compliments the Count's "known munificence" (49) and then mentions the "dowry" (51) that will be part of the bargain. He is cold and calculating and feels that his "nine-hundred-years-old name" (33) should bring him anything he wants. He values status and money more than he values positive human qualities, and that makes it easy for the reader to dislike him.

Topic Sentence *Through the Duke's description of his last Duchess's personality and his response to it, Browning brings out the theme that pride leads to moral decay.* Because of his sense of superiority and his refusal "to stoop" to talk to his wife about how he perceives her actions, the Duke orders her death. He tells the Count's representative, "I gave commands; / Then all [her] smiles stopped together. There she stands / As if alive" (45–47). The Duke obviously feels that he is above the law. Since he cannot possess his wife completely, he decides that she is unworthy of life, so he has her killed. By telling this to the emissary, he is actually telling him what behavior he expects from his future wife. His pride demands that he be the master and she be the slave. This can be seen in his mentioning one last work of art to his listener before their departure: "Notice Neptune . . . / Taming a sea-horse / Which Claus of Innsbruck cast in bronze for me!" (54–56). This suggests that the Duke thinks of himself as a god—like Neptune—and he plans to tame and control his future wife so that she will worship him alone. His overwhelming pride has corrupted him to the point where he will kill to maintain superiority, and he will do it again if necessary to satisfy his ego.

Concluding Topic Sentence *Thus Browning's use of first person point of view in his poem is very effective.* As the Duke speaks, the reader feels as if he is there, watching the Duke's politeness to the emissary but sensing beneath it his cruelty and pride. The Duke teaches us that how we talk about and how we treat others reveal the state of our hearts and our souls. Sadly, the Duke is heartless, and his soul has been destroyed by his pride. He is not a human being—he is truly the deadly duke.

Michael Kubiak

Try to pay attention to your own use of point of view as you talk to your family and friends. As you describe your activities, notice how you can produce emotional responses in your audience, such as making them laugh or perhaps even making them cry. You can also communicate the message you want by picking and choosing the details you include and emphasize. These same principles govern the stories told by fictional characters or outside narrators.

❧ Point of View Analysis Plan Sheet ❧

Author: _____ Title: _____

Thesis: _____

_____

_____

_____

_____

Topic sentence: _____

_____

_____

           Supporting quote: page or line _____

           Supporting quote: page or line _____

           Supporting quote: page or line _____

Topic sentence: _____

_____

_____

           Supporting quote: page or line _____

           Supporting quote: page or line _____

           Supporting quote: page or line _____

Topic sentence: _____

_____

_____

           Supporting quote: page or line _____

           Supporting quote: page or line _____

           Supporting quote: page or line _____

Topic sentence: _____

_____

_____

Supporting quote: page or line _____

Supporting quote: page or line _____

Supporting quote: page or line _____

Topic sentence: _____

_____

_____

Supporting quote: page or line _____

Supporting quote: page or line _____

Supporting quote: page or line _____

Topic sentence: _____

_____

_____

Supporting quote: page or line _____

Supporting quote: page or line _____

Supporting quote: page or line _____

Concluding points: _____

_____

_____

_____

_____

_____

_____

_____

❧ Peer/Self-Evaluation of a Point of View Analysis Essay ❧

> **Directions:** Make specific suggestions about each part of the essay, pointing out particular areas that the writer could improve. Keep in mind the qualities of good writing: unity, organization, development, clarity, and coherence.

I. Introduction

Is the lead relevant and interesting?

Are the author's full name and the title of the work correctly spelled and punctuated?

Does the brief plot summary include an identification of the point of view?

Does the thesis name the point-of-view character and list his or her character traits?

Does the thesis describe the reader's emotional response to the characters and state the theme in the work produced by the point of view?

II. Body Paragraphs

Do the topic sentences contain the key points about the character of the narrator, the reader's emotional response, and the theme as listed in the thesis?

Are the supporting quotations properly introduced?

Are the supporting quotations relevant to the topic sentence of the paragraph?

Are the analysis sections adequately developed?

Do the body paragraphs follow the order of the thesis?

Are the body paragraphs unified and coherent?

III. Conclusion

Is a signal word included somewhere in the paragraph?

Is the effectiveness of the choice of point of view stated and explained?

Is the final sentence an effective clincher?

IV. Expression

Are all the ideas expressed in complete sentences?

Are the sentences clear and correctly punctuated?

Are there any problems with subject-verb or pronoun-antecedent agreement?

Are all the words correctly spelled?

V. Overall Evaluation

Most effective part of the essay:

Least effective part of the essay:

List three specific actions which could be taken by the writer to improve this and future papers:
1.

2.

3.

Evaluator's name: _____ Date: _____

Name_____ Section _____ Date_____

❧ Exercise on Point of View ❧

> Read the following excerpts from short stories and then identify the point of view being used in each one. Circle the clue words that led to your decision.

1. "The American and the girl with him sat at a table in the shade, outside the building. It was very hot and the express from Barcelona would come in forty minutes. It stopped at this junction for two minutes and went on to Madrid.
    'What should we drink?' the girl asked. She had taken off her hat and put it on the table.
    'It's pretty hot,' the man said." From "Hills Like White Elephants" by Ernest Hemingway.[1]

    Point of View: _____

2. "Well, the Fourth of July is over! The people are all gone and I am tired out. John thought it might do me good to see a little company, so we just had mother and Nellie and the children down for a week." From "The Yellow Wallpaper" by Charlotte Perkins Gilman.[2]

    Point of View: _____

3. "As Gregor Samsa awoke one morning from uneasy dreams he found himself transformed in his bed into a gigantic insect. He was lying on his hard, as it were armor-plated, back and when he lifted his head a little he could see his dome-like brown belly divided into stiff arched segments.
    What has happened to me? he thought. It was no dream." From "The Metamorphosis" by Franz Kafka.[3]

    Point of View: _____

4. "Leo hurried up to bed and hid under the covers. Under the covers he thought his life through. Although he soon fell asleep he could not sleep her out of his mind." From "The Magic Barrel" by Bernard Malamud.[4]

    Point of View: _____

---

[1] Reprinted with permission of Charles Scribner's & Sons, an imprint of Macmillan Publishing Company, from MEN WITHOUT WOMEN by Ernest Hemingway. Copyright 1927 by Charles Scribner's Sons. Copyright renewed 1955 by Ernest Hemingway.
[2] In *An Introduction to Literature*, ed. Sylvan Barnet, Morton Berman, and William Burto, 8th ed. (Boston: Little, 1985), 107.
[3] in *An Introduction to Literature*, 158.
[4] in *An Introduction to Literature*, 333.

5.   "She had sort of oaky hair that the sun and salt had bleached, done up in a bun that was unraveling, and a kind of prim face. Walking into the A & P with your straps down, I suppose it's the only kind of face you *can* have." From "A & P" by John Updike.[5]

Point of View: _____

6.   "'Mummy,' I said, 'do you know what I'm going to do when I grow up?'
      'No, dear,' she replied. 'What?'
      'I'm going to marry you,' I said quietly." From "My Oedipus Complex" by Frank O'Connor.[6]

Point of View: _____

[5] in *An Introduction to Literature*, 390.
[6] in *An Introduction to Literature*, 311.

Symbolism Analysis

Overview

Symbolism is a much discussed concept in art, music, literature—in all of the humanities. The reason is that man—the only animal capable of using symbols—delights in his power to create them. A symbol is something (it can be a person, an object, an action, a place, a color) that can stand for or represent something else in addition to its literal meaning. As an artistic device, symbolism adds depth and complexity of meaning to many works of literature.

Understanding Symbolism

A symbol is generally defined as something which can stand for or represent something beyond itself. It operates on two levels: it is itself (particular, literal), and it can be something more than itself (universal, figurative). The heart, for example, is a particular muscle of the body that has a particular purpose—the circulation of the blood. It is literally—really—necessary to the continuation of life. On a symbolic level, it is universally considered to be the seat of emotions, the figurative—unreal—source of love. Another example is the flag. It is a particular type of cloth of specific colors and design, but on a universal, figurative level, it is a symbol of the nation, the country, the people, and the ideals it represents.

Types of Symbols

A writer may sometimes use an isolated symbol—like the heart or a ring—in a story, but more often he or she will use a pattern or a group of symbols which may fall into various types or categories. These may be **symbolic characters, names, objects, actions, places,** and **colors.** A specific character—who may represent a universal type—may perform symbolic actions with symbolic objects in a symbolic place to convey an idea on a symbolic level. For example, a bullfighter (a brave man) moves gracefully (bravely) and waves a red cape (a sign of his courage) before a bull (danger, death) in an arena (any battleground or even life itself) to convey the idea that bravery is "grace under pressure." (Thanks, Hemingway!) In her short story "The Lottery," Shirley Jackson uses each type of symbol to convey her theme about the power of tradition. Old Man Warner (a symbolic name) is the oldest man in the town, and he warns the townspeople about the dangers of changing the town's tradition of a yearly lottery. His name and his words tie him to the past and the importance of maintaining tradition. Tessie (a symbolic character) is the townswoman who becomes the victim of tradition and functions as the scapegoat, sacrificed so that the town will have a good corn crop. She is chosen because she has picked the slip with the black mark (a symbolic object and color) from the black lottery box (another object also symbolically black and old). The sacrifice of Tessie occurs in the town's square (a symbolic place), which symbolizes that the entire population of the town is controlled by the pressure to conform. As the townspeople stone Tessie (a symbolic action), they are carrying on tradition in a town trapped in the past. Such patterns may not be clearly labeled by the author, but they can be spotted and identified by the careful and critical reader.

Universal and Personal Symbols

Some symbols that have been used repeatedly by writers with the same cultural background come to have a clearly understood universal significance. The color black, for example, is usually associated with death, so when the box used in "The Lottery" by Shirley Jackson is black, it suggests the ritual death that will soon follow. The snake has been a symbol for Satan since he took on the form of a serpent in the Garden of Eden to tempt Eve, so when Young Goodman Brown in Nathaniel Hawthorne's short story of the same name meets a traveller in the forest whose staff looks like "a great black snake, so curiously wrought that it might almost be seen to twist and wriggle itself like a living serpent,"[1] readers immediately associate the traveller with Satan and evil.

Other symbols, however, have a personal significance created by an author to suggest his or her own feelings about an object, action, or character. While water or rain is universally a symbol of life, Hemingway used rain as a symbol of death in his novel *A Farewell to Arms*. The book begins with a description of death in battle in the rain, Catherine Barkley talks about her fear of dying in the rain, and the book ends with her death and Frederic's returning to the hotel in the rain. Hemingway seems to relate the darkness and gloominess that accompany rain to the depression and sadness that surround death. To decide whether a symbol is a universal or a personal one, you need to consider its use within the work as a whole.

Clues to Symbolism

There are, generally speaking, some clues that symbolism may be present in a work of literature. If you have the overwhelming feeling that this work is "very strange" or that the events could never happen in real life, the author probably intends that the work be read on a symbolic level rather than a literal one. Such a work might be Shirley Jackson's short story "The Lottery." It seems inconceivable that in our day the people of a small town would still sacrifice human life for a good corn crop; literally, we say, it could not happen, but on a figurative or symbolic level, the human spirit is often sacrificed in the name of tradition and "what's always been." Other stories may not be so obviously strange, but they may leave you with a sense of uneasiness, with the feeling that you haven't discovered the depths of the author's perceptions. For example, in D. H. Lawrence's short story "The Horse Dealer's Daughter," the love relationship of Mabel Pervin and Jack Fergusson develops so quickly that it is hard to believe in and accept. The sense that this is an improbable love story would lead the informed reader to look for symbols that could relate to a universal idea.

If something is operating as a symbol, the author may emphasize its importance in different ways, perhaps through detailed description, repetition, word choice, or even direct statement. In "The Horse Dealer's Daughter," D. H. Lawrence uses the pond in which Mabel tries to kill herself as a symbol of death and rebirth. He describes it in four very detailed paragraphs that include repeated references to death and coldness. He also uses forms of the verb *to rise* when he describes Jack's rescue of Mabel, suggesting that both of them have risen from death and have been reborn to new lives. The devices that Lawrence uses to give emphasis to the pond also signal its symbolic meaning in the work.

---

[1] In *An Introduction to Literature*, ed. Sylvan Barnet, Morton Berman, and William Burto, 10th ed. (New York: Harper, 1993) 75.

Archetypal Symbolism

The theory of archetypal symbolism, originated by Swiss psychologist Carl Jung, holds that there are recurring characters and actions—universals—that appeal to our "collective unconscious," those subliminal memories shared by all members of the human race. Jung believed that certain symbols—which he called archetypes—call forth these memories because they reflect universal aspects of the human condition. Some archetypal characters are the savior, the innocent youth, the wise old man, the domineering father, the evil stepmother, the hero, the *femme fatale*, the saint, the scapegoat, and the outcast. Archetypal actions include the journey, the quest, the initiation, the loss of innocence, the descent into hell, and death and rebirth, while archetypal elements include water, earth, sky, desert, heat, cold, darkness, and light.

These symbols have appeared over and over again in literature. They are popular with writers and readers alike because they crystallize meaningful human experiences. Most people have encountered the scapegoat—like Tessie in "The Lottery" by Shirley Jackson—or have taken the journey from innocence to experience—like young Robin in Hawthorne's "My Kinsman, Major Molineux." When you encounter archetypal characters, actions, or elements in a story, try to trace their symbolic significance throughout the work.

Symbolism and Allegory

One type of symbolic narrative is the allegory in which the writer creates one set of characters and events that have direct one-to-one equivalents. Allegories often take place in invented worlds, are easily paraphrased, and usually deal with spiritual questions. Fables and parables—types of allegories—are short narratives with a "moral" or lesson about life.

Nathaniel Hawthorne's "Young Goodman Brown" has allegorical overtones. Young Goodman Brown (a good man) is married to Faith (virtue), but he is still impelled to leave her and take a journey (from innocence to experience, from ignorance to knowledge, from appearance to reality). He leaves the town (the domain of goodness) and enters the forest (the domain of evil), and on his journey, he encounters Satan (the embodiment of evil), his grandfather (evil in the family), the governor and court members (evil in the state), and Goody Cloyse, Deacon Gookin, and the minister (evil in the church). At the witches' sabbath (the acknowledgment of evil), the worshippers (all human classes) undergo a baptism of evil (the appearance of evil in man's nature). Hence Goodman's journey represents any person's psychological journey from innocence to the acceptance of evil in mankind and in oneself.

Interpreting the Symbolism

A good way to start your symbolic analysis of a work is to pick one major symbol (usually a central character) and identify a possible symbolic interpretation. Then check to see if the other symbols can be related to that one and its interpretation. For example, R. P. McMurphy in Ken Kesey's *One Flew Over the Cuckoo's Nest* helps the inmates of a mental institution help themselves. He saves them from the forces that fight against them, and it is easy to see him as a savior, a Christ figure. He is a major symbolic character; once his significance is identified and interpreted, it is possible to look for symbolic objects and actions that relate to him and this interpretation. Big Nurse, Miss Ratched, might represent the forces of evil that work against the patients to keep them from achieving their manhood. As McMurphy battles against her to save the men who become his followers (his disciples), he takes them on a fishing trip (does that sound Biblical?), and as a result of that victory over Big Nurse, he is forced to undergo shock treatment. The shock treatment table is in the form of a cross, and the electrodes are reminiscent of the crown of thorns that Christ wore when he was being punished before his actual death. McMurphy's lobotomy and death relate to Christ's crucifixion and death so that mankind (the patients) might live.

This process of identifying and interpreting the symbols can also be illustrated by considering Shirley Jackson's "The Lottery." As the story unfolds, it becomes evident that Old Man Warner is the strongest supporter of the ritual of the lottery which is being carried out. It is easy to see, from his words and actions, that he speaks out in favor of tradition, and hence he can be identified as the spokesman or the voice of tradition. After his significance is determined from, of course, what he says and does in the story, it is possible to relate all of the other symbolic characters, objects, and actions to some aspect of tradition.

If you are having difficulty getting started with your interpretation of the symbols in a work, you will be glad to learn that your library has reference works that can help you in your quest for meaning. Quite probably it has several dictionaries of symbols which will list all of the generally accepted universal meanings for common symbols. Two works in this area are *The Dictionary of Symbols* by Jean Chevalier (Viking Penguin, 1997) and *Dictionary of Symbolism: Cultural Icons and the Meanings Behind Them* (NAL/Dutton, 1993). The librarian can help you locate additional reference works to help you gain insight into the symbolic meaning of the work you are analyzing. Remember, however, that interpretations are not simply pulled out of the air (or out of a reference work); they are related to the subject matter, to the characters' words and actions, and to what happens in the work as a whole.

Finding the Symbolic Theme

The last part of symbolism analysis involves "adding up" the interpretations of the symbols to see what theme or meaning the author is conveying. It is usually some idea that is universally applicable to the human condition. In Hemingway, we often find the theme that man faces many dangers in the game of life—some that he cannot overcome—but he should still face them with courage the way that Santiago does in *The Old Man and the Sea*. Ken Kesey tells us in *One Flew Over the Cuckoo's Nest* that human beings can support and save each other and that love often demands sacrifice. Shirley Jackson tells us in "The Lottery" that tradition is not always good and that custom should be examined before it is accepted. The symbolic themes vary, of course, depending on the subject matter and on the author's view of life; the alert reader will perceive them and evaluate their usefulness in his or her own value system.

Writing about Symbolism: Step by Step

Try to follow these steps as you plan your essay on symbolism analysis.

1. Not every work of literature has a symbolic level, so try to choose a work which appears to have more than just a literal level of meaning. Clues to this type of work might be a sense of strangeness or a feeling that there is more to the work than the obvious interpretation.
2. Pick out the characters, the names, the objects, the actions, the places, and the colors which seem especially important in the work. Remember, however, that it is not necessary to mention or interpret every symbol that you can identify. Here are some organizational options to consider:
   a. one, several, or all of the symbolic characters;
   b. one or more of the symbolic characters and their actions with the symbolic objects;
   c. one, several, or all of the symbolic objects;
   d. one, several, or all of the symbolic actions;
   e. one, several, or all of the symbolic objects and actions;
   f. symbolic names of characters and/or places;
   g. symbolic places where significant actions occur;
   h. symbolic colors.
   i. any combination of symbols that work together to convey a theme.

Some writers may choose to analyze just one character, one object, or one action in great detail, while others may choose to analyze several symbols from each type to give a more comprehensive picture of the pattern of symbols used by the author. The choice is yours as to the type and number of symbols you plan to analyze.

3. To begin your interpretation of the symbols you plan to discuss, choose a major character (this is usually a good place to start) and review the character's words and actions—his or her role in the work. Your explanation of his or her symbolic meaning is not arbitrary; it is directly related to what the character says and does in the work as a whole. Having arrived at a possible interpretation, return to the other characters and see how they relate to the symbolic meaning you have established. Most of them should fit into a pattern of meaning around your interpretation of the central character. Having interpreted the symbolic characters, proceed to the symbolic objects and try to relate them to the main idea or theme which ties the symbolic characters together. Now move to the symbolic actions by relating them to your interpretation of the symbolic objects. Continue the same process with any other symbolic groups you plan to discuss. All of the symbols should fall into place around one central theme or idea.

4. The types of symbols you plan to analyze in your essay (symbolic characters, symbolic objects, symbolic actions, symbolic places, symbolic colors) or the specific symbols you have chosen are listed in the introduction as the first part of the thesis statement. The second part of the thesis is a statement of the theme to which the symbols relate.

5. Each type of symbol or each specific symbol is interpreted and explained in a separate body paragraph. The topic sentence names the symbolic type and then lists the specific symbols to be analyzed. Each symbol is then interpreted by using the literary analysis pattern. State what the symbol represents, provide introductory material for a supporting quotation, quote from the work, and then explain how the quotation supports your interpretation of the symbol.

6. The conclusion is a thorough discussion of the theme listed in the thesis in the introductory paragraph. The topic sentence clearly states the theme and the rest of the paragraph shows how the theme relates to the work and then explores the theme's universal significance. Consider how the ideas relate to everyone's life—not just to the specific situation presented in the work.

The following diagram, model essays, and plan sheet will help you organize and write a well developed essay on symbolism in a work of literature.

Diagram of the Structure of a Symbolism Analysis Essay

Title

Introductory Paragraph:

Open with interesting lead material.

Name the work and the author.

Give a brief summary, working down to the idea that symbolism is present in the work.

List the types of symbols or the specific symbols you plan to discuss: characters, names, objects, actions, places, or colors.

State the theme that is communicated through the symbols.

Thesis

Body Paragraphs:

In the first part of the body, interpret the first type of symbol listed in the thesis. The topic sentence names the symbolic type and then lists the specific symbols to be discussed in the paragraph. Each symbol is interpreted/explained in the order listed. State the meaning of the symbol, introduce a supporting quotation, quote it, and then in your analysis explain *how* the quotation supports that interpretation.

The second part of the body interprets the second type of symbol listed in the thesis statement. The topic sentence includes the name of the type and then a list of the symbols to be analyzed. Each symbol's interpretation is followed by introductory material for a quotation, the quotation itself, and then analysis.

The third type of symbol listed in the thesis is explained in the third part of the body. It should be organized in the same way as the preceding paragraphs. Direct quotations preceded by introductory material should be used to support your interpretations, and the quotations should be followed by analysis which explains how the quotation justifies the stated symbolic meaning.

Concluding Paragraph:

Begin with a signal word, and in the topic sentence restate the symbolic theme. Then briefly show how the theme evolves from and relates to the symbols in the work. The rest of the paragraph explains the theme's universal meaning by showing how it relates to everyone's life because of the universal human condition.

Model Essay One

This student-written essay analyzes one symbolic character.

Our Old Friend

Death is a certainty of life, but the time of its arrival is often uncertain. Death wears many disguises, and though dark and sometimes ugly, it can also be seen as a friend, for death is often the vehicle of escape from a painful, futile existence. Early in Joyce Carol Oates' short story entitled "Where Are You Going, Where Have You Been?"[1] Connie, a typical fifteen-year-old girl, wishes that "she herself was dead and it was all over" (35). Her careless wish is fulfilled when she meets a character named Arnold Friend.

Thesis Statement → *His untimely arrival, his appearance and that of his companion Ellie, and his offer to Connie of a ride in his vehicle give evidence of his true identity: Arnold Friend symbolizes death.*

Topic Sentence → *Since each of us is certain of someday meeting with death, Arnold clearly states his mission in Connie's life at their first meeting at the drive-in.* He appears at the moment when she is experiencing "the pure pleasure of being alive" with Eddie, her latest beau (37). Though at times in each our lives death would seem a welcome relief, its arrival is usually at a time when life seems a precious gift. Even Arnold's first words to Connie are a prophetic "'Gonna get you, baby,'" (37). As death personified, he reminds Connie of the inevitability of her demise. There is no way she can escape.

Topic Sentence → *Just as death often comes disguised, Arnold's appearance belies his true identity.* When he shows up—uninvited—in Connie's driveway, she quickly sizes him up: "his face was a familiar face, somehow: the jaw and chin and cheeks slightly darkened [. . .] sniffing as if she were a treat he was going to gobble up and it was all a joke" (42). Connie, probably having been exposed to death in some form, recognizes it in Arnold Friend. The darkness of death is prevalent in his appearance, and Connie fears she is a treat for his consumption. She sense what we all know: death is a joke, life's bad punchline. Another thing Connie notices is Arnold's unmistakable resemblance to a cadaver. When he removes his sunglasses, Connie notes "how pale the skin around his eyes was" (43). His skin tone is the pallor of death. Even his friend Ellie bears a striking resemblance to one who has passed on with his "pale, bluish chest" (45) as he sits in the back seat of Arnold's car in "a kind of daze" (45). Arnold has brought an accomplice from the land of death to help him bring Connie home. The sight of these two strangers causes Connie to become frightened. When Arnold's whole face suddenly appears to Connie to be "a mask," (48) she becomes hysterical facing uncertainty about her passage from this life. She does not know what awaits.

Topic Sentence → *Arnold's offer to Connie is a ride in his omnious-looking vehicle.* The car is painted a gold that hurts Connie's eyes with "the numbers 33, 19, 17"

---

[1] Joyce Carol Oates, "Where Are You Going, Where Have You Been?" *The Wheel of Love and Other Stories* (New York: Vanguard Press, a division of Random House, Inc., 1970). Used by permission of Vanguard Press, a division of Random House, Inc.

painted on one side along with Arnold's name "in tarlike black letters" (41). The fact that Connie's eyes hurt to see the car suggests that death is often painful to view. Although she can't decipher the secret code on his car, Arnold gives a direct hint when he says, "'Around the other side's a lot more—you wanta come and see them?'" (41). As death is often referred to as "the other side," Arnold directly invites Connie to meet his other victims. The numbers tell us that death is indiscriminate of age. Even after Connie has considered escape by picking up the phone, Arnold tries to persuade her to accompany him on his "ride" (42) by telling her, "'The place where you came from ain't there any more, and where you had in mind to go is canceled out. This place [. . .] is nothing but a cardboard box I can knock down any time'" (52). Arnold Friend reminds Connie that one's situation or location makes absolutely no difference to death. While every individual may have a concept of her own destiny, be it heaven, hell, or otherwise, death need only be concerned with one's passage to the destiny that awaits. Connie finally succumbs to the "vast sunlit reaches of the land behind [Arnold]" and watches her "body and [her] head of long hair moving out into the sunlight where Arnold Friend waited" (54). She accepts death's offer of escape from a life of darkness and leaves her past behind to discover a new level of existence with Arnold.

Restatement of Thesis

And so death with all of its certainty and its many disguises sometimes becomes our friend because it helps us escape the pain and futility of life. Connie knew what she was doing when she sacrificed her brief existence in order to accept a ride with an old friend. She wanted to escape from her unhappy family life the way that many teenagers do who do not see a way out of their situation. Perhaps that's why many of them choose suicide rather than facing their pain. Unfortunately, like Connie, they don't seem to realize that life can change, but their choice is forever.

Kathie Markezinis

✁ Model Essay Two

This student essay analyzes several symbolic characters.

Murder in the Name of Tradition

Traditions are practices passed down from generation to generation. Although they can be political, social, or religious, most involve family and friends who gather together to participate in some familiar ritual. Usually these regular occurrences are happy occasions, but in Shirley Jackson's short story "The Lottery,"[1] one particular yearly tradition meant to insure

[1] Shirley Jackson, "The Lottery" *An Introduction to Literature,* ed. Sylvan Barnet, Morton Berman, and William Burto, 8th ed. (Boston: Little, 1985). All parenthetical page numbers refer to the text in this edition.

a good harvest is anything but a joyous occasion. Each year, the towns-people gather to draw the name of a victim to be offered for their sacrifice. Ultimately, for all of them, it is a chance taken that may preserve their life or assure their death. "A hush [falls] on the crowd" (338) as names are called to draw a paper from the black box. The person drawing the paper with the black dot becomes the next victim to give up his or her life for the sake of carrying out this horrible tradition. *Jackson uses the symbolic characters of Old Man Warner, Bill Hutchinson, and Davy Hutchinson to convey her theme that customs should be examined before they are accepted and passed on to the next generation.*

Thesis Statement

Topic Sentence

For seventy-seven years, Old Man Warner has been a willing participant and a staunch believer in the yearly ritual of the lottery; he symbolizes the voice of tradition. When one of the townspeople points out that another village is considering quitting the lottery, Warner answers, "'Pack of crazy fools [. . .]. Next thing you know, they'll be wanting to go back to living in caves'" (339). Because the lottery has been part of the culture of the town for generations, he believes that not participating in it would be barbaric. Warner tries to discourage the townspeople from having such crazy ideas because, to him, the lottery is the civilized thing to do. He also believes that because of the "'Lottery in June, corn [will] be heavy soon'" (339). This is the cornerstone on which Old Man Warner bases his traditional beliefs: without the lottery, there would be no assurance of a good harvest. He definitely feels there is "'Nothing but trouble in [stopping the lottery],'" and because "'There's always been a lottery'" (339), he is positive that any break from this old tradition would have disastrous consequences for the town and its people.

Topic Sentence

While Old Man Warner represents the voice of tradition, Bill Hutchinson symbolizes the ultimate follower of tradition. After Bill draws the paper with the black dot indicating that he or one of the members of his family is doomed to death, his wife shouts words of protest to the people of the town who run the lottery. He tells her coldly, "'Shut up, Tessie'" (340). Even in the face of death, Bill unquestioningly goes along with the procedures of this ritual; he does not analyze its senselessness, nor does he offer any objection. In fact, telling his wife to be quiet indicates that he does not agree with her feelings about the fairness of the lottery. He is blind to any thought that this tradition could not possibly be valid or that it should be reconsidered as an unnecessary or gruesome part of the culture of the town. As each progressive step of the lottery brings death closer to someone in his family, Bill, again, "with one quick glance at his wife and children" (341), proudly takes part in the drawing of the papers. When Tessie refuses to open her hand holding her slip of paper, "Bill Hutchinson [goes] over to his wife and [forces] the slip of paper out of her hand" (341). He obviously feels it is unthinkable not to submit willingly to this practice; he never once stops to consider whether following this ritual is the right thing to do. Bill Hutchinson truly represents the ultimate follower of tradition.

Topic Sentence

Davy Hutchinson symbolizes the assurance that the tradition of the lottery will be passed on to the next generation of followers. As he watches each member of his family draw a paper from the black box, little Davy, in turn, "[comes] willingly [. . .] up to the box" (341) and takes a paper out. No one draws for him; he does it himself. By doing this, he is being indoctrinated into the tradition. He is learning that no one is exonerated from taking part in the ritual, but because he is so young, he does not realize the significance or the consequences of the custom that he is participating in. To him, this yearly event is part of the everyday life of the people of the town. Also, he is not encouraged to question the necessity of the tradition; he is only taught to follow and accept the terms of the ritual. When his mother is the person who draws the paper with the black dot, she automatically becomes the next victim of this dreadful tradition, and again, the townspeople do not shelter Davy from this final step of the lottery. In fact, "someone [gives] little Davy Hutchinson a few pebbles" (342) to hurl at his mother. Giving the child the pebbles insures that the tradition will be carried on by the next generation. Davy learns that the lottery must continue and he must participate—no matter who draws the black dot. Unfortunately, like his father, Davy follows blindly.

Restatement of Thesis

Jackson, then, shocks us into realizing that traditions should not be followed blindly. By using the symbolic character of Old Man Warner, she emphasizes how entrenched some traditions can become in a person's life, and because of this, they are hard to break. In the character of Bill Hutchinson, she reveals how rituals foster a person to follow obediently, never questioning the validity of the custom. Through Davy Hutchinson, we are shown how subtly traditions are taught. Without being given an opportunity to decide for themselves, young children are drawn into carrying on traditions. Although we all have certain rituals we follow without question, Jackson urges us to think about them and reconsider their necessity and validity. Whether they are political, social, religious, or family traditions, we should be aware that all rituals need to be subjected to a prudent review for their practicality. To blindly follow tradition can have devastating consequences.

Anna Cellini

Model Essay Three

Here is a student-written essay that focuses on several different types of symbols.

The Rebirth of Mabel and Jack

When two people get married, they unite to form one; they become one body, one soul. There is a sequence of events that precede marriage, though. The two people meet, fall in love, and get married, and this process takes place over a length of time. In the short story "The Horse Dealer's Daughter"[1] by D. H. Lawrence, the events leading to the marriage of Mabel Pervin and Dr. Jack Fergusson occur in one day. The suddenness of this

[1] D. H. Lawrence, "The Horse Dealer's Daughter" *The Complete Short Stories,* Volume II (New York: Viking, 1961). All parenthetical page numbers refer to the text in this edition.

Thesis Statement	process suggests that symbolism is present in the story. *Lawrence uses symbolic characters, symbolic places, and symbolic objects to convey his theme that there must be an equilibrium of emotion and reason in a person's life in order for that person to attain a sense of wholeness. Also, a person can be reborn through love, and the combination of the two people can help create the essential balance needed for happiness.*
Topic Sentence	*One of the symbolic characters in the story is Mabel Pervin.* She symbolizes the emotional side of human nature. Even though her mother died when Mabel was fourteen, she still grieves over the tragedy and "lives in the memory of her mother" (447). She cannot accept the reality of her mother's death. She endures from day to day, and her only joy in life comes from thinking about her own suicide. She feels she will "be coming nearer to her fulfillment, her own glorification, approaching her dead mother, who was glorified" (447). She is contemplating suicide because she feels that there is nothing to live for without her mother. She feels that happiness can only be reached through her death. These are obviously thoughts that are characteristic of a person who is highly emotional, irrational, and unstable, a person who cannot keep problems in proper perspective. Mable's strong emotions are also revealed to Jack after he saves her from her attempted suicide. She "shuffled forward on her knees, and put her arms around him [. . .] clutching him with strange convulsive certainty [. . .] passionately kissing his knees [. . .] as if unaware of everything" (452–453). Mabel lets her inner passion explode in gestures that are animalistic and uncontrolled. Once again she is extremely emotional, almost irrational.
Topic Sentence	*In contrast, Jack Fergusson, another symbolic character, represents the rational side of human nature.* He is very logical and is always thinking. Even when Mabel is throwing herself at him, Jack is trying to reason it out: "He had never thought of loving her [. . .]. He had no single personal thought of her" (453). Only a person who is an intelligent, reasoning, and cautious individual would weigh the odds and logically try to reason out this emotional situation instead of letting his feelings govern his actions. Jack seems to be emotionless; he has a hard time expressing his feelings and believes that he must bury them in the deep recesses of his soul. Jack is also cautious in what he does because he is worried about what others might think of his relationship with Mabel: "That this was love! That he should be ripped open in this way! Him, a doctor! How they would all jeer if they knew! It was agony to him to think they might know" (455). Jack is more concerned about the opinion of others than he is about his own feelings. He is unable to let himself go, and he needs to bring out his emotions and passions. He needs someone to help control the intellectual quality in him.
Topic Sentence	*The symbolic places are the pond and the fireplace.* The pond is where Jack and Mabel are first actually in close contact with one another. It symbolizes their grave and their death. When Jack tries to rescue Mable, "the water clasped dead cold round his legs" (450). The pond seems to pull him under, to bury him in the "wet, gray clay" (450). He is powerless and he struggles for "what seemed an eternity" (450). Both Mabel and Jack are symbolically buried in the pond, but when they rise to the surface, they are cleansed of their old images. They are given another chance to live. The fireplace, another symbol, represents the passion that is buried and just waiting to flare within Mabel and Jack. Even though Jack tries desperately to

conceal his passion, Mabel seems to bring it out. She has a power over him that makes him feel "warm inside himself [. . .] [and] his heart seemed to burn and melt away in his breast" (454). Mabel touches his heart, and her fire melts the wall around his emotions. On the other hand, Jack brings out the passion and love hidden in Mabel. There is a "faint delicate flush [. . .] [a] terrible shining of joy in her eyes" (454). Jack gives Mabel a new life, and she is reborn. The fire, then, symbolizes the new life of Jack and Mabel and the warmth of love that is now burning within them.

The symbolic objects are Mabel's and Jack's clothes and Mabel's eyes. Mabel's clothes symbolize her emotional state throughout her life. She is always dressed in black. When Jack looks toward the pond on his way home from his rounds, he sees "a figure in black" (449). Mable's black clothing symbolizes her depression and coming death. Even when she changes her clothes after the incident at the pond, she wears "her best dress of black voile" (456). It is hard for Mabel to completely break loose from her depression even though Jack tells her he loves her and wants her. She still has doubts and fears and feels that she isn't good enough for him. Jack's clothes symbolize the shedding of his old image to become a new person. The old clothes that smell of "the dead clayey water" (451) symbolize Jack's death. He constantly wants to remove his old clothes and put on something fresh and new. He wants to shed his past image and look ahead to the future and a new life. Mabel's eyes are the most important symbolic element in the story. They symbolize the power of life and love. When Jack looks at Mabel fixing her mother's grave in the cemetery, "there was a heavy power in her eyes which laid hold of his whole being [. . .]. He had been feeling weak and done before. Now life came back into him, he felt delivered from his own fretted daily self" (448). Before Jack sees those powerful eyes of Mabel, he is weak, but her eyes make him strong, ready to live life. Her eyes give him the spark he needs to continue on. Mabel's eyes are also the element that attracts Jack to her. She looks "at him with large, portentous eyes [. . .] [that] seemed to mesmerize him" (448). Jack is spellbound every time he looks into Mabel's eyes. They seem to contain a certain power that possesses him and makes him feel and act unlike himself. They hold the love and passion that Jack is craving, so he finally surrenders to Mabel and falls in love with her.

And so the symbols Lawrence uses reveal his message that through love, a person can be reborn, that a wholeness and a balance of emotions and logic can be attained. When love is not a part of a person's life, he becomes lonely and depressed, just as Mabel and Jack are before they find each other. They feel as though something is missing from their lives; there is an emptiness that needs to be filled. Finally the powerful emotion of love overtakes them and fills that gap, making them whole, creating that balance that is needed for humans to survive. Through Jack and Mabel's love, Lawrence tells us that there is always hope, that through love people can be changed and become happier than they are. If we are unhappy or lonely, we can reach out to others in love. When that love is returned, we can be reborn and begin to live again. And when two people in love complement each other, they become one in body and soul—which is what love and marriage are all about.

Debbie Burns

Model Essay Four

This student-written essay focuses on symbolism in a poem by William Blake.

The Sick Rose

O rose, thou art sick!
The invisible worm
That flies in the night,
In the howling storm,

Has found out thy bed
Of crimson joy,
And his dark secret love
Does thy life destroy.

The Death of a Rose

Roses are the flower of choice on Valentine's Day because they are generally accepted as symbols of love, fragrant and beautiful. In William Blake's poem "The Sick Rose,"[1] however, he presents a rose about to be destroyed, not enjoyed. *Blake uses four symbols—the rose, the worm, the storm, and the bed—to convey his theme that love cannot last if it is weakened by negative emotions.*

Thesis Statement

Topic Sentence

The rose is almost universally accepted as a symbol of love. The speaker addresses the flower, saying, "O rose, thou art sick!" (line 1). On a literal level, it appears to the speaker that the rose has begun to wilt or darken, suggesting it is showing signs that it is no longer perfect. On a symbolic level, the rose represents a love that has begun to wilt, that is no longer beautiful or perfect. When love is fading, there are usually visible signs that feelings have changed, from a lack of loving smiles to a lack of physical contact. If this cooling of passion is evident to outsiders, it is surely evident to those involved in the dying relationship.

Topic Sentence

The worm is a symbol of disease in the relationship, an insidious devouring force that is attacking the love the couple have for each other just as the literal worm is attacking the rose. Love is being threatened by an "invisible worm / That flies in the night" (2–3). The darkness of the night suggests the coming death of the relationship caused by perhaps distrust, perhaps jealousy, perhaps fear of being consumed and controlled by the lover. These darker "invisible" emotions sicken relationships because they subtly eat away at the heart, the seat of love.

Topic Sentence

The "storm" (4) symbolizes the passion these lovers should feel for each other, but the fact that the speaker describes it as a "howling storm" (4) suggests that the feelings are not joyous and life-filled but mournful and death-filled. A howl is a sad, plaintive sound, symbolizing pain, sorrow, or anger. Perhaps the relationship is beset by these negative emotions because of a

[1] In *An Introduction to Literature*, ed. Sylvan Barnet, Morton Berman, and William Burto, 10th ed. (New York: Harper, 1993) 470.

	lack of fideltiy or a lack of deep commitment to each other. Their stormy love affair is on a rocky course, threatened by darkness and emotional pain.
Topic Sentence	*The lovers' "bed / Of crimson joy" (5–6) is a symbol of their past love-making when their feelings for each other brought pleasure and delight rather than pain.* The crimson color suggests that their love was once new and vivid and the blush was on them, but now their feelings for each other have turned into a "dark secret love / [that] Does [their love's] life destroy" (7–8). All of the "dark," negative, painful emotions that undermine love—distrust, jealousy, possessiveness—have sickened the lovers' relationship to the point that their love is dying. What was once alive and beautiful has become dark and dead because negative emotions have wormed their way into the lovers' hearts and consumed the joy that love once held.
Restatement of Thesis	*Through the symbols, then, Blake communicates his theme that love is beautiful, but it can be destroyed by the dark side of this emotion.* The rose, a thing of beauty, is destroyed by a natural predator, the worm, that works its way into the heart of the rose and then consumes its very existence. In the same way, love, a thing of beauty, is destroyed by its natural predators—distrust, jealousy, possessiveness—which work their way into the hearts of the lovers and then consume and destroy the relationship. Just as the rose needs light to blossom and bloom, so love needs the light of trust and understanding to be radiant and alive.

Jeanette Aler

JUST ONE MORE THING

Once you become aware of symbols, you will find them everywhere, and you will begin to appreciate their role in our culture. From the Easter bunny to hearts and flowers, they add special meaning to our holidays, our family celebrations, and our religious ceremonies.

❧ Symbolism Analysis Plan Sheet ❧

Author: _____ Title: _____

Thesis: _____

_____

_____

_____

_____

Topic sentence: _____

_____

_____

                Supporting quote: page or line _____

                Supporting quote: page or line _____

                Supporting quote: page or line _____

Topic sentence: _____

_____

_____

                Supporting quote: page or line _____

                Supporting quote: page or line _____

                Supporting quote: page or line _____

Topic sentence: _____

_____

_____

                Supporting quote: page or line _____

                Supporting quote: page or line _____

                Supporting quote: page or line _____

Topic sentence: _____

_____

_____

        Supporting quote: page or line _____

        Supporting quote: page or line _____

        Supporting quote: page or line _____

Topic sentence: _____

_____

_____

        Supporting quote: page or line _____

        Supporting quote: page or line _____

        Supporting quote: page or line _____

Topic sentence: _____

_____

_____

        Supporting quote: page or line _____

        Supporting quote: page or line _____

        Supporting quote: page or line _____

Concluding points: _____

_____

_____

_____

_____

_____

_____

_____

⚜ Peer/Self-Evaluation of a Symbolism Analysis Essay ⚜

> **Directions:** Make specific suggestions about each part of the essay, pointing out particular areas that the writer could improve. Keep in mind the qualities of good writing: unity, organization, development, clarity, and coherence.

I. Introduction

Is the lead relevant and interesting?

Are the author's full name and the title of the work correctly spelled and punctuated?

Does the plot summary lead into the idea that symbolism is present in the work?

Does the thesis name the specific symbols or list the types of symbols to be discussed in the body?

Does the thesis also state the symbolic theme that the symbols convey?

II. Body Paragraphs

Do the topic sentences contain the name of a specific symbol or state the type of symbol discussed in the paragraph?

Are the supporting quotations properly introduced?

Are the supporting quotations relevant to the interpretation of the symbols?

Are the analysis sections adequately developed?

Do the body paragraphs follow the order of the thesis?

Are the body paragraphs unified and coherent?

III. Conclusion

Is a signal word included somewhere in the final paragraph?

Is the symbolic theme rephrased in the topic sentence?

Does the rest of the paragraph relate the theme to the work and then to everyone's life?

Is the clincher sentence effective?

IV. Expression

Are all the ideas expressed in complete sentences?

Are the sentences clear and correctly punctuated?

Are there any problems with subject-verb or pronoun-antecedent agreement?

Are all the words correctly spelled?

V. Overall Evaluation

Most effective part of the essay:

Least effective part of the essay:

List three specific actions which could be taken by the writer to improve this and future papers:

1.

2.

3.

Evaluator's name: _____ Date: _____

❧ Exercise on Symbolism ❧

Completing this worksheet on symbolism will make you aware of some of the symbols in your daily environment. Next to the object, character, action, and color, briefly explain the symbolic meaning generally agreed upon by our culture.

Symbolic Objects:

Heart	Diamond ring
Flag	Wedding ring
Cross	Rocks
Water	Ashes
Flowers	Butterfly
Snake	Dove
Fire	Mink
Sun	Pearls
Moon	Blood
Sky	Tree
Lily	Christmas tree

Symbolic Characters:

Soldier	Baby
Policeman	Old man
President	Pope

Symbolic Actions:

Exchanging rings

Throwing rice at a wedding

Catching the bouquet or the garter

Breaking a glass at a Jewish wedding

Carrying the bride over the threshold

Pouring of water in baptism

Placing ashes on foreheads

Sprinkling dirt on a coffin

Kissing on both cheeks

Symbolic Colors:

Black

Yellow

White

Red

Blue

Green

Purple

Analyzing Poetry

Overview

Poetry, one of the major forms of literature, intimidates many readers because they are convinced it is more difficult to understand than short stories, novels, or plays. However, once one realizes that poetry, despite its different appearance on the page, is also written in sentences that can be analyzed and understood, it is easy to begin to enjoy its richness of form and meaning.

Poets and Poems

William Wordsworth, an English poet who revolutionized poetry as part of the Romantic Movement in England in the nineteenth century, describes a poet as "a man [or woman] . . . endued with more lively sensibility, more enthusiasm and tenderness, who has a greater knowledge of human nature, and a more comprehensive soul, than are supposed to be common among mankind. . . ."[1] All of these wonderful qualities—identified, of course, by a poet—suggest that poets are sensitive people who experience life very deeply, and they wish to share their feelings with us through their poetry. Perhaps that's why Wordsworth defines poetry as "the spontaneous overflow of powerful feelings."[2]

Percy Bysshe Shelley, another English Romantic poet, defines a poem as "the very image of life expressed in its eternal truth."[3] This definition suggests that poets capture the universal and unchanging aspects of the human condition in their work, and if we study poetry, we will actually be studying life itself. And, Shelley insists, since "poetry is ever accompanied with pleasure,"[4] the task will be doubly rewarding.

Types of Poems

The word "poet" comes from the Greek word *poietes* which literally means "maker." As "makers" of a literary work, poets have a variety of tools at their disposal. They will not, however, use all of them

---

[1] From "Preface to *Lyrical Ballads*" *The Norton Anthology of English Literature*, ed. M. H. Abrams, 5th ed. (New York: Norton, 1987) 1388.

[2] Wordsworth 1388.

[3] From *A Defence of Poetry* in *The Norton Anthology*, 1809.

[4] Shelley 1810.

in every poem; their choices will depend on the effect they want to achieve, the message they want to communicate, the experience they want us to share, or the emotions they want us to feel.

Poets write poems, but they do not speak in them. Poets create masks, *personas,* that they assume in different poems, and these personas are labeled in different ways, depending on the type of poem the poet has chosen to write.

If poets want to recreate an experience, to tell a story, they will write a narrative poem and create a narrator to describe the action; therefore the voice speaking in the poem is that of the narrator. Thomas Hardy's "The Man He Killed" on page 165 is a narrative poem about an infantry man's experience with killing an enemy soldier in battle.

If, on the other hand, poets want to express an emotion or share an idea, they will write a **lyric** poem and create a speaker to convey their thoughts and feelings. "The World Is Too Much with Us" by William Wordsworth on page 162 is a lyric in which the speaker conveys his thoughts and feelings about man's separation from nature. The speaker in a lyric poem is generally ascribed the same gender as that of the poet, so the speaker in Wordworth's poem is referred to with the masculine *he,* while the speaker in a lyric by Elizabeth Barrett Browning is referred to with the feminine *she.*

If poets want to create a dramatic scene as a background for their insights, they will write a **dramatic monologue,** with the voice in the poem belonging to an identifiable character or to an unnamed one. "Ulysses" by Alfred Lord Tennyson records Ulysses farewell to his people as he sets off on his last great journey, while Matthew Arnold in "Dover Beach" records the words of an unnamed man as he laments the loss of religious faith in a world struggling to make sense of new scientific discoveries and the terrible effects of war.

These three types of poems, then, the narrative, the lyric, and the dramatic monologue, are conveyed to us through different voices to produce different effects.

Poetry and Fiction

Poetry shares some common elements with fiction, such as plot, character, setting, and theme. **Plot,** a series of related incidents in fiction, may be just that in a narrative poem as the action that the narrator is describing unfolds. In a lyric poem in which the speaker is expressing an emotion or sharing an idea, the plot is the series of connected feelings or thoughts that move through the work.

Character in a poem refers to the nature of the narrator in a narrative poem or of the speaker in a lyric poem. By the way the narrator tells the story or describes a series of events, he or she reveals a personality, attitudes, and values. These can be inferred by the narrator's word choice, the details emphasized, even by the details that are omitted. The characters in the narrative itself will reveal their personalities through their words, actions, choices, thoughts, and feelings.

In a lyric poem, the speaker reveals his or her personal qualities—character—through the emotions that are expressed or the thoughts that are shared. These emotions can range from happiness, joy, and love to fear, frustration, anger, and so on endlessly. Once you detect these emotions and decide why the speaker is expressing them, you can infer some of his or her personal qualities. As you think along with the speaker as he or she shares thoughts and ideas, you can also make inferences about character by analyzing the subjects he or she thinks about, the order in which the thoughts progress, and the conclusion that is reached. If these emotions or thoughts are addressed to a specific person who is clearly identified or to a person who is unnamed, as in a dramatic monologue, that person—referred to as the listener—can also be analyzed the way the speaker is. If the listener is capable of sharing emotions or following a thought process, then he or she is probably like the speaker in terms of personal qualities.

The **setting**—the time and place of the poem—may be explicitly described, or it may be implied by the details that the narrator or speaker describes. This aspect of the poem is important because the setting helps to create atmosphere, to increase the probability of certain events occurring, to reveal the personality of the narrator or of the speaker, and to communicate the theme. If the speaker is standing alone by the quiet seashore during sunset or is in the midst of an early morning battle watching soldiers being killed by a gas attack, it is easy to see how the environment would produce different thoughts and feelings.

Because poets are sharing their values, their views and ideas about life, poems—like fiction—also have a **theme.** It is communicated through the subject of the work, through what is said about the subject, and through the poet's use of poetic devices. This message about life is an idea, an insight that the poet has had and wants to share with us. Whether we accept or reject it, it has enlarged our minds by making us evaluate the poet's idea and its place in our value system. Any time that we think critically about an experience or an idea, we become more sensitive and thoughtful human beings.

In addition to these shared elements of literature, poets also have other tools—poetic devices—to help them "make" a poem.

Poetic Devices

When poets decide to share their insights into life in the form of a poem, they have many poetic devices to choose from to convey their ideas. Two devices most frequently associated with poetry are rhythm and rhyme. **Rhythm** is the beat that we hear in a line of poetry, the pattern created by the sound of the accented syllables in the poet's words, while **rhyme** is the repetition of the end sound in words. These qualities we discovered as children when we enjoyed learning and reciting nursery rhymes the way preliterate cultures used rhythm and rhyme as memory devices to pass on stories as part of their oral tradition. Since rhythm and rhyme are not a natural part of our use of language, their presence suggests that words have been manipulated in a special way to convey the pleasure of sound along with their meaning.

The rhyme scheme in a poem is identified by assigning the same letter of the alphabet to each similar sound at the end of a poetic line. Thus the rhymes in the first stanza of William Blake's poem "The Lamb"[5] would be analyzed this way:

The Lamb

Little Lamb, who made thee?	a
Dost thou know who made thee?	a
Gave thee life, and bid thee feed	b
By the stream and o'er the mead;	b
Gave thee clothing of delight,	c
Softest clothing, wooly, bright;	c
Gave thee such a tender voice,	d
Making all the vales rejoice?	d
Little Lamb, who made thee?	a
Dost thou know made thee?	a

The repetition of the rhyming pattern helps to give unity to the stanza and to the poem as a whole when similar sounds are repeated in following stanzas. Rhyme also helps to highlight or emphasize key words and ideas in a work.

---

[5] In *An Introduction to Literature*, ed. Sylvan Barnet, Morton Berman, and William Burto, 10th ed. (New York: Harper, 1993) 569.

While most people associate poetry with rhythm and rhyme, poets do not always employ these devices because they may not contribute to the effect they wish to achieve. They may choose, for example, to use **free verse,** unrhymed rhythmical lines which vary in length but which often employ the repetition of images, phrases, and parallel grammatical structure.

Other aspects of the pleasing sounds of poetry are such devices as **alliteration,** the repetition of the initial consonant sound in words as in "silent snow"; **assonance,** the repetition of vowel sounds as in the repeated long *e* in "see the team"; and **consonance,** the repetition of consonant patterns as in "rude-ride." **Onomatopoeia,** the use of words that sound like their meaning as in "moan" or "murmuring," can also contribute to the pleasure produced by the sound of the language. To appreciate the effects of these sound devices, poetry should be read aloud, for it truly is the combination of the sound and the sense of the lines that makes poetry the art form that it is.

The sense of poetic lines is often expressed in figures of speech, the two most common being the simile and the metaphor. The **simile** is a comparison that uses the words "like" or "as" to establish the likeness between two different terms as in "He is as brave as a lion." The comparison focuses on just one quality that the two share, but there is a richness of meaning evoked when the lion's bravery is translated into human terms: man can be as unyielding as the king of beasts. The **metaphor,** an implied comparison, also establishes likenesses between distinctly different things but without using "like" or "as" in the equation. The statement "He is a lion in battle" is a metaphor that suggests the warrior is brave, as in the simile, but it also encompasses other qualities the lion would exhibit in battle, such as power, strength, fierceness, and persistence. While the metaphor seems to carry more complexity of meaning, it is not inherently better than the simile; the poet's choice depends upon the point he or she wishes to convey, the effect he or she wants to produce.

When poets use **personification,** they attribute human qualities to inanimate objects. Wordsworth, the English Romantic poet, personified the daffodils when he described them as "Tossing their heads in sprightly dance" in his poem "I Wandered Lonely As a Cloud." Daffodils do not dance, but by suggesting that they do through personification, Wordsworth depicts liveliness, happiness, and joy, qualities evidenced by human beings when they dance.

Organization in Poetry

Poets often organize their poems into stanzas, poetic paragraphs. The most common stanzaic forms are the couplet, the tercet, and the quatrain. The **couplet** consists of two lines with the same end rhyme, while the **tercet** consists of three rhyming lines. The **quatrain** is a four-line stanza which may contain no end rhymes or may rhyme in a variety of ways, such as *abab, aabb,* or even *abcb.*

A popular structure or organization for lyric poems is the **sonnet,** consisting of fourteen lines. The two major types of sonnets are the Italian (Petrarchan) and the English (Shakespearean). The Italian sonnet is divided into two parts, the octave which presents the subject or issue of the work, and the sestet, which comments on the ideas presented in the first eight lines. The Shakespearean sonnet consists of three quatrains which present the central idea and a couplet which comments on it. Some modern poets have varied the divisions and usual rhyme schemes of these sonnet forms, but the number of lines is never varied.

Poets choose the poetic devices and the stanzaic patterns that will express their ideas most effectively. They combine the pleasure of sound with their ideas to produce a wonderful blend of sound and sense.

Symbolism in Poetry

Another device that poets use to convey meaning is symbolism. A **symbol** is something—a person, place, object, action, color, or event—that has two levels of meaning. It is itself on the literal, particular level, but it also signifies something beyond itself on a figurative, universal level. For example, the rose is a particular flower noted for its beauty and its thorns. On the figurative level, it is often a symbol of love because love is a beautiful experience that—in certain circumstances—can also cause us pain. William Blake uses the rose as a symbol of love in his poem "The Sick Rose" to convey his ideas about the forces that destroy the beauty of love. Our culture employs symbols during important life events like baptism, marriage, and death, and these symbols—water, rings, and flowers—can frequently be found in poetry, but authors are also free to create their own symbols to help communicate their message. Poets use symbols for the same reason that writers of fiction and drama do—to add complexity and richness to their work.

Imagery in Poetry

One of the most often used devices in poetry is **imagery,** words and phrases conveying sensory impressions that help us recreate the work in our imaginations. Most imagery is visual in nature because our sense of sight is the one that we depend on most frequently to learn about our environment. In her poem entitled "Barbie Doll," Marge Piercy describes the central character after her death with images that make it easy to imagine the scene: "In the casket displayed on satin she lay / . . . / dressed in a pink and white nightie."[6] If we are participating in the work, we can visualize the wake scene and see the girl in her shroud, and our memories of similar scenes stir our emotions and help us "feel" the poet's message about what is important in life.

Imagery is important in poetry because it draws the reader into the poem by appealing to the senses and to the imagination. When it is responded to, imagery can help to stir one's emotions, create the atmosphere or background for the action, reveal the character of the speaker, and communicate the theme. If you try to "see" the scene and to "hear" the voice of the speaker (that's why it's important to read poetry aloud), you will enhance your understanding and your appreciation of the poems that you read.

Tone in Poetry

Tone is defined as the author's attitude toward the subject, and it is described by adjectives that we apply to our own wide-ranging attitudes, from caring, affectionate, and loving to demeaning, critical, sarcastic and so on. These feelings are expressed by the speaker's choice of words (both their denotation—the dictionary meaning—and their connotation—their emotional overtones), word order, use of metaphor, simile, or symbol, and use of imagery. All of these aspects of style convey the speaker's attitude, and of all the possible attitudes that could be expressed, it is absolutely essential to recognize an ironic one. **Irony** is a figure of speech in which the expressed meaning is the opposite of the intended meaning. For example, W. H. Auden seems to be praising "The Unknown Citizen" for his exemplary life but is actually criticizing the fact that he conformed to the point of never developing a personal identity. Other aspects of verbal irony are **understatement** in which something is represented as less than it is and **hyperbole** or **overstatement** in which exaggeration is used to heighten the poem's effect or to help communicate its meaning. Obviously, if one misinterprets the tone, one may miss the meaning of the poem, for one of the important functions of tone is to convey the theme.

Explicating Poetry

The verb *to explicate* comes from the Latin *explicat(us)* which means to "set forth" or "unfold." Therefore, when you explicate a poem, your job as a writer is to explain, comment on, and analyze each line, describing how the poet's use of words, rhyme, rhythm, poetic devices, figurative language, imagery, and tone help produce the meaning and the effect of the work. Beginning with the first line and moving through the poem to the end, you quote from and analyze every line to show how the poet com-

---

[6] From *CIRCLES ON THE WATER* by Marge Piercy. Copyright © 1982 by Marge Piercy.

municates the theme in the work. You do not need, however, to follow the exact order of the lines if clarity or emphasis can be achieved by reordering them.

❧ Writing an Explication: Step by Step

When preparing to write an essay which explicates a poem, try to keep these steps in mind:

1. Begin by reading the poem a sentence at a time, making sure that you understand the meaning of each word. Poets choose each word carefully, depending on both denotative and connotative meaning. The denotation can be found in the dictionary, but since some words may have several meanings—some obsolete—be sure to choose the meaning that is appropriate to the context in the sentence. The connotation relates to the emotions that the word may evoke because of our past experiences.

2. Once you understand the meaning of the poem, read it again to identify words that rhyme or that contain alliteration, assonance, or consonance. Mark any examples of similes, metaphors, or symbols, and note any images and the sensory impressions that they convey. Also decide on the tone of the work based on the subject, the word order, and the poet's overall style.

3. The first part of the introduction should include the following:
   a. the author's full name and the title of the poem;
   b. the type of poem—narrative, lyric, or dramatic monologue;
   c. the voice in the poem—the narrator, the speaker, or an identifiable character;
   d. the setting in time and place if it is stated or can be inferred from the text;
   e. a brief summary of what the poem is about.

4. The thesis—the last part of the introduction—is a statement about the poet's use of specific poetic devices to convey the theme which is clearly stated.

5. As you start the body paragraphs, begin with the first stanza of the poem, explaining the meaning of each line by paraphrasing and quoting and by pointing out and explaining the effect of any poetic devices that the poet employs. Remember that each line of the poem must be explained because each line contributes to the total effect of the work; you may, however, explicate line four before line three, for example, if that approach would help clarify the poet's intent.

6. To paragraph the body effectively, it is usually most practical to keep the discussion of each stanza in the same paragraph. If, however, your discussion becomes lengthy because of all of the poetic devices that the poet has used, break the discussion into at least two parts at a logical point, such as at the end of a sentence in the stanza.

7. In the conclusion, comment on the poet's effective use of poetic devices to convey his or her meaning and then discuss that meaning as it relates to the universal human experience.

The following diagram, model essays, and plan sheet will help you write a thorough and effective explication of a poem.

Diagram of the Structure of a Poetry Explication

Title

Introductory Paragraph:

Open with interesting lead material.

Name the work and the author.

Briefly summarize the work and identify the type of poem, the voice in the poem, and the setting.

State that the poet uses a variety of poetic devices or list the specific devices used to convey the theme which is expressed in a sentence or two.

Body Paragraphs:

The first body paragraph explicates the first stanza or the first part of the poem (if it is not divided into stanzas) by explaining the meaning of *each* line, using quotations to prove your analysis, and by pointing out the poetic devices the poet uses and commenting on their effect.

The second and all succeeding body paragraphs follow the same pattern of explaining and commenting on each line by quoting frequently to support your interpretation. Try to keep the discussion of each stanza in a single paragraph; if, however, the stanza is packed with poetic devices, it may become necessary to break the paragraph into two parts at a logical transition point.

Concluding Paragraph:

Use a signal word, comment on the poet's effective use of poetic devices to convey his or her theme, and then fully discuss the theme as it relates to everyone's life.

The following student-written essay explicates a sonnet by William Wordsworth.

The World Is Too Much with Us

The world is too much with us; late and soon,
Getting and spending, we lay waste our powers;
Little we see in Nature that is ours;
We have given our hearts away, a sordid boon!
This Sea that bares her bosom to the moon,
The winds that will be howling at all hours,
And are up-gathered now like sleeping flowers,
For this, for everything, we are out of tune;
It moves us not.—Great God! I'd rather be
A Pagan suckled in a creed outworn;
So might I, standing on this pleasant lea,
Have glimpses that would make me less forlorn;
Have sight of Proteus rising from the sea;
Or hear old Triton blow his wreathed horn.

Out of Tune with Nature

Much is written about people's interest in possessions, about materialism, about lack of interest in the environment. These are not new problems as William Wordsworth's Italian sonnet entitled "The World Is Too Much with Us,"[1] written in 1807, points out. *He uses visual and auditory images to convey his theme that man has lost his soul by separating himself from nature.*

In the first four lines of the octave, the speaker states his proposition that people are more interested in materialism than in nature. He complains that "The world is too much with us" (line 1), suggesting that acquiring the things of the world like money, power, and status consume all of our time and energy. By doing so, according to the speaker, "we lay waste our powers" (2), squandering them on things that have little real value. He decries our "late and soon, / Getting and spending," wasting all of our time working making money that we can then spend on luxuries. We are focused on things, and as a result "Little we see in Nature that is ours" (3). We have given up the peace, tranquility, and beauty that nature offers and have "given our hearts" (4) to the god of materialism. The speaker is saddened by this "sordid boon" (4) or despicable gift of ourselves in worship of materialistic values.

The second quatrain in the octave is filled with visual and auditory images of nature as the speaker describes what people are missing by turning their backs on nature. He states that we are "out of tune" (8) with beauty and do not appreciate the "Sea that bares her bosom to the moon" (5). This

Thesis Statement

Topic Sentence

Topic Sentence

[1] In *An Introduction to Literature*, ed. Sylvan Barnet, Morton Berman, and William Burto, 10th ed. (New York: Harper, 1993) 571.

visual image suggests a loving encounter between these elements of nature as the sea responds to the moon's effects on the tides. In an auditory image, the speaker states that we are also unaware of the power of "The winds that will be howling at all hours / And are up-gathered now like sleeping flowers" (6–7). The speaker appreciates both the powerful and the gentle aspects of the wind that can howl or, as the simile points out, be as gentle as "sleeping flowers." We have become so jaded that nothing "moves us" (9). In the speaker's eyes, we are missing out on "everything" (8) if we spend all our time in the world of materialism rather than in the world of nature.

Topic Sentence

The dash in the middle of line nine indicates the actual end of the octave and the beginning of the sestet in which the speaker suggests his solution to the new religion of materialism. His exclamation "Great God!" (9) is both a cry of dismay and a plea for a return to a former way of looking at the world. He would "rather be / A Pagan suckled in a creed outworn" (9–10) than be a man who makes money and possessions his god. If his heart and his values are in the right place, he can appreciate the gifts the natural world has to offer, like "standing on [a] pleasant lea, / [and having] glimpses that ... make [him] less forlorn" (11–12). In a beautiful meadow, he can see and experience the peace that nature has to offer and return to a time when man worshipped natural gods like "Proteus rising from the sea" or "Triton [blowing] his wreathed horn" (13–14). The images of the sea gods suggest that the speaker sees God in nature rather than in money, possessions, and political power.

Restatement of Thesis

Through his use of imagery, then, Wordsworth communicates his views on a society that seeks material things rather than the natural beauty of nature. In his eyes, if we are unmoved by the sight of the sea or the sound of the wind, we are wasting our energies on things that cannot really satisfy our souls. If, on the other hand, we can see God in the tides or hear God's voice in the wind, we are in tune with nature and can enjoy her gifts of beauty, tranquility, and peace.

Mary O'Brien

✥ Model Essay Two

The following student-written essay illustrates the process of explicating this sonnet by Shakespeare:

Sonnet 18

Shall I compare thee to a summer's day?
Thou are more lovely and more temperate:
Rough winds do shake the darling buds of May,
And summer's lease hath all too short a date:
Sometime too hot the eye of heaven shines,
And often is his gold complexion dimmed;
And every fair from fair sometime declines,
By chance or nature's changing course untrimmed:
But thy eternal summer shall not fade
Nor lose possession of that fair thou ow'st,

Nor shall Death brag thou wand'rest in his shade,
When in eternal lines to time thou grow'st.
So long as men can breathe or eyes can see,
So long lives this, and this gives life to thee.

Beauty and Art

Have you run out of ways to compliment the person you love? If you have, perhaps you should try writing a poem the way Shakespeare did in "Sonnet 18."[1] *In this fourteen-line poem written in iambic pentameter, he uses a variety of poetic devices to convey his theme that while physical beauty fades, the beauty of a poetic compliment will last forever.*

In the first quatrain, the speaker is considering ways to compliment his love. He asks her, "Shall I compare thee to a summer's day?" (line 1) because summer is thought to be the loveliest season of the year. The word "compare" suggests that the speaker will enumerate his love's similarities to a beautiful summer's day, but he goes on to point out contrasts because she is "more lovely and more temperate" (2). His use of the word "more" indicates that the speaker is aware of summer's loveliness and warmth, but he believes that his love is even more spectacular. The colon at the end of line two shows that the following lines will explain the speaker's reasons for his feelings. He recognizes that "Rough winds do shake the darling buds of May" (3), suggesting that storms can mar May's beauty. He also realizes that "summer's lease hath all too short a date" (4) and that its beauty will quickly be gone. The metaphor "summer's lease" compares summer to a transient who is only a temporary resident of the lovers' world.

In the second quatrain, the speaker continues to point out reasons why his love is more beautiful than a "summer's day." He uses a metaphor for the sun by referring to it as "the eye of heaven" (5), and he complains that "Sometime [the sun is] too hot . . . / And often is his gold complexion dimmed" (6) by clouds that obscure the sun's golden rays. The implication is that his love's eyes never create discomfort and that her complexion is always clear and bright. In the next line, however, the speaker acknowledges that "every fair from fair sometime declines" (7), suggesting that all natural loveliness is rooted in time, a fact he emphasizes by using the word "sometime" twice in the quatrain. Time is one factor that affects all of life; neither nature nor man escapes time's "changing course untrimmed" (8). Natural beauty is always temporary because of the aging process and because it can be affected "by chance" or fate. The speaker seems to be focusing on the negative aspects of nature's beauty—its flaws and its fading—to lead into a contrast in the third quatrain.

As the speaker begins the next part of the sonnet, he seems to contradict some of his earlier statements about physical beauty. Now when he addresses his love, his tone is very positive:

Thesis

Topic Sentence

Topic Sentence

Topic Sentence

[1] William Shakespeare, "Sonnet 18" *William Shakespeare: The Complete Works*, ed. Peter Alexander (London: Collins, 1970) 1311.

But thy eternal summer shall not fade
Nor lose possession of that fair thou ow'st,
Nor shall Death brag thou wand'rest in his shade. (9–10)

The speaker's use of the words "eternal summer" contrasts with his use of words like "sometime" and "decline" in the second quatrain to emphasize the fact that his love's beauty will last forever because she will never lose the loveliness she owns—unlike summer's beauty that will fade and lose its "lease." She will even escape Death and its darkness because "in eternal lines to time [she] grow'st" (12). Death is personified as a braggart who will never have the chance to boast about his conquest because the lines of the speaker's sonnet have immortalized his love's beauty, and rather than fade, it will continue to increase through time.

Topic Sentence

The couplet shows the speaker's confidence in the eternal beauty of his love and of his artistic compliment. He boldly states, "So long as men can breathe or eyes can see / So long lives this, and this gives life to thee" (13–14). And he was right, for the beauty of the woman he loved can still be seen in his description of her loveliness more than 400 years later. The speaker's overall use of end rhyme in the first and third and the second and fourth lines of each quatrain and in the couplet shows that he has carefully crafted his compliment and designed it to stand in permanent form as a testament to the loveliness of his love.

Restatement of Thesis

And so, Shakespeare's use of metaphor, personification, tone, and rhyme helps to establish the contrast between the transcience of physical beauty and the permanence of artistic beauty. While the speaker acknowledges the beauty of his beloved as being greater than the beauty of summer, he does admit that all natural beauty fades because it is eventually touched by time and death. However, what escapes these aspects of life is art, for as long as the human race appreciates art, the beauty captured within it will live on. The mortal body of the woman complimented in the sonnet has long been in Death's "shade," but her beauty will be forever bright in the eyes of those who read Shakespeare's immortal poem.

Robert Sanders

Model Essay Three

Here is an explication of the following poem by Thomas Hardy:

The Man He Killed

'Had he and I but met
By some old ancient inn,
We should have sat us down to wet
Right many a nipperkin!

'But ranged as infantry,
And staring face to face,
I shot at him as he at me,
And killed him in his place.

'I shot him dead because—
Because he was my foe,
Just so: my foe of course he was;
That's clear enough; although

'He thought he'd 'list, perhaps,
Off-hand like—just as I—
Was out of work—had sold his traps—
No other reason why.

'Yes; quaint and curious war is!
You shoot a fellow down
You'd treat if met where any bar is,
Or help to half-a-crown.'

The Folly of War

As America basks in the patriotic glow of its triumphant win in the Persian Gulf War, one wonders about the feelings of those who actually fought and killed others in combat. When Thomas Hardy wrote "The Man He Killed,"[1] he created a narrator who was still haunted by thoughts of the human life he destroyed while serving in the infantry. *Through Hardy's use of rhyme, rhythm, and tone, he communicates the theme that soldiers must continually rationalize their actions in war in order to live with their memories.*

Thesis

Topic Sentence

As the narrator begins his story about the man he killed in battle, he seems to be in control of his emotions as the regular patterns of rhyme and the iambic rhythm suggest. He tells his listener,

'Had he and I but met
By some old ancient inn,
We should have sat us down to wet
Right many a nipperkin!' (lines 1–4)

The narrator creates the friendly and familiar image of an inn to suggest that if he and his victim had "met" there, they would have "sat . . . down" to enjoy "many a" glass of ale. The inn image appeals to the reader's sense of sight, hearing, and taste and reveals that the narrator is an open and friendly man who mixes easily with strangers and enjoys their company.

Topic Sentence

The opening of the second stanza with the word "But" prepares the reader for the contrasts of setting and actions that follow. Instead of sitting next to each other in an inn, the narrator and his victim are "ranged as infantry, / And staring face to face" (5–6). The battlefield image establishes them as enemies looking at each other from opposite sides. Then the narrator describes their unfriendly actions: "I shot at him as he at me, / And killed him in his place" (7–8). Rather than sharing a cup, they are swapping bullets, and it was the narrator who was the better shot. He has now become a killer because he carried out his responsibilities as an infantryman. In the first two stanzas of the poem, the lines flow smoothly, with just com-

[1] Thomas Hardy, "The Man He Killed" *The Complete Poetical Works of Thomas Hardy*, Vol. I, ed. Samuel Hynes (Oxford: Clarendon, 1982) 344–345.

mas to mark brief pauses in the narrator's description of the action, and each stanza is a separate sentence. The tone is matter-of-fact as he describes—in words of one syllable in lines seven and eight—the past and its unchangeable deed.

Topic Sentence

In the third stanza, however, as the narrator attempts to explain his motives for the killing, his thoughts are marked by long pauses and repetition. When he says, "I shot him dead because—" (9), the hesitation created by the dash suggests his mind is searching for the words that will help him face his deed. He then rationalizes that his victim was his "foe, / Just so" (10–11), and in an effort to convince himself of that, he repeats, "my foe of course he was; / That's clear enough;" (11–12). The repetition and the lack of commas around "of course" make it seem that the narrator has settled the question in his own mind and does not want to examine his conclusions, but he then immediately adds "although" which runs on into the next stanza: "He thought he'd 'list, perhaps, / Off-hand like—just as I—" (13–14). Now the narrator has gone beyond the idea of an unknown "foe" to the man behind the label and is considering his victim's reason for becoming involved in the war in the first place. Maybe his decision was not based on his political beliefs at all, but on an "off-hand" action. Like the narrator, he, too, may have been "out of work [and] had sold his traps—" (15), and that was the "reason why" (16) he was on the front line.

Topic Sentence

The change in the rhythm because of the narrator's frequent and heavy pauses suggests the movement of his thoughts as he tries to deal with the frequent and heavy feelings of guilt at the memory of his deed. He painfully recognizes and states that he and his victim were really kindred souls, men very much alike in their efforts to make a life for themselves. The narrator's tone is melancholy as he remembers the circumstances that brought him to that dramatic moment in time.

Topic Sentence

The beginning of the last stanza with the word "Yes" shows that the narrator's thought processes have brought him to a moment of insight into the events that led him to kill another man. When he says, "Yes; quaint and curious war is!" (17), he seems to have realized that he, like the man he killed, was also a victim of war. It was war that caused him to "shoot a fellow down / [He'd] treat if met where any bar is / Or help to half-a-crown" (18–20). War creates enemies among men who—in another time or place—would otherwise be friends one would "treat" or "help"—surely not kill. As the narrator arrives at this insight of how the common man is trapped by the political decisions of governments and kings, his speech patterns become again more rhythmic and regular. He seems to have absolved himself of guilt as he recognizes that war, with its strange and meddlesome powers, is the real killer.

Restatement of Thesis

Hardy, then, through his use of poetic devices, has brought out his theme about war. By focusing on the men who are caught up in its awesome and frightening power, he shows us the tragedies of war. Some men are killed—lost forever—while others are haunted by their memories and driven by their need to understand their actions. War turns possible friends into certain "foes," yet despite the suffering it causes, men still continue to use war as a means to achieve peace. Indeed, war is "quaint and curious."

Donna Stewart

Here is poet James Dickey's[1] advice on how to experience poetry:

"The beginning of your true encounter with poetry should be simple. It should bypass all classrooms, all textbooks, courses, examinations, and libraries and go straight to the things that make your own existence exist: to your body and nerves and blood and muscles. Find your own way—a secret way that just maybe you don't know yet—to open yourself as wide as you can and as deep as you can to the moment, the *now* of your own existence and the endless mystery of it, and perhaps at the same time to one other thing that is not you, but is out there: a handful of gravel is a good place to start. So is an ice cube—what more mysterious and beautiful *interior* of something has there ever been?

As for me, I like the sun, the source of all living things, and on certain days very good-feeling, too. 'Start with the sun,' D. H. Lawrence said, 'and everything will slowly, slowly happen.' Good advice. And a lot *will* happen."

Go ahead—give it a try.

---

[1]James Dickey, "How to Enjoy Poetry" (New York: International Paper Company, 1982).

❦ **Poetry Explication Plan Sheet** ❦

Author: _____ Title: _____

Thesis: _____

_____

_____

_____

_____

Topic sentence: _____

_____

_____

Supporting quote: page or line _____

Supporting quote: page or line _____

Supporting quote: page or line _____

Topic sentence: _____

_____

_____

Supporting quote: page or line _____

Supporting quote: page or line _____

Supporting quote: page or line _____

Topic sentence: _____

_____

_____

Supporting quote: page or line _____

Supporting quote: page or line _____

Supporting quote: page or line _____

Topic sentence: _____

_____

_____

                    Supporting quote: page or line _____

                    Supporting quote: page or line _____

                    Supporting quote: page or line _____

Topic sentence: _____

_____

_____

                    Supporting quote: page or line _____

                    Supporting quote: page or line _____

                    Supporting quote: page or line _____

Topic sentence: _____

_____

_____

                    Supporting quote: page or line _____

                    Supporting quote: page or line _____

                    Supporting quote: page or line _____

Concluding points: _____

_____

_____

_____

_____

_____

_____

_____

Peer/Self-Evaluation of a Poetry Explication Essay

> **Directions:** Make specific suggestions about each part of the essay, pointing out particular areas that the writer could improve. Keep in mind the qualities of good writing: unity, organization, development, clarity, and coherence.

I. Introduction

Is the lead relevant and interesting?

Are the author's full name and the title of the work correctly spelled and punctuated?

Does the summary of the work include the type of poem, the voice in the poem, and the setting?

Does the thesis identify the poetic devices used in the work and state the theme communicated through them?

II. Body Paragraphs

Do the topic sentences indicate the part of the poem to the explicated in the paragraph?

Are the supporting quotations properly introduced?

Do the supporting quotations illustrate the poetic devices used in the stanza?

Do the analysis sections explain/comment on the effects of the poetic devices? Are the analysis sections adequately developed?

Are the body paragraphs unified and coherent?

III. Conclusion

Is a signal word included somewhere in the paragraph?

Is the use of the poetic devices related to the poet's theme?

Is the theme discussed in terms of its universal application to everyone's life?

IV. Expression

Are all the ideas expressed in complete sentences?

Are the sentences clear and correctly punctuated?

Are there any problems with subject-verb and pronoun-antecedent agreement?

Are all the words correctly spelled?

V. Overall Evaluation

Most effective part of the essay:

Least effective part of the essay:

List three specific actions which could be taken by the writer to improve this and future papers:

1.

2.

3.

Evaluator's name: _____ Date: _____

❧ Exercise on Explicating a Poem ❧

> In the following poem by William Wordsworth, circle all of the poetic devices and explain how they help convey the meaning of the work.

I Wandered Lonely as a Cloud[1]

I wandered lonely as a cloud
That floats on high o'er vales and hills,
When all at once I saw a crowd,
A host of golden daffodils;
Beside the lake, beneath the trees,
Fluttering and dancing in the breeze.

Continuous as the stars that shine
And twinkle on the milky way,
They stretched in never-ending line
Along the margin of a bay:
Ten thousand saw I at a glance,
Tossing their heads in sprightly dance.

The waves besides them danced; but they
Out-did the sparkling waves in glee:
A poet could not but be gay,
In such a jocund company:
I gazed—and gazed—but little thought
What wealth the show to me had brought:

For oft, when on my couch I lie
In vacant or in pensive mood,
They flash upon that inward eye
Which is the bliss of solitude;
And then my heart with pleasure fills,
And dances with the daffodils.

Type of Poem:_____

Rhyme Scheme: _____

_____

_____

_____

---

[1] From *The Norton Anthology of English Literature*, ed. M. H. Abrams, 5th ed. (New York: Norton, 1987) 1426.

Setting: _____
_____
_____
_____

Figures of speech: _____
_____
_____
_____
_____
_____
_____
_____

Symbols: _____
_____
_____
_____
_____
_____
_____
_____

Images: _____
_____
_____
_____
_____
_____
_____
_____

Tone: _____
_____
_____
_____
_____

Imagery Analysis

Overview

Imagery can be defined as words or phrases which evoke *sensory* impressions in the reader. It contributes to the richness of a work because it appeals to our imagination (note the root *image* in imagination) and most often enables us to visualize the scene we are reading about. Through his choice of words, an author can make us *see* the rugged coast, *hear* the ocean crashing against the shore, *feel* the sand beneath our feet, and *smell* the salty, wind-whipped air. If we recognize and respond to images, we will find new levels of emotional depth and meaning in any literary work.

Imagery and Its Effects

Imagination is one of our greatest gifts, and images—words or phrases which evoke sensory impressions—appeal to that faculty. Words like "green," "bang," "soft," "sweet," and "sour" appeal respectively to our sense of sight, hearing, touch, taste, and smell. Our imaginations can help us vicariously experience these sensations and enable us to participate more concretely and more fully in a work of literature. We think *and feel* with the author as we recall personal experiences related to common images.

Imagery is one of the main devices used by a poet because he wants us to respond imaginatively and sensually to his words. When Shakespeare describes "the lark at break of day arising / From sullen earth, [singing] hymns at heaven's gate,"[1] he wants us to visualize the small songbird in flight and to hear its melodious song. In the same way, writers of prose fiction and drama want us to respond imaginatively and sensually to their words as well. For example, in the short story "The Short Happy Life of Francis Macomber," Hemingway describes Robert Wilson's "extremely cold blue eyes."[2] While this phrase helps us to visualize Wilson, it also suggests his cold, steely personality and his ability to remain cool and calm under pressure. In the novel *Ordinary People* by Judith Guest, Conrad, the central character, says that Berger, his psychiatrist, has "the look of a crafty monkey."[3] This image, besides describing

[1] "Sonnet 29" *William Shakespeare: The Complete Works* (London: Collins, 1970) 1313.

[2] Reprinted with permission of Charles Scribner's Sons, an imprint of Macmillan Publishing Company, from THE SHORT STORIES OF ERNEST HEMINGWAY. Copyright 1936 by Ernest Hemingway. Copyright renewed © 1964 by Mary Hemingway.

[3] From ORDINARY PEOPLE by Judith Guest. Copyright © 1976 by Judith Guest. Used by permission of Viking Penguin, a division of Penguin Books USA Inc.

Berger, suggests that he is a primeval man, one who uses his instincts to complement his intelligence in dealing with his patients. In the drama *The Glass Menagerie*, Tennessee Williams refers to Laura Wingfield with the image of "Blue Roses" (Scene II). This image emphasizes the unreal aspects of Laura's personality since, as she says, ". . . blue is wrong for—roses . . ." (Scene VII).[4] All of these images add levels of meaning to a work as they appeal to our minds and our imaginations.

✛ Analyzing Imagery

Images can be divided into types based on the sense to which they appeal. **Visual** images present pictures of people, places, objects, or events that appeal to our sense of sight, while **auditory** images appeal to our sense of sound and bring the memory of a sound into our consciousness. **Tactile** images, **gustatory** images, and **olfactory** images appeal respectively to our sense of touch, taste, and smell. Images can also relate to our sense of motion and to our feelings of heat or cold, our **thermal** sense. By helping us recreate pictures or sensations in our imaginations, images make a work more real, more concrete, more alive.

Since an author usually relies primarily on his sense of sight to perceive elements in his environment, most of the imagery in a work tends to be visual in nature. The author helps us "see" his work; he doesn't simply "tell" us what happens next. Sometimes he will use a single image to convey an idea, but most often he will use **a pattern or cluster of images** that all relate to one main idea or concept. For example, in the first six lines of "Dover Beach,"[5] Matthew Arnold uses a cluster of visual and auditory images to present a beautiful picture of the sea coasts of France and England that prompts him to philosophize about life and love:

> The sea is calm to-night
> The tide is full, the moon lies fair
> Upon the straits:—on the French coast the light
> Gleams and is gone; the cliffs of England stand,
> Glimmering and vast, out in the tranquil bay.
> Come to the window, sweet is the night air!

The speaker begins by using images that describe the tranquility of the scene. The "calm" sea is serene and "full" at high tide, bathed in the light of the "moon." Across the English Channel, the speaker sees "light [that] / Gleams and is gone," suggesting the presence of life which is then extinguished by the darkness. The white cliffs of Dover, "glimmering and vast," complete the picture of the "tranquil bay." The speaker is obviously an observant man whose use of images helps us appreciate the natural beauty of the scene. Then we realize that he is not alone when he asks his companion to "come to the window" to enjoy the "sweet . . . night air." The visual images of the tranquil sea are heightened by the sweet smells of a beautiful summer evening that waft through the windows of a retreat on Dover Beach.

The image pattern changes, however, as the speaker focuses his and his companion's attention on the sound of the sea:

> Only, from the long line of spray
> Where the sea meets the moon-blanched land,
> Listen! you hear the grating roar
> Of pebbles which the waves draw back, and fling,

[4] Tennessee Williams, *The Glass Menagerie*, Copyright © 1945 by Tennessee Williams and Edwina D. Williams and renewed 1973 by Tennessee Williams. All parenthetical scene numbers refer to the text published by Random House, Inc. Reprinted by permission.

[5] Matthew Arnold, "Dover Beach" *The Portable Matthew Arnold*, ed. Lionel Trilling (New York: Viking, 1949) 165–167.

At their return, up the high strand,
Begin, and cease, and then again begin,
With tremulous cadence slow, and bring
The eternal note of sadness in.

As they stand at the window, they hear "the grating roar / of [the] pebbles" as the waves come in and then recede with a "tremulous cadence slow." The sound—which we also hear through the imagery—stirs feelings of sadness within the speaker. Apparently he associates the eternal rhythm of the sea and its soulful sound with feelings of melancholy and sorrow.

In the second and third stanzas, the speaker objectifies these feelings of sadness by relating them to auditory images of the past and the present, to Sophocles and himself:

Sophocles long ago
Heard it on the Ægean, and it brought
Into his mind the turbid ebb and flow
Of human misery; we
Find also in the sound a thought,
Hearing it by this distant northern sea.

The Sea of Faith
Was once, too, at the full, and round earth's shore
Lay like the folds of a bright girdle furled.
But now I only hear
Its melancholy, long, withdrawing roar,
Retreating, to the breath
Of the night wind, down the vast edges drear
And naked shingles of the world.

The image of Sophocles, the Greek dramatist, listening to the same sound more than two thousand years ago on the shore of the Ægean emphasizes the eternal nature of the sea and the eternal nature of life and its recurring problems. The "ebb and flow / Of human misery" suggest mankind's endless struggles with pain, pestilence, famine, war, and death. Sophocles' comparison of the movement of the sea to the movement of human history prompts the speaker to compare it to the present state of the "Sea of Faith." It, too, was once "full," clothing the "round earth's shore" like a "bright girdle furled." This image implies that religious faith encircled the earth, bringing hope and comfort to a confused world. Unfortunately, Faith, like the sea and its tides, is now "retreating"; its sound has become a "melancholy . . . roar" as it departs, leaving mankind in a state of emptiness and despair. The image of the "night wind" suggests the darkness and the chill that fill the void as the loss of Faith exposes the "naked shingles of the world." The absence of the bright robe of faith that was once a source of comfort has left mankind unprotected in a cold and uncaring world.

As the speaker realizes his own vulnerability, he seeks a substitute for Faith that will enable him to deal with life and its problems, and he finds it in love. In the last stanza, images of romantic beauty contrast with images of war and battle:

Ah, love, let us be true
To one another! for the world, which seems
To lie before us like a land of dreams,
So various, so beautiful, so new,
Hath really neither joy, nor love, nor light,
Nor certitude, nor peace, nor help for pain;

                    And we are here as on a darkling plain
                    Swept with confused alarms of struggle and flight
                    Where ignorant armies clash by night.

The speaker's addressing his companion as his "love" reminds us of the romantic scene created by the images in the first stanza. He is asking his beloved to "be true" so that his lost religious faith can be replaced by their faith in each other. He argues that the world which appears to be a "land of dreams" because it seems "so beautiful, so new" is really an empty fantasy that has nothing of lasting value to offer mankind. The material world holds "neither joy, nor love, . . . / . . . nor help for pain." The values that used to be based on faith in God have been lost, and now, the speaker contends, there is nothing to cling to but each other. The image of the world as a place of "light" and "peace" is destroyed by the speaker's description of it as a "darkling plain / Swept with confused alarms of struggle and flight." Darkness is a symbol of the hopelessness that is caused by a world at war "where ignorant armies clash by night." The speaker believes that the sights and sounds of battle can only be relieved by the sight of a loved one and the sound of loving words vowing faith and commitment to one another.

By using images based on the sight and sound of the sea and by relating them to human misery, faith, love, and war, Arnold helps us share a romantic scene and understand the speaker's need for peace and his plea for fidelity. The strong sensory appeal of the images draws us into the work and makes it come alive for us because we can *see* the scene in our imagination.

Imagery and Atmosphere or Mood

When authors use imagery in their work, they do so because imagery can produce several important effects in a work of literature. One of its effects is to produce an appropriate atmosphere or mood for the situation presented in the work. The atmosphere is generally described by adjectives, and it is created by the types of images the writer employs. In "Dover Beach," the images of the "calm" sea and the "full" tide create a feeling of peacefulness, and the moonlight hints at romance, suggesting a love-filled atmosphere. This is confirmed in the image of the speaker and his "love" together at the window enjoying the beauty of the scene. This peaceful, romantic mood becomes more thoughtful, more melancholy, however, as the speaker hears the sound of the sea and its "tremulous cadence slow" which evoke a sense of "sadness."

As the speaker recalls Sophocles' thought about "human misery" and then states his own thought about the retreat of Faith, the melancholy atmosphere is reinforced. His view of the world as a "land of dreams" without "joy," "love," "light," "certitude," "peace," or "help for pain" leads to his sense of despair and hopelessness. The cause of these feelings—a world at war—adds to the gloomy atmosphere created by the depressing images. Against this background, it is easy to understand the urgency of the speaker's plea for fidelity from his love. He needs that love to serve as a ray of hope in a darkening world. The atmosphere in a work, then, is a product of the kinds of images the writer chooses.

Imagery and Emotion

A writer usually tries to produce a particular emotional effect in the reader, and if the reader is imaginatively responding to a work of literature, the chances are good that he or she will experience some emotion. These emotional effects may range from joy and happiness to pity and fear, depending on the nature of the subject matter and the writer's theme. Imagery helps to make these emotions more real by relating them to sensory impressions. In "Dover Beach," Arnold's use of imagery to stir our emotions is very effective. As the speaker begins his description of a beautiful romantic scene, we may experience some envy, wishing to be there with a loved one to enjoy the romantic mood. That envy turns to empathy, however, as the speaker recalls life's sadness and relates it to the problems man faces without the support of religious faith. We can share in this sadness because there are times in everyone's life when "human misery" and despair surface. When the speaker asks his love to "be true" and to serve as his source of light and peace in life, we empathize with his need for certainty in a world of "struggle and flight." We, too, have probably experienced the need for closeness and commitment to help us deal with life's conflicts and difficulties. If we feel the support and fidelity of our loved ones, we feel sympathy for those who are still searching for security in life. Imagery always helps us imagine and share the speaker's situation, and when that happens, the emotional impact of the work is much more effective.

Imagery and Character

The images that an author chooses can help us determine the personality traits of a character in fiction or drama or of the speaker in a poem. For example, as the speaker in "Dover Beach" uses images to describe the beauty of the natural scene, we can see that he is an observant man. When he says, "The sea is calm to-night," he implies that this is not always the case and shows that he has observed this scene when the natural conditions were obviously different. His comments on the sweetness of the air and the "grating" sound of the pebbles are other indications that he is sensually in tune with his environment.

When the speaker becomes more reflective and mentions the "sadness" he perceives in the sound of the sea, he reveals his sensitivity and thoughtfulness. His image of Sophocles shows that he is a learned man who understands and appreciates what history and literature can teach us about the human condition. The speaker's concern about the loss of faith which he depicts in the image of a "withdrawing" sea shows that he has a spiritual side to his nature that needs a source of nourishment and fulfillment.

The images of the final stanza in the poem show that the speaker is a realist who recognizes that while the world may seem "so beautiful, so new," there is a darker side which man must inevitably face on his "darkling plain." In searching for a solution, the speaker turns to love, suggesting that he is also a romantic who sees intimate love as a refuge in a hostile world.

Images, then, help us see how characters in literature perceive the world and what is important in it. Since their character shapes their perceptions, analyzing them can help us get into the mind and heart of fictional beings.

Imagery and Theme

Each work of literature communicates an idea about some aspect of life. As the author plans his or her work, he or she arranges its elements to bring that idea to the reader. One of those elements is imagery. It appeals to the reader's senses by helping him to visualize the scene and to imagine himself a part of it. This involvement helps the reader perceive the message in the work. The message in Arnold's "Dover Beach," for example, is brought out by the use of contrast in the image patterns. The beautiful visual images that describe the "land of dreams" contrast with the "grating roar" created by the sound of the sea. This contrast is reinforced by the difference in Sophocles' and the speaker's interpretation of this "eternal note of sadness." While it reminds Sophocles of the recurring pattern of "human misery," it reminds the speaker of the once comforting faith in God which has been lost in a world torn apart by war. These contrasts help to communicate the theme that man must have faith in something—in another human being if not in God—to deal with the problems life brings. Love for and faith in an eternal God can act as an anchor in life, but if that love and faith are lost for whatever reason, steadfast love for and faith in another human being can be comforting. Love can, in fact, make "human misery" bearable, and in a world united by love, war would be an outmoded solution to human problems.

Seeing and sensing the speaker's situation and sharing his reflections on life and love help us to understand the meaning of Arnold's thought-provoking poem. In almost every work where imagery is an important element, the theme is made more vivid and more real for us as we respond to the sensory impressions conveyed through the images.

Imagery's Importance

To appreciate imagery, it is necessary to recreate—in the mind's eye with the help of your imagination—the scene/situation/emotion presented by the writer through his use of words with sensory appeal. This vicarious participation in the work truly makes literature more real and more meaningful.

Writing about Imagery: Step by Step

As you prepare to write your imagery analysis essay, try to follow these steps:

1. When selecting a work to analyze, choose one that contains words or phrases (images) which appeal to your five senses: sight, hearing, touch, taste, and smell. Begin by circling all the images you can identify.

2. Check to see if there are several images that all relate to one main subject or idea. This series of related images is called an image pattern or cluster. Identify and label these patterns throughout the work. Some of them could be more extensive or more important than others, so try to choose patterns that you can explain, expand, and analyze in the body paragraphs of your essay. This list of image patterns is the first part of the thesis in the introductory paragraph.

3. The second part of the thesis lists the specific effects of the image patterns which will be discussed in detail in the concluding paragraph. You may choose one primary effect, you may choose to explain two or three effects, or you may even discuss all four:

    a. the images produce an appropriate emotional atmosphere or background for the events in the work;

    b. the images produce an emotional response or reaction based on the events in the work;

    c. the images reveal the personality of the speaker or of a character in the work;

    d. the images make the theme or message in the work easier to perceive and understand.

4. There should be at least one body paragraph for each image pattern listed in the thesis. As you write the body paragraphs, remember that the topic sentence introduces the image pattern and then the development of the paragraph includes quotations of the images which are followed by analysis that explains the meaning, the significance, the effectiveness of the images. Follow the image pattern through the work, discussing and analyzing as many images as possible to build a strong paragraph.

5. The concluding paragraph is not just a brief summary of the effects of the imagery. It is a thorough discussion of only the effects you listed in the thesis. If appropriate, explain *how*—in detail—the images produced an emotional atmosphere or background, what emotions you felt as a result of the images, what qualities in a character were brought out through the images, and what themes were communicated through the image patterns. Try to end with a broad generalization about the overall effectiveness of imagery in the work as a whole.

The following diagram, model essays, and plan sheet will help you organize and write an essay on imagery in a work of literature.

Diagram of the Structure of an Imagery Analysis Essay

Title

Introductory Paragraph:

Open with interesting lead material.

Name the work and the author.

Briefly summarize the work and list the image patterns that will be explored and explained in the body paragraphs.

State the effects of imagery, i.e., atmosphere, emotional response, character development, theme, that you will explain in the concluding paragraph.

} Thesis

Body Paragraphs:

The first part of the body relates to the first image pattern identified in the thesis. The topic sentence introduces the image pattern and then quotations of the images and analysis of them follow. The quotations of the images can be worked into your paraphrased explanation of the work, and the analysis explores and expands the meaning and significance of the images.

The second part of the body explores and explains the second image pattern listed in the thesis. The topic sentence introduces the image pattern, and then quotations of the images are followed by analysis which explains the effectiveness and the significance of the images.

The third part of the body expands upon the third image pattern identified in the thesis. Name the pattern in the topic sentence, and then trace the images through the work, using direct quotations and analyzing the images by describing their connotations, their significance, their meaning.

If you listed additional image patterns in the thesis, trace their development in separate body paragraphs that also use the literary analysis pattern.

Concluding Paragraph:

Use a signal word and then explain only the effects of imagery you listed in the thesis. If appropriate, describe how the imagery produced an emotional atmosphere in the work by presenting the subject matter vividly and concretely, how it increased the emotions experienced by the reader, how it revealed character, and how it helped to communicate the theme(s) in the work.

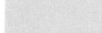

Model Essay One

This student-written essay analyzes imagery and its effects in the following poem by Randall Jarrell.

The Death of the Ball Turret Gunner[1]

From my mother's sleep I fell into the State,
And I hunched in its belly till my wet fun froze.
Six miles from earth, loosed from its dream of life,
I woke to black flak and the nightmare fighters.
When I died they washed me out of the turret with a hose.

The Nature of War

Thesis Statement

When conflicts arise between governments, war is too often the result. Those who have been caught in its clutches know that war is hell; it cares not how or how many it kills. Such is the message of Randall Jarrell's poem "The Death of the Ball Turret Gunner."[1] *He uses images of sleep, the State, and war to create a chillingly impersonal atmosphere and to convey his theme that the State kills coldly and impersonally to maintain its supremacy over others.*

Topic Sentence

In the first two lines, the speaker—the ball turret gunner—uses images of sleep and the State to describe his birth and his citizenship. His entry into this world occurs during his "mother's sleep" (line 1). Her state of restful peacefulness contrasts with the speaker's "who fell into the State" (1). His birth is a fall—obviously not a choice—from the peace and comfort of his mother's womb into a cold and impersonal "State" (1). His citizenship begins at birth, and he immediately becomes a social security number and then a number on a dogtag in the military. The "State" takes control of the gunner's life. At the choice of the "State," he finds himself in the "belly" (2) of a fighter plane where he is "hunched" (2) and uncomfortable. No longer does he have the security and warmth of his mother's womb, for this "belly" is not warm and comforting; it is, in fact, so "wet" and cold that his military "fur" (2) jacket "froze" (2). He is trapped like an animal whose cage is made of plexiglass and is fastened to the underside of a plane. His position makes him vulnerable, but it is what the "State" demands—his very life if necessary for victory.

Topic Sentence

In the next two lines, the image of war and its terrible consequences is a gunfight that takes place "six miles from earth" (3). The peace and quiet of space are shattered as is the gunner's "dream of life" as he awakes to the reality of war in the cold and impersonal guise of "black flak" (4) from the enemy's planes. Black is the color of death, and the word "flak" almost imitates the sound of anti-aircraft artillery shells hitting the plane. They pierce the womb-like turret and destroy all the possibilities the gunner's future holds. His dreams have become a "nightmare" (5) from which he will never awaken.

[1] "The Death of the Ball Turret Gunner" from *The Complete Poems* by Randall Jarrell. Copyright © 1969, renewed 1997 by Mary von S. Jarrell. Reprinted by permission of Farrar, Straus and Giroux, LLC.

Topic Sentence

The gunner's death is presented through the image of an abortion: "When [he] died they washed [him] out of the turret with a hose" (5). The procedure is conducted on an airfield—not in a comfortable hospital—by soldiers routinely performing their jobs. "They" are nameless automatons trained by the "State" to do a job in order to keep the war going, for the dead gunner lies in the way of getting the plane back in the air. His body is treated like an unborn fetus that is "washed" from the womb-like turret. There is no human touch—just the powerful force of water to wash away any signs of his existence. His life has been aborted just as he reaches the prime of his life, and there is no one there to mourn his loss. The "State" has demanded the ultimate sacrifice, and he has become yet another number— a wartime statistic.

Restatement of Thesis

And so as the images move from the peace of his mother's sleep to the terrible sounds of his death from anti-aircraft artillery in just five short lines, the ball turret gunner speaks volumes to us about the horror of war. The "State" is cold and impersonal as it takes him into the military where he is trained to kill or be killed. He becomes a number to keep track of, an instrument of the "State" designed to destroy the enemy. His human value is compromised, however, because he is dispensable, and when he dies, his body is hosed away quickly to expedite the arrival of the next ball turret gunner who will probably meet the same fate. Will we ever learn?

M. Eileen Duncan

Model Essay Two

The following student-authored essay analyzes the images in William Ernest Henley's poem "Invictus" published in 1875.

Invictus[1]

Out of the night that covers me,
Black as the pit from pole to pole,
I thank whatever gods may be
For my unconquerable soul.

In the fell clutch of circumstance
I have not winced nor cried aloud.
Under the bludgeonings of chance
My head is bloody, but unbowed.

Beyond this place of wrath and tears
Looms but the Horror of the shade,
And yet the menace of the years
Finds, and shall find, me unafraid.

It matters not how strait the gate,
How charged with punishments the scroll,
I am the master of my fate:
I am the captain of my soul.

[1] Max Eastman, ed. *Anthology for Enjoyment of Poetry* (New York: Scribner's, 1951) 295.

"Invictus": A Terrorist's Creed

When Timothy McVeigh faced execution for the bombing of the Murrah Federal Building in Oklahoma City, he chose William Ernest Henley's "Invictus"[1] for his last words. While many view the poem as a work that glorifies courage in the face of difficulty, its imagery reveals another interpretation. *The poem is spoken by an unnamed narrator who uses images of darkness and pain to reveal his negative view of life. His attitude toward suffering communicates the theme that a man can become incapable of human feelings.*

In the first stanza, the speaker uses images of darkness to reveal his dark and twisted view of life. His voice arises "out of the night that covers [him]" (line 1). He is a creature of the darkness which he describes as "black as the pit from pole to pole" (2). He seems to be at the bottom of the pit, at the low point of his life. He sees no hope, for in his eyes the entire world is enveloped in darkness. Yet out of this despair, he searches for meaning, saying, "I thank whatever gods may be / For my unconquerable soul" (3–4). He is uncertain about the power behind the universe but covers his doubt by claiming to be undefeated by the blackness, by his lack of control over the universe. While he claims that he is superior to any circumstance he has encountered, his credence is weakened by his use of negative images. They reveal that, to him, life is dark and dead and filled with pain.

To strengthen his steely self-image, the speaker continues to deny the darkness and his real problems and brags about his ability to conquer life. He hints at the "fell clutch of circumstance" (5) that he has endured. Obviously he has been caught in cruel and difficult situations from which he has been unable to free himself, but he claims he has "not winced or cried aloud" (6). He gives no visual or verbal hint of the pain he has internalized. By hiding his pain, however, he permits it to twist his ego into believing that pain does not exist. By denying his feelings, he kills them and buries them deep within himself. He sees whatever happens to him as "the bludgeonings of chance," (7) denying any connection to his own actions. The image of "bludgeonings" suggests violent beatings, yet he just coldly states that his "head is bloody, but unbowed" (8). He has apparently suffered physically and emotionally, but by refusing to acknowledge his pain, he has become a cold, unfeeling machine, a heartless empty shell of a man.

In the third stanza, the speaker reinforces his negative view of life through images of pain that describe his present circumstances as a "place of wrath and tears" (9). "Wrath" connotes rage, violence, and anger, and "tears" connote sadness, suffering, and pain. The darkness is unrelieved, and the only thing the speaker has to look forward to is "the Horror of the shade" (10). The capital letter on the word "Horror" emphasizes the feelings of terror and fear that the speaker refuses to verbalize, but they emerge subconsciously as he describes his attitude toward death and darkness. His use of the phrase "menace of the years" reprieves the earlier images of life as dark and dangerous. The negative images are unrelieved, but again, the speaker denies any negativity and claims to be "unafraid" (12). He refuses to deal with his feelings and boasts about being above fear and pain which he ironi-

Thesis

Topic Sentence

Topic Sentence

Topic Sentence

[1] Max Eastman, ed. *Anthology for Enjoyment of Poetry* (New York: Scribner's, 1951) 295.

cally acknowledges by using words like "wrath," "tears," "Horror," and "menace" to describe his experiences. He has built a wall around his heart to block out his feelings.

Topic Sentence   *In the last stanza, the speaker's images reveal his uncertainty about the ultimate pain and fear—death.* In the first stanza, it appears that he isn't sure if a power greater than himself exists, but now he dwells on possible problems with his entry into eternity when he says, "It matters not how strait the gate / How charged with punishments the scroll" (11–12). He admits that there may be a narrow passage he must enter, a type of judgment he may face, one that he may find difficult to get through because of past actions; in fact, he suggests that he may even deserve "punishments" because of his deeds. Despite this possibility, he claims, "I am the master of my fate: I am the captain of my soul" (17–18). In his self-talk, he tries to reassure himself that he is in control of his destiny, but actually he has not mastered life or feelings—he has killed them. He has turned himself into a monster devoid of human emotion. He is an empty shell of a man who has kept such a stiff upper lip that he has become unable to feel anything and therefore is incapable of the most basic of human feelings. His heart is dead.

Restatement of Thesis   *And so while the speaker claims to be strong in the face of suffering, his use of imagery reveals the theme that suffering can actually cause a man to become inhuman.* By denying that his own pain exists, he has become unable to feel anything, including the pain of others. Unwilling or unable to learn acceptance, he has sacrificed his humanity and become a cold and heartless machine. While the human condition is filled with suffering and pain, it is also filled with happiness and joy. If all one sees is the dark side of life, then there is nothing to live for. True courage, on the other hand, embraces all that life offers and faces the light, not the darkness.

Justin McQuillan

❧ Model Essay Three

This student-written essay analyzes imagery and its effects in the following poem by Marge Piercy:

What's That Smell in the Kitchen?[1]

All over America women are burning dinners.
It's lambchops in Peoria; it's haddock
in Providence; it's steak in Chicago;
tofu delight in Big Sur; red
rice and beans in Dallas.
All over America women are burning
food they're supposed to bring with calico
smile on platters glittering like wax.
Anger sputters in her brain pan, confined
but spewing out missiles of hot fat.
Carbonized despair presses like a clinker from a
barbecue against the back of her eyes.

[1] From CIRCLES ON THE WATER by Marge Piercy. Copyright © 1982 by Marge Piercy. Reprinted by permission of Alfred A. Knopf, Inc.

If she wants to grill anything, it's
her husband spitted over a slow fire.
If she wants to serve him anything
it's a dead rat with a bomb in its belly
ticking like the heart of an insomniac.
Her life is cooked and digested,
nothing but leftovers in Tupperware.
Look, she says, once I was roast duck
on your platter with parsley but now I am Spam.
Burning dinner is not incompetence but war.

To Honor and Obey: A Wife's Servitude

Who ever came up with the wife's marital vow "to honor and obey"?
In addition, the saying "A woman's place is in the kitchen" is as restrictive
and stifling as telling a dog to "Sit and stay." Unfortunately, wives are often treated like trained dogs. In the poem "What's That Smell in the
Kitchen?"[1] Marge Piercy describes the plight of the American wife. It is one
shared by all wives, and it revolves around their husbands' lack of appreciation of them. Wives across the country rebel against this image of the happy
homemaker by burning dinner. If "A woman's place is in the kitchen," then
she will use the weaponry provided there. She is extremely disgruntled, and
Piercy uses many metaphorical images to express the wife's anger and de-
Thesis Statement scribe what is left of her self-esteem. *By creating images of the typical
American wife, food preparation, and leftovers, Piercy creates an emotional
atmosphere filled with anger and despair. In addition, the imagery illustrates
her theme that these wives are being oppressed and neglected by their husbands and society.*

Topic Sentence *In the beginning of the poem, Piercy creates images of the American
wife in her role as cook.* The typical image is that of June Cleaver or Betty
Crocker who would be happily and lovingly preparing dinner for her family. Piercy, however, creates a picture riddled with irony: "All over America
women are burning dinners. / . . . it's haddock / in Providence; it's steak in
Chicago;" (lines 1–3). Each wife is preparing the dish appropriate to her location. This demonstrates her conformity to society's expectations. The
twist, however, is that the wife is not trying to excel in the kitchen but is
instead staging a rebellion. She and many other wives across the country are
". . . burning / food they're supposed to bring with calico / smile on platters glittering like wax" (6–8). The smile and the shiny platters fit the familiar image of a pretty woman serving her beautiful dinner to her eager family. Her hair is perfect, her makeup fresh, her smile sincere, her ironed dress
unstained. It is seemingly an effortless and enjoyable feat. In Piercy's poem,
though, the women are not enjoying their role. The clincher is that the food
is burned intentionally. Incompetence would not damage the image of the
perfect wife as much as defiance would.

[1] From CIRCLES ON THE WATER by Marge Piercy. Copyright © 1982 by Marge
Piercy. Reprinted by permission of Alfred A. Knopf, Inc.

Topic Sentence   *Piercy continues building an image of the angry and rebelling wife by comparing her emotions to food preparation.* She is truly frustrated with her role as cook: "Anger sputters in her brainpan, confined / but spewing out missiles of hot fat" (9–10). This is an effective and vivid metaphor. "Sputters" and "spewing" are particularly descriptive of both an angry reaction and hot fat frying. There is pressure building up, and the anger and hot fat are almost explosive. Then Piercy discloses the cause of the woman's animosity: "If she wants to serve [her husband] anything / it's a dead rat with a bomb in its belly . . ." (15–16). Piercy's twist on the word "serve" implies that the wife resents being treated like a servant to her husband. If there is anything she would *happily* serve him, it would be something lethal. Barbecued rat-on-a-skewer paints an ominous picture of the night's dinner special, but it is even more frightening if you are the one considered to be the rat. The woman's anger is obviously deep-seated because she apparently does not feel any remorse about her hostile schemes against her husband.

Topic Sentence   *Piercy concludes her picture of the American wife by comparing her life to images of leftovers.* Not much remains of her glorious dreams of marriage and equality: "Her life is cooked and digested, / nothing but leftovers in Tupperware" (18–19). Everyone knows what event physiologically follows digestion. The wife sees her life as a type of "human waste" as undesirable as the leftovers. Being sealed in Tupperware adds to the image of her being trapped and suffocated. Her self-image is squashed, and there is no hope in sight. She believes that "once [she] was roast duck / on [her husband's] platter with parsley but now [she is] Spam" (20–21). She has gone from being an elegant gourmet feast to the closest thing to dog food. With a heart filled with dismay and rejection, she turns to "burning dinner" (22) in an effort to wage "war" (22) upon her husband and his thoughtlessness.

Restatement of Thesis   *Piercy, then, has masterfully used imagery to create an emotional atmosphere of anger and oppression and to convey her theme that the American wife is trying to fight against her oppression.* Although society's prize homemaker cooks what she is supposed to, she always burns it. The burning is not due to an honest mistake or to her lack of culinary ability, however. She intentionally burns her husband's food to vent her anger, for "Burning dinner is not incompetence but war" (22). Throughout the poem, she is either burning food or imagining revenge on her husband, for she does not dare to outwardly defy society's expectations. If she did, she would be considered a complete failure and a bad wife; therefore, she has to covertly rebel. At least she is not alone. Whether she knows it or not, wives all across America are suffering the same plight and burning their husband's dinners to express their frustration over being taken for granted. Meanwhile, their unwitting or uncaring husbands continue to ask, "What's that smell in the kitchen?" Will they ever learn?

Ann M. Conway

Model Essay Four

This student essay analyzes the use of imagery in a short story:

The Gift of Uniqueness

Thesis Statement

In literature, a character's appearance is often a clue to his or her personality. This is especially true in "Gift of Grass"[1] by Alice Adams. Cathy, the central character, is a confused sixteen-year-old who has refused to return to school in the fall. Her mother, Barbara, and her step-father, Bill, want her to see a psychiatrist to help her sort out her goals in life. *As Adams describes each of these characters, she uses image clusters to reveal their basic personalities and to communicate the theme that each person is unique and should not be forced to follow in another's footsteps.*

Topic Sentence

Cathy is a teenager who does not want to grow up and face the adult world. Her childishness is evident in the images that Adams chooses for her description. Cathy's "rather squat, short body," her "jeans and black turtleneck sweater," and her "perfectly round brown eyes in a pale, round face" suggest that she is still a "little girl" (376). These images showing Cathy's size and style of dress, her innocent eyes, and her baby face are signs that she is still physically and emotionally immature. Her plain appearance shows that she lacks adult sophistication, and her statements to Dr. Fredricks, her psychiatrist, about her goals in life reveal that she also lacks direction and motivation: "'I'm not interested in standards, or school or earning money or getting married'" (376). Obviously Cathy is not yet ready to grow up and enter the adult world since she rejects the goals that most adults strive for in our society. This is emphasized by what she says she is interested in: "'Clouds. . . . And foghorns. I wonder where they all are'" (377). These images show that Cathy is lost in the "clouds" and that she is looking for direction the way that foghorns give direction to ships' pilots who are unable to see things clearly in the fog. To escape her confusion, Cathy has turned to drugs, and before she returns home from the doctor's office, she smokes "a very mashed joint. . . . She sucked in and waited for the melting of her despair" (379). This image suggests that she is sucking on the cigarette the way a child would suck on a bottle; it gives her comfort and reduces her sense of hopelessness in life. Drugs help her forget her fear of growing up, getting a job, and forming relationships. She would rather stay a child.

Topic Sentence

Perhaps Cathy's problems are created in part by her mother, Barbara. The images that Adams uses to describe Barbara show that she and Cathy are alike in some ways but different in others. Barbara also has "round eyes," but hers are "often opaque," (380), suggesting that she is not as open as Cathy. Although Barbara's shape is also "childlike," she has a sense of style that is evident in her "smart gray wool dress" (380). These images show that Barbara is sophisticated and knows how to dress for success.

---

[1] Alice Adams, "Gift of Grass" *An Introduction to Literature*, ed. Sylvan Barnet, Morton Berman, and William Burto, 8th ed. (Boston: Little, 1985). All parenthetical page numbers refer to the text in this edition.

And she is a successful "interior decorator" (376) who likes to use "cool blues and greens" (379) which reflect her desire for control, for perfection. In fact, she wants everything "to be perfect—her house, her husband, her daughter and especially herself" (380). This puts a tremendous pressure on all of them, and since Cathy feels less than perfect when she compares herself to her mother, she would rather drop out than compete. Unfortunately, there is no real communication between Barbara and Cathy as seen in the way they sit "at opposite ends of the sofa, facing Bill rather than each other" (380). This image emphasizes the emotional as well as the physical distance between mother and daughter. The contrasts between them—illustrated by the images—reveal that Barbara is unhappy because Cathy isn't perfect, and Cathy is unhappy because she feels that she cannot live up to her mother's expectations.

Topic Sentence

The differences in Barbara and Cathy parallel the differences in Bill, Barbara's husband, and his father. The images that Adams uses to characterize Bill emphasize his somewhat effeminate nature. He is "a very thin, narrowly built man with delicate bones and sparse blondish hair" (380). The "delicate" image emphasizes his slight build, and his thinning hair contrasts with the male image of hairiness. Bill's image differs sharply from that of his father's; he "had been a mighty hunter . . . with rather Bunyanesque notions of manhood . . ." (380). The Paul Bunyan image brings to mind a well built giant of a man with macho characteristics. Bill's appearance is one of the reasons why he has "had trouble from time to time believing in himself as a man" (380). This lack of confidence in his manhood has weakened his self-concept, and to prove to himself that he is truly male, he "played around" (380) with other women while he was married to his first wife and to Barbara, his second. The playboy image seems to build his confidence, but he confesses to Cathy that he still has problems with "booze" and sees himself as "a fatuous drunk" (382). Like Cathy, Bill has problems accepting himself as he is because of a deep-seated sense of inadequacy that stems from his relationship with his father. He tells Cathy that he "'was very much afraid of'" his father (380), and that probably created communication problems between them. Their differences are brought out by the activities each liked to engage in. Bill "liked to wash dishes, which his father had seen to it that he was not allowed to do" (381), while his father preferred "hunting" (380). These images reveal the void that existed between father and son. A man's washing dishes projects a sissified image to Bill's father, while hunting projects the image of "coarse, red-faced, hunting cretins" to Bill (380). Obviously, Bill could not live up to his father's expectations for him, and that has caused him to find life "confused and difficult" (382). He could never truly become his own person.

Restatement of Thesis

And so, through her use of imagery, Adams has characterized Cathy, Barbara, and Bill and has emphasized her theme that each person should be allowed to develop as a unique individual. Cathy is a teenager who is afraid to grow up because she feels that she cannot become the perfect person that her perfect mother wants her to be. As a result, she has turned to drugs and has refused to face life's challenges. Barbara is uptight because she has not learned to face the fact that people are human beings with imperfections that can be accepted through unconditional love. Bill, a man who could not live up to his father's expectations, has also had problems accepting himself and has turned to affairs and alcohol to help himself cope. If only parents could accept themselves and their children as unique individuals, there would be fewer people who need psychiatrists, drugs, or extramarital affairs to help them deal with life. Destroying another's uniqueness is a terrible waste of human potential; accepting it is the highest wisdom.

Regina Lang

JUST ONE MORE THING

"Imagine" is a wonderful word with endless possibilities. It permits us to experience vicariously anything we wish. The writer who uses sensory appeals (images) asks us to enter into a work with our minds **and** our imaginations. In the words of John Lennon, "It's easy if you try."

❧ Imagery Analysis Essay Plan Sheet ❧

Author: _____ Title: _____

Thesis: _____

_____

_____

_____

_____

Topic sentence: _____

_____

_____

Supporting quote: page or line _____

Supporting quote: page or line _____

Supporting quote: page or line _____

Topic sentence: _____

_____

_____

Supporting quote: page or line _____

Supporting quote: page or line _____

Supporting quote: page or line _____

Topic sentence: _____

_____

_____

Supporting quote: page or line _____

Supporting quote: page or line _____

Supporting quote: page or line _____

Topic sentence: _____

_____

_____

Supporting quote: page or line _____

Supporting quote: page or line _____

Supporting quote: page or line _____

Topic sentence: _____

_____

_____

Supporting quote: page or line _____

Supporting quote: page or line _____

Supporting quote: page or line _____

Topic sentence: _____

_____

_____

Supporting quote: page or line _____

Supporting quote: page or line _____

Supporting quote: page or line _____

Concluding points: _____

_____

_____

_____

_____

_____

_____

❦ Peer/Self-Evaluation of an Imagery Analysis Essay ❦

> **Directions:** Make specific suggestions about each part of the essay, pointing out particular areas that the writer could improve. Keep in mind the qualities of good writing: unity, organization, development, clarity, and coherence.

I. Introduction

Is the lead relevant and interesting?

Are the author's full name and the title of the work correctly spelled and punctuated?

Does the summary of the work end with the list of image patterns (the first part of the thesis) that will be discussed in the body paragraphs?

Does the thesis also state the effects of the image patterns that will be discussed in the conclusion?

II. Body Paragraphs

Do the topic sentences name the image pattern to be discussed in the paragraph?

Are the supporting quotations properly introduced?

Do the supporting quotations illustrate the image pattern?

Do the analysis sections explain/comment on the images?

Are the analysis sections adequately developed?

Are the body paragraphs unified and coherent?

III. Conclusion

Is a signal word included somewhere in the paragraph?

Does the topic sentence rephrase the effects of the images as stated in the thesis?

Is the discussion of each of the effects specific in detail and adequately developed?

IV. Expression

Are all the ideas expressed in complete sentences?

Are the sentences clear and correctly punctuated?

Are there any problems with subject-verb or pronoun-antecedent agreement?

Are all the words correctly spelled?

V. Overall Evaluation

Most effective part of the essay:

Least effective part of the essay:

List three specific actions which could be taken by the writer to improve this and future papers:
1.

2.

3.

Evaluator's name: _____ Date: _____

❧ Exercise on Imagery ❧

> In the following poem by Marge Piercy, circle the images (words or phrases with sensory appeal) and then explain how they help to reveal character, create atmosphere or mood, produce an emotional response, and communicate the theme.

Barbie Doll[1]

This girlchild was born as usual
and presented dolls that did pee-pee
and miniature GE stoves and irons
and wee lipsticks the color of cherry candy.
Then in the magic of puberty, a classmate said:
You have a great big nose and fat legs.

She was healthy, tested intelligent,
possessed strong arms and back,
abundant sexual drive and manual dexterity.
She went to and fro apologizing.
Everyone saw a fat nose on thick legs.

She was advised to play coy,
exhorted to come on hearty,
exercise, diet, smile and wheedle.
Her good nature wore out
like a fan belt.
So she cut off her nose and her legs
and offered them up.

In the casket displayed on satin she lay
with the undertaker's cosmetics painted on,
a turned-up putty nose,
dressed in a pink and white nightie.
Doesn't she look pretty? everyone said.
Consummation at last.
To every woman a happy ending.

Character of the girlchild: _____

_____

_____

_____

_____

_____

_____

_____

Atmosphere in the beginning, middle, and end of the poem: _____

_____

_____

_____

_____

_____

_____

_____

Emotional response toward the girl and her associates: _____

_____

_____

_____

_____

_____

_____

_____

_____

Theme: _____

_____

_____

_____

_____

_____

_____

Structural Analysis

Overview

A work of fiction, a poem, or a drama makes its impact upon us as a whole because the whole is usually greater than the sum of its parts. It should be recognized, however, that many works are separated into parts by the author. As we move from chapter to chapter in a novel, from one verse to another in a poem, or from one act to another in drama, we are seeing the structure of a work unfold, for structure is the order of the parts and the relationship of the parts to each other and to the whole work. Understanding how the parts fit together and relate to each other can add to our understanding and appreciation of the work as a whole.

Analyzing Structure

Every literary work has an underlying structure. It is the organizing principle in a work that determines the order of the parts and their relationship to each other and to the work as a whole. Writers choose a structure, an order, that will convey the ideas, the themes, that they want their readers or their audience to consider.

When analyzing the structure of a work, there are three basic steps: identifying the main parts, deciding why the author has divided his work at a particular point, and showing how the organizing principle (the structural device) strengthens and reinforces the work's theme.

Often the author simplifies **the first step** of the process—identifying the main parts—by dividing his work into chapters, stanzas, or acts and scenes. These divisions function as the major parts; when works are not divided into parts, we can look for internal clues to structure—a change in the thought pattern, a new complication in the plot, or the introduction of a new character. As each new part is added to a work, its structure becomes more involved and complex. It would be accurate to say that, generally, a novel of thirty chapters or a poem of ten stanzas is more complex—structurally—than a novel of fifteen chapters or a poem of two stanzas.

The second step in structural analysis is trying to decide why the author chose to divide his work in the precise places that he did. In attempting to answer "Why the division here?" one is really asking, "What is the connection (relationship) between the first part and the second part? How does the second part relate to the third part?"—and so on until all the pieces have been fit into the puzzle. There are many possible reasons for dividing a work at a particular point. Some simple organizing principles might be time (change in the day, a season, or a lifetime), contrast, comparison, example, cause/effect, logical process (step-by-step), logical argument, space (a change in location), size, proximity (a change in distance or a change in a relationship), order of importance, parts of the plot pattern, repetition, and so on endlessly.

In trying to identify the structural principle involved in a story, poem, or drama, one might ask, "How does part one *differ* from part two? What is *new* in part two or in part three that would demand a new chapter or a new stanza?" It is safe to assume that a new part in a story, poem, or play is comparable to a new paragraph in prose. Some new aspect of an idea or a totally new but related idea is being introduced. Deciding what is new and how it relates to what precedes it is deciding upon structural principles.

The third step of structural analysis is showing how the structure strengthens and supports the overall theme of the work. This relationship is usually not as obvious as the relationship between each of the parts. It generally requires a more reflective thought process which involves (1) the formulation of a general idea (theme) that the work seems to be conveying about life and (2) a determination of how that idea fits into the structure that was identified in step two.

Structure in Poetry

Let's look at Elder Olson's "Directions to the Armorer" so we can apply the three-step structural analysis process:

Directions to the Armorer[1]

All right, armorer,
Make me a sword—
Not too sharp,
A bit hard to draw,
And of cardboard, preferably.
On second thought, stick
An eraser on the handle.
Somehow I always
Clobber the wrong guy.

Make me a shield with
Easy-to-change
Insignia. I'm often
A little vague
As to which side I'm on,
What battle I'm in.
And listen, make it
A trifle flimsy,
Not too hard to pierce.
I'm not absolutely sure
I want to win.

Make the armor itself
As tough as possible,
But on a reverse

[1] By Elder Olson: Copyright © 1963 by Elder Olson. Reprinted by permission.

Principle: don't
Worry about it
Saving my hide:
Just fix it to give me
Some sort of protection—
Any sort of protection—
From a possible enemy
Inside.

In this poem, we can see that there are three major parts as determined by the three stanzas. As we read each stanza, we should also note that it divides into three internal parts: the identification of the piece of armor, a description of how it should be made, and a reason for its construction in that manner. This pattern is used consistently in each verse.

In the second step of the structural analysis process—explaining why the poet divided his work into three parts and what structural principle is being employed—we can see that when the poet orders a new piece of armor, he begins a new stanza. He starts with the sword in the first stanza, moves to the shield in the second, and ends with the armor itself in the third. As we consider the armor and the order, we note that each piece is held or worn progressively closer to the body. If a person in armor were defending himself, the sword would be held away from the body to fend off any would-be attackers. The shield would be held closer to the body to protect the part which is under attack. Lastly, the armor would be worn against the body itself—over the heart—to protect its most vulnerable part. Since each piece of armor gets progressively closer to the body, one possible interpretation of structure is a spatial order based on proximity or closeness to the speaker.

The third step of the structural analysis process involves relating the theme to the structural device. In "Directions to the Armorer," the speaker seems to be saying that he often makes mistakes and that he isn't sure about his judgments or his values. This leads to the theme or main idea that a man sometimes needs protection from himself because he is often his own worst enemy. This theme is reinforced and strengthened by the structure. As each piece of armor comes closer to the speaker, the realization becomes clearer that the real source of danger is not from the outside—but from the inside—from the speaker himself. The closeness or proximity of the enemy is reinforced by the increasing proximity of each piece of armor until the armor covers the speaker's heart—often the source of man's weakness as well as his strength.

The subtle relationship of theme and structure adds depth and complexity to a work. Analyzing this connection involves explaining how the way the parts are ordered reinforces the message in the work. Assume, for example, that an author uses the structural device of time in a poem about love whose theme is that love has deep roots. Appropriate questions to ask would be what is the function of roots, or how does time relate to love and to its roots? What happens to the roots of anything over time—especially at different times of the year? Answers to questions like these would reveal how the time structure helps to being out the theme of the work and why the author's choice of structure was an effective one.

Structure in Fiction

Structure is especially easy to see in poetry, but keep in mind that it is also present in prose fiction and drama. The end of one chapter and the beginning of another in a novel indicate some type of change in the structure, usually a change of focus from one character to another, a change of time or place, a change in the conflict, or a change from one part of the plot to another. This approach to structure is also evident in some short stories. For example, Frank O'Connor divides his short story "Guests of the

Nation"[2] into four distinct parts or mini-chapters. The first three parts begin with Bonaparte and Noble, the young Irish soldiers, playing a friendly game of cards with their English prisoners, Belcher and Hawkins. Jeremiah Donovan, the older, experienced Irish soldier, enters the cottage each night, and each time his presence becomes more of a threat. At first, he seems friendly enough, but in part two, he warns Bonaparte that the Englishmen will be shot if Irish prisoners are killed, and later, in part three, he brings the word that the Englishmen will be shot to avenge Irish losses. Each of Donovan's pronouncements strikes a blow against Bonaparte's innocence and naiveté about war, so it is easy to understand part four's dramatic and traumatic conclusion. When Donovan coldly murders the prisoners, Bonaparte's life is changed. He moves from innocence to experience, and he tells us that "anything that happened to [him] afterwards, [he] never felt the same about again" (16).

The change in Bonaparte's perceptions of reality was prepared for by the way O'Connor structured his story. Donovan's changing attitude toward the prisoners paralleled Bonaparte's changing attitude toward war. At first it seemed patriotic to be involved, but when Bonaparte discovered that war meant killing other human beings, he felt "very small and very lost and lonely like a child astray in the snow" (16). The parallel structure emphasizes the theme that the coldness and impersonality of war change innocent young men into confused and lost souls.

While O'Connor uses a straightforward time line to move us through the work, another writer might change the usual structure or order of the plot to emphasize an event, a character's development, or the theme. Hemingway in the "The Short Happy Life of Francis Macomber" shows the effects of Francis's cowardly act of running from the wounded lion at the beginning of the story, long before he describes the actual event. By using a **flashback**—a twist of time in which past actions are introduced into present events—Hemingway reveals what the characters are like by showing first their reaction to this key event. Francis is apologetic, his wife is angry and cruel, and Wilson, the white hunter, thinks Francis is a "bloody coward." By not describing Francis's fear-filled flight until the night before he faces and stands firm before the wounded buffalo, Hemingway uses the contrast of the two scenes to emphasize the character change in Francis and to reveal his theme about what constitutes a happy life. The placement of this key scene is a choice Hemingway made about the structure of his plot.

Another structural option for a writer is a **repetitive structure** in which certain events or images are repeated at key points in the work. William Faulkner uses this structure as well as the flashback in his short story "A Rose for Emily." Emily's refusal to bury her dead father for three days is repeated later in the story in her decision not to bury Homer Barron after she poisons him, thus bringing the reader full circle. The story itself is an extended flashback with Miss Emily's death announced in the first line and then her life described in the first four parts of the work. Not until Part V does Faulkner satisfy the curiosity he created in the first paragraph about the inside of Miss Emily's house. When authors put important events in unusual places in a work, critical readers notice the structure and ask what the author gains from his creative choices.

Structure in Drama

Structure is also present in drama, and the parts are most often identified for us by the playwright's division of his work into acts or scenes. Tennessee Williams divides *The Glass Menagerie* into seven scenes, and by analyzing the dramatic action in each scene, it is easy to see the structural device of contrast in operation. In Scenes I and II, we can see the underlying frustrations of Amanda, Laura, and Tom. Amanda is frustrated by her husband's desertion, her lost youth and popularity, and Laura's shyness. Laura contrasts with her mother because of her lack of confidence and her lack of gentlemen call-

---

[2] Frank O'Connor, "Guests of the Nation" *Stories by Frank O'Connor* (New York: Vintage, 1956). All parenthetical page numbers refer to the text in this edition.

ers. Tom's anger contrasts with Laura's submissiveness in relation to Amanda, and his presence contrasts with his father's absence.

Scene III in the play contrasts Tom's open hostility toward his mother over her interference in his life with his tentative reconciliation with her at the end of Scene IV. His agreement to look for a gentlemen caller for Laura brings us to the main contrast of the play in Scenes V, VI, and VII. In Scene V, Tom announces that he has invited a caller, Jim O'Connor, over for dinner, and this raises the hope that Laura may find a future and a life of her own in marriage. This increasing hope brings us to the climax of the play as Jim, free of his old high school sweetheart, praises Laura's prettiness and kisses her. This high point contrasts with the despair and disappointment brought out by Jim's painful announcement that he is engaged to another girl, Betty, and that he cannot return. Amanda's great plans and Laura's hopes are shattered, and the play ends in darkness and despair.

Williams use of contrast in the structure of the play emphasizes the contrast between illusion and reality that forms one of his main themes. The Wingfields have difficulty facing present reality so they live in worlds of illusion built around the past or a hoped-for future. Because they cannot face their problems, they cannot solve them; therefore, they are unhappy. Williams' crafting of the structure of his drama—the arrangement of the order of the scenes—helps to communicate his themes and to make his work effective.

In each successful work of literature, there will be a structure, a skeleton, a principle of organization which can be identified by the critical reader. Each work will have a unique structure which will be evident only upon study and scrutiny, for the good writer so intertwines the theme and the structure that only the analytical reader will be able to see the part that each plays in a successful work. Try to become a structural sleuth. It can be a real challenge to your logical (and creative) mind.

❧ Writing about Structure: Step by Step

As you plan to write your structural analysis essay, try to keep these points in mind:

1. When choosing the subject of your analysis, keep in mind that the number of major parts in the work will determine the number of body paragraphs since each part is analyzed in a separate paragraph in the body of the essay. Remember, too, that the greater the number of parts, the more complex the work, so to make your analysis clear and easy to follow, it's best to choose a work with from two to five major parts.
2. The structural device or organizing principle is easier to identify in some works than in others, so try to choose a work that has an identifiable and easy-to-label structure. Some structural devices which are relatively easy to spot in a work are time order, comparison, contrast, cause/effect, spatial order, and logical argument.
3. The thesis contains the following information:
   a. the number of major parts in the work;
   b. the structural device the author uses to organize and unify the work, i.e., time, contrast, comparison, example, cause/effect, logical process, logical argument, space, size, proximity, order of importance, flashbacks, repetition, archetypal characters, actions, or elements, or other organizing principles;
   c. an explanation of how the structural device relates to and helps communicate the theme which is stated.
4. The first body paragraph in the essay explains the opening situation in the work by identifying the characters involved and their relationships, by describing their setting in time and place, and by interpreting the content (ideas) in the first major part. This interpretation must be supported by direct quotations from the work and by an analysis of them.

5. All succeeding body paragraphs (one for each remaining part) must begin with a topic sentence which points out how this new part is related to the preceding part. What follows is an analysis of the content in this new part based, of course, on the literary analysis pattern of generalization, introductory information for a quotation, the direct quotation itself, and explanation/analysis.

6. The conclusion is a thorough discussion of how the structural device relates to and reinforces the theme in the work. The topic sentence expresses this relationship and clearly states the theme. The remainder of the paragraph explores and explains the theme in terms of its universal applications and in terms of how the structural device helps to communicate and emphasize those ideas.

The following diagram, model essays, and plan sheet will help you organize and write an essay on structure in a work of literature.

Title

Introductory Paragraph:

Open with interesting lead material.

Name the work and the author.

Briefly summarize the work and then identify the number of major parts and name the structural device.

Indicate that the structure of the work reinforces its theme and then explain the theme in a sentence or two.

} Thesis

Body Paragraphs: There will be at least one body paragraph on each major part.

In body paragraph one, describe the opening situation in the work by identifying the characters, their relationships, and their setting. Then explain the content or main ideas in part one by using the literary analysis pattern (generalizations, introductory information for a quotation, the direct quotation, and analysis) to support your explanation/interpretation.

All other body paragraphs on the remaining parts begin with a topic sentence that shows the relationship of each new part to the one preceding it by pointing out how the structural device is used. The sentences which follow interpret the content in the new part by using introductory information for a quotation, the quotation itself, and analysis to support the generalizations about structure.

Concluding Paragraph:

Use a signal word in your topic sentence which relates the structural device to the theme, and then explain—in detail— how the structural device communicates or helps to reinforce the theme—which is fully discussed and analyzed. The paragraph should be approximately five to seven sentences in length to insure a thorough discussion of the relationship between the structure and the theme in the work.

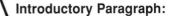

Model Essay One

The following student essay analyzes the structure in a poem by Philip Booth.

First Lesson[1]

"Lie back, daughter, let your head be
tipped back in the cup of my hand.
Gently, and I will hold you.

Spread your arms wide, lie out on the
stream and look high at the gulls.

A dead-man's float is face down. You will
dive and swim soon enough where this
tidewater ebbs to the sea. Daughter,
believe me, when you tire on the long
thrash to your island, lie up, and survive.

As you float now, where I held you and
let go, remember when fear cramps your
heart what I told you: lie gently and
wide to the light-year stars, lie back,
and the sea will hold you."

Life's Important Lesson

Learning to swim can be frightening, but if the teacher is your father whom you love and trust, it can be a beautiful and reassuring experience. That is the situation in "First Lesson"[1] by Philip Booth. The poem is an extended metaphor in which the father who is teaching his daughter to swim actually teachers her about life. *By using a time structure throughout the lesson, Booth conveys the theme that with guidance from a loving father, a child can develop the ability to face any situation in life.*

Thesis Statement

In the first stanza, the father begins by teaching his daughter to float, a basic skill that leads to confidence in the water. He tells her to "lie back" (line 1) as he supports her head "in the cup of [his] hand" (2). His presence and his strength give her the confidence to stretch out on the water because she knows that he is there to support her; she has nothing to fear. He then tells her to lie "gently" (3) on the water, and he "will hold" her (3). His use of the word "gently" reveals his sensitivity and his experience in the water. He knows that fear and struggle make floating much more difficult. His holding her head in his hand is a birth image that shows the beautiful connection between father and daughter. Her trust begins at birth and is strengthened by the experiences they share.

Topic Sentence

The second stanza is related to the first as the father continues instructing his daughter during the time of the lesson. His advice to "spread [her] arms wide" (4) implies that she should be open to life and experience. By

Topic Sentence

[1] "First Lesson," from *Letter from a Distant Land* by Philip Booth, copyright © 1975 by Philip Booth. Used by permission of Viking Penguin, a division of Penguin Putnam Inc.

embracing life, she will live it to the full. When he tells her to "lie out on the / stream and look high at the gulls" (4–5), he is telling her to live life with her eyes open, to recognize and be receptive to all opportunities in life. The sky is the limit if she sets her goals "high" (5) and does not give in to fear or discouragement. The gulls fly high above the sea, so if the daughter looks upward and focuses on things above, she will achieve more in life; it will be much easier to stay afloat.

Topic Sentence *The third stanza relates to the first two as a continuation of the lesson.* The father contrasts what he has just told the daughter, "to look high" (5), with a description of "A dead-man's float [that] is face down" (6). The dead man sees nothing; his vision of life is filled with darkness. The daughter's vision, however, is full of light and expectation, for she "will / dive and swim soon enough where [the] / tidewater ebbs to the sea" (6–8). Floating is just the beginning skill and symbolizes the daughter's innocence and youth, while diving and swimming symbolize her maturing and moving into adulthood. She will have the opportunity to "dive" into life and achieve her goals, but the father does not want her to rush into things that she may not be able to handle. Knowing how difficult life can be, he offers her advice on how to deal with adversity: "Daughter, / believe me, when you tire on the long / thrash to your island, lie up, and survive" (8–10). The father knows that there will be times when his daughter will want to give up as she works toward her goals, her "island," but he knows that if she will "lie up" or just float rather than "thrash" or struggle, she will be able to survive. The father has probably experienced some difficult times and has learned that acceptance, going with the flow, and time solve some of life's problems.

Topic Sentence *The last stanza relates to the first three as the daughter begins to "float" away from "where [her father] held [her] and / "let [her] go" (11–12) on her own.* She has learned the basic skills necessary for survival in the water and in life, but her father knows that there will be times of doubt and fear, so he gives her one last piece of advice:

> [. . .] remember when fear cramps your
> heart what I told you: lie gently and
> wide to the light-year stars, lie back,
> and the sea will hold you." (12–16)

The daughter is leaving the safety of her father's support, for he knows that he must "let go" if she is to develop her independence and her life skills. There will be times when she is afraid, but if she follows the loving advice of her father, she will be a survivor. His repetition of the word "gently" emphasizes the importance of acceptance and looking up at the eternal and steadfast stars, unlike the dead man who looks downward. The "sea" symbolizes life, and there are times when not struggling makes life easier to accept. If the daughter knows when to "swim" and when to "float," she will be able to endure and overcome all of life's challenges.

Restatement of Thesis *And so Booth's use of time as a structural device helps to communicate the theme that just as a child must learn how to float and swim in order to survive in the sea, she must also learn when to float or swim to survive in the sea of life.* The father begins with the basic floating position on the water and holds his daughter "gently" as she opens her arms and lifts her eyes to watch the high-flying gulls. He knows that once she masters this basic skill, she will gain confidence and be ready to "dive and swim" in the sea. He also knows that she will tire as she swims in the deeper water, so he reminds her of the importance of floating and of letting the sea support her until she regains her strength and is ready to go on. This same principle applies to life. Fathers need to teach their children that life requires basic skills, too, like moving "gently" into life, like not rushing too quickly into the complex world of adulthood—into deeper water—until they are ready. Then they will be safely launched into life, knowing when to swim and when to float—when to survive and when to accept whatever life brings their way. Understanding the difference is an important lesson to learn.

Diane Piper

Model Essay Two

This student essay is a structural analysis of a sonnet by John Keats:

Bright Star, Would I Were Stedfast as Thou Art[1]

Bright star, would I were stedfast as thou art—
Not in lone splendor hung aloft the night,
And watching, with eternal lids apart,
Like nature's patient, sleepless eremite,
The moving waters at their priestlike task
Of pure ablution round earth's human shores,
Or gazing on the new soft-fallen mask
Of snow upon the mountains and the moors—
No—yet still stedfast, still unchangeable,
Pillow'd upon my fair love's ripening breast,
To feel for ever its soft swell and fall,
Awake for ever in a sweet unrest,
Still, still to hear her tender-taken breath,
And so live ever—or else swoon to death.

Time for Love

The saying "Time waits for no man" reminds us that time is fleeting and man can never make it stand still. However, that doesn't stop him from wishing that the best moments in life could go on forever. This is the wish expressed by the speaker in John Keats' Italian sonnet entitled "Bright Star, Would I Were Stedfast as Thou Art."[1] *Keats uses the structural device of*

Thesis

[1]John Keats, "Bright Star, Would I Were Stedfast as Thou Art" *The Complete Poetical Works of Keats,* Cambridge Edition (Boston: Houghton, 1899) 232.

contrast to convey the theme that if love's fleeting passion could be made eternal, it would make life—or even death—a lastingly beautiful experience.

In the octave of the sonnet, the speaker addresses a "Bright star" and expresses his wish to be as "stedfast" (line 1) as it is. He recognizes the brevity of human life and would like to share the star's eternal nature. He, too, wants to be unchanging but not to perform the star's tasks which he then describes. The speaker does not want to spend his time in "lone splendor" eternally "watching" the "moving waters" as they wash against the earth's "shores" (2–6). He sees the star in religious terms, describing it as a "sleepless eremite" or religious hermit performing "priestlike task[s]" for the "human" earth (4–6). Nor does the speaker want to be like the star "gazing on the new soft-fallen mask / Of snow upon the mountains and the moors" (7–8). While the star, with "eternal lids apart" (3), spends its time looking down on earth's beauty in the seas and the snow-covered landscape, the speaker would like to spend eternity enjoying a contrasting type of beauty—that of his beloved.

In the sestet of the sonnet, the speaker explains why he wants to be "unchangeable" like the star and contrasts his ideal activities with those of the star. He would like to spend eternity in the passionate embrace of his love. He wants to be forever "pillow'd upon [her] ripening breast" (10) so that they will never be separated from each other. Their closeness will allow him "To feel for ever [her breast's] soft swell and fall" (11). Held in her embrace, he will feel each breath she takes and be comforted by her presence and her physical beauty. He does not want their passionate love for each other ever to diminish; he wishes to be "Awake for ever in a sweet unrest" (12) to feel each pang of pleasure and "to hear her tender-taken breath" (13). The speaker's images depict a passionate love scene that he wants to last "for ever" (12), and if he were like the "stedfast" (1) star, he would experience unchanging, undying love. He would like to "live ever" in that state or, if that is not possible, to "swoon to death" (14) at the moment of the most intense passion and love.

Keats' use of contrast as a structural device, then, helps to communicate the theme that life—and even death—would always be beautiful if they could be spent in the arms of one's beloved. The speaker, looking at one of the "bright" stars in the universe, envies its eternal nature and wishes to be like it. He is obviously a finite being, a victim of time, and when he contrasts his human nature with the star's, he, too, wants to be "stedfast." His activities in his "unchangeable" state, however, would contrast with those of the star; he wants closeness with his love so he can enjoy her beauty and share her passion. The speaker has obviously been in this state with his love, but he knows how passion passes and how life's pain and sorrow contrast with its fleeting pleasures. If he could just live in a permanent state of passion or else die in its throes, he would be happy. Sadly, the speaker's lifetime is limited, but at least he can—through love—share bright and beautiful moments with his beloved. He, like all of us, needs time for love.

Mary Cappello

Model Essay Three

The following student-authored essay is an analysis of the structure in Robert Hayden's poem "Those Winter Sundays."

Those Winter Sundays[1]

Sundays too my father got up early
and put his clothes on in the blueblack cold,
Then with cracked hands that ached
from labor in the weekday weather made
banked fires blaze. No one ever thanked him.

I'd wake and hear the cold splintering, breaking.
When the rooms were warm, he'd call,
and slowly I would rise and dress,
fearing the chronic angers of that house,

Speaking indifferently to him,
who had driven out the cold
and polished my good shoes as well.
What did I know, what did I know
of love's austere and lonely offices?

Acts of Love

Our attitudes toward our parents change with time. As young children, we have a tendency to ignore their love; however, as adults, we understand and appreciate it. The three-stanza narrative poem "Those Winter Sundays"[1] by Robert Hayden is about such a late-blooming love. The narrator describes how, as a child, he took his father for granted and now as an adult *Thesis Statement* regrets his lack of appreciation for his father's love. *Using the structural device of time, Hayden conveys the theme that only with the passage of time do we truly appreciate all our fathers have done for us.*

Topic Sentence   *The narrative is spoken by a man who is thinking about his childhood and his relationship with his father.* In the first stanza, he recalls that "Sundays too [his] father got up early" (line 1). He is dutiful, for the well being of the family is his first priority. In spite of the fact that he has "cracked hands that ached / from labor in the weekday weather" (3–4), he fulfills his obligations. This father, hardworking during the week, does not even think about himself on Sunday, his day of rest, so he rises early to make "banked fires blaze" (5) and drive out the "blueblack cold" (2) that fills the house. Sadly, "No one [in the family] ever thanked him" (5) for his hard work on their behalf. Despite deriving benefits from the obvious commitment of their father, the family is cold and ungrateful.

[1] Reprinted from ANGLE OF ASCENT: New and Selected Poems by Robert Hayden with the permission of Liveright Publishing Corporation. Copyright © 1966 by Robert Hayden.

The second stanza is a continuation of the first in that it is later that same Sunday morning and now the narrator is awakened by "the cold splintering, breaking" (6) due to his father's early activity. The narrator is well taken care of and treated with kindness by his father. First he makes sure that the "rooms were warm" (7), and then "he'd call" (7). All the father's efforts served one purpose: to provide for his son's comfort. The narrator rises "slowly" (8), however, "fearing the chronic angers of that house" (9). Something is missing in this family, for the physical warmth contrasts with the cold and angry atmosphere that the narrator does not want to face. Obviously, there are serious problems, problems that are always there because communication and appreciation are lacking among family members.

The third stanza completes the first two and is enriched by the narrator's insight and mature reflection now that he is older. The narrator describes how as a child he spoke indifferently to [his father] / who had driven out the cold / and polished [his] good shoes as well (10–12). Acknowledging that he was insensitive and indifferent, the narrator describes his lack of appreciation for his father's acts of devotion. Somehow this humble, hardworking, and caring man got nothing but his son's coldness in return for his loving actions. With the passage of time, however, the narrator has come to realize the depths of his father's love, and he asks regretfully, "What did I know, what did I know / of love's austere and lonely offices?" (13–14). Now that the narrator is older, he realizes how demanding and sometimes unrewarding parental love can be, and he finally recognizes and appreciates his father's love. The recognition has come late, but hopefully it is not too late to thank his father for his loving care.

And so, through his structural device of time, Hayden conveys his theme that sincere appreciation for a father's love often takes time to develop. Hayden uses three stanzas to describe the amount of time needed by the narrator to recognize the love that motivated his father's actions. Those little acts of love done behind the scenes like warming the house and polishing shoes often go unnoticed by children who take so much for granted. Sometimes, in fact, they do not understand the demands of fatherly love until they have children of their own. It becomes important, then, to thank our fathers before it is too late. That way we will never have to regret our indifference or our lack of gratitude for their love the way the speaker regrets not appreciating his father's acts of love.

Steve Lewis

Model Essay Four

This student essay is a structural analysis of a short story.

Structural Analysis of "My Kinsman, Major Molineux"

Thesis Statement

In Nathaniel Hawthorne's short story "My Kinsman, Major Molineux,"[1] Robin, the young protagonist, is searching a colonial town for his uncle, Major Molineux. *Hawthorne's use of the search motif reinforces the theme of a dependent youth becoming an independent adult. Hawthorne's story can be broken into three major divisions. The first part is Robin's arrival in the colonial town, which signifies Robin's naive and dependent nature. The second part is Robin's search for Major Molineux, which shows Robin's loss of confidence and his realization that life is very complex and not simple, as he originally believed. Finally, the third part of Hawthorne's story, the discovery of Major Molineux, illustrates Robin's initiation into adulthood and his gaining of independence.*

Topic Sentence

While Robin is entering the town by way of a ferry, Hawthorne stresses Robin's innocence and dependence. His "brown, curly hair . . . and bright cheerful eyes" (229) give an air of confidence to the adolescent, confidence that life, like his eyes, is also bright and cheerful. Of course, when the evil hostility of the New England town is considered, it is easy to see that Robin's confidence is not due to shrewdness, as Hawthorne ironically suggests, but rather to his ignorance. In fact, Robin's innocent nature is so obvious that even the ferryman could accurately survey the youth as being "country-bred, and . . . upon his first visit to town" (229). Robin's innocence, however, is not the only factor that stands out in the opening scene. Robin is also a very dependent youth. His blue stockings "were the incontrovertible work of a mother or a sister" and his three-cornered hat "had perhaps sheltered the graver brow of the lad's father" (229). Although these articles of clothing strongly suggest Robin's family dependence, they don't suggest it as strongly as the oak cudgel which has retained "part of the hardened root" (229). Hawthorne uses these words as if to say that the sapling may be out of the ground, but it has never let go of its dependence on the root. This image of the sapling is used to symbolize Robin's status as he enters the town. He is introduced in the story as a country youth away from home, yet he is still dependent upon his family and still dependent upon the simplicity of the country.

Topic Sentence

Hawthorne uses the search portion of the structure to break down Robin's "bright and cheerful" confidence (229). When Robin gets off the ferry to begin his quest for the Major, he suddenly realizes "he knew not wither to direct his step" (230). This fact coupled with Robin's overpayment of the ferryman implies that young Robin does not know much of anything. His lack of city experience, however, does nothing to diminish his confidence. He looks at the small wooden houses and thinks "this low

[1] Nathaniel Hawthorne, "My Kinsman, Major Molineux" *The Snow Image and Other Twice-Told Tales* (New York: Books for Libraries, 1970).

hovel cannot be my kinsman's dwelling" (230). This thought not only adds to Robin's naive confidence, but also to his feeling of dependence on the Major because Robin has come to rise in the world, and if his kinsman did live in such a "low hovel," poor Robin might not have anyone to depend on. Early in his search, the naive youth is given many clues that reality is not what he thinks it is. At this point, however, the over-confident youth experiences only what he wants to experience. When the first man Robin asks directions from angrily tells him he will be "'acquainted with the stocks by daylight,'" Robin simply thinks "this is some country representative . . . who has never seen the inside of my kinsman's door" (231). Of course, it is ironic that Robin should accuse the civilian of this because Robin himself fits the accusation perfectly.

Topic Sentence *The town continues to treat Robin in a harsh manner, but the innocent youth rationalizes the citizens' strange behavior.* When Robin meets the maiden in the scarlet petticoat, he still feels everything is all right because he "knew nothing to the contrary" (237). This is not very sound logic for a young man about to rise in the world because just seeing nothing to the contrary doesn't mean there isn't that possibility. However, after his encounter with the night watchman, Robin begins to lose his blind confidence. He "now roamed desperately, and at random through the town" (240). Young Robin is beginning to realize that he is on his own. He doesn't have his family or the Major to help. He begins to feel a "sensation of loneliness stronger than he had ever felt" (243). The youth now begins to dream of home to rid himself of the loneliness, but it doesn't work because when Robin tries to enter the door, "he was excluded from his home" (245). It is at this point that Robin cries, "'Am I here or there?'" (245). He truly is neither. He is no longer a naive and innocent child because he knows something is wrong, but he is not yet an adult because he doesn't know what is wrong. He is also not independent quite yet, but he is not dependent either because he has no one to be dependent on. Robin is truly in a state of transition.

Topic Sentence *Robin's discovery is used by Hawthorne to show Robin's initiation into adulthood.* He learns from his new friend that a man may "have several voices . . . as well as two complexions" (248). He is actually telling Robin that reality is really more intricate and involved than he once thought. At this point, Robin is still neither here nor there, but when he finally sees the Major "in tar and feathery dignity" (251), Robin arrives into adulthood. He now knows what a fool he's been and lets out a tremendous laugh. The laugh symbolizes his knowledge of reality and the evil of reality. More importantly, however, Robin gains his independence. He is told he cannot go back home, back to innocence, back to dependence. Robin must stay and "rise in the world without the help of [his] kinsman, Major Molineux" (253).

Restatement of Thesis *Hawthorne, with fine use of structure, shows the growing up of Robin Molineux.* A change from innocence to experience, from dependence to independence, is a theme Hawthorne stresses throughout the structure of the story. Even through the setting, Hawthorne develops a sense of independence. The colonists, like Robin, gain their independence after leaving "home," and their rebellion against the Major shows longing for that independence. Robin's story, in fact, can be used to symbolize young America. Based on Robin's search for independence, Hawthorne's story carries a great deal of meaning. It's a story with a moral, a moral that a young man, in order to truly rise in the world, must do so without the help of others.

Mark Doczy

JUST ONE MORE THING

Have you ever felt the need to get organized, to establish priorities, to put things in order? Writers feel the same need when they are sorting out ideas, trying to establish a logical progression of thought to communicate their theme. If you are a logical thinker, you'll enjoy the challenge of following their line of thought through a work, and when you discover the organizing principle, you will appreciate their ability to blend structure and theme.

❧❧ Structural Analysis Essay Plan Sheet ❧❧

Author: _____ Title: _____

Thesis: _____

_____

_____

_____

_____

Topic sentence: _____

_____

_____

Supporting quote: page or line _____

Supporting quote: page or line _____

Supporting quote: page or line _____

Topic sentence: _____

_____

_____

Supporting quote: page or line _____

Supporting quote: page or line _____

Supporting quote: page or line _____

Topic sentence: _____

_____

_____

Supporting quote: page or line _____

Supporting quote: page or line _____

Supporting quote: page or line _____

Topic sentence: _____

_____

_____

        Supporting quote: page or line _____

        Supporting quote: page or line _____

        Supporting quote: page or line _____

Topic sentence: _____

_____

_____

        Supporting quote: page or line _____

        Supporting quote: page or line _____

        Supporting quote: page or line _____

Topic sentence: _____

_____

_____

        Supporting quote: page or line _____

        Supporting quote: page or line _____

        Supporting quote: page or line _____

Concluding points: _____

_____

_____

_____

_____

_____

_____

❧ Peer/Self-Evaluation of a Structural Analysis Essay ❧

> **Directions:** Make specific suggestions about each part of the essay, pointing out particular areas that the writer could improve. Keep in mind the qualities of good writing: unity, organization, development, clarity, and coherence.

I. Introduction

Is the lead relevant and interesting?

Are the author's full name and the title of the work correctly spelled and punctuated?

Does the summary of the work include the number of major parts and identify the structural device?

Does the thesis also state that the structure of the work reinforces the theme which is explained in a sentence or two?

II. Body Paragraphs

Does the first topic sentence describe the opening situation in the work by identifying the characters, their relationship, and the setting?

Does the rest of the first paragraph explain what happens in the first part by using the literary analysis pattern?

Do the other body paragraphs begin with topic sentences that show how each part relates to the part before it?

Does the rest of each paragraph interpret the content in the new part through the use of the literary analysis pattern?

III. Conclusion

Is a signal word included somewhere in the paragraph?

Does the topic sentence restate how the structural device relates to the theme?

Is the discussion of this relationship fully developed?

IV. Expression

Are all the ideas expressed in complete sentences?

Are the sentences clear and correctly punctuated?

Are there any problems with subject-verb or pronoun-antecedent agreement?

Are all the words correctly spelled?

V. Overall Evaluation

Most effective part of the essay:

Least effective part of the essay:

List three specific actions which could be taken by the writer to improve this and future papers:
1.

2.

3.

Evaluator's name: _____ Date: _____

⊱⊰ **Exercise on Structural Analysis** ⊱⊰

> Analyze the structure in the following poem by Walt Whitman. What is the structural device? How does it complement and reinforce the meaning of Whitman's poem?

A Noiseless Patient Spider[1]

A noiseless patient spider,
I mark'd where on a little promontory it stood isolated,
Mark'd how to explore the vacant vast surrounding,
It launch'd forth filament, filament, filament, out of itself,
Ever unreeling them, ever tirelessly speeding them.

And you O my soul where you stand,
Surrounded, detached, in measureless oceans of space,
Ceaselessly musing, venturing, throwing, seeking the spheres to
   connect them,
Till the bridge you will need be form'd, till the ductile anchor
   hold,
Till the gossamer thread you fling catch somewhere,
   O my soul.

Number of major parts:_____

_____

_____

Structural device:_____

_____

_____

Theme:_____

_____

_____

Relationship of the structure to the theme:_____

_____

_____

_____

_____

_____

_____

---

[1] Walt Whitman, "A Noiseless Patient Spider" *The Works of Walt Whitman*, Vol. I (New York: Funk and Wagnalls, 1948) 391.

Tone Analysis

Overview

In literature, tone relates to the means by which the author conveys his or her attitude toward the subject and the audience. In the spoken language, it is easy to pick up the speaker's attitude by the tone of voice used and by the emphasis or inflection placed on certain words. In the written language, however, tone is conveyed by the complex interactions of such elements of style as word choice, usage levels, imagery, figurative language, sentence structure, rhythm, irony, and overstatement or understatement. Tone is important because understanding the author's tone is essential to understanding the meaning of the work.

The Importance of Tone

We quickly learn as we master language that tone of voice can affect the meaning of a given statement. The words "I hate you" can actually mean "I love you" if spoken in the right tone of voice. Tone is extremely critical when we speak, and the listener responds to it almost on an instinctual level. We can all remember times when our parents were angered not so much by what we said but because they did not like the way we said it; they did not like our tone.

In literature, tone refers to the means by which the author conveys his or her attitude or feelings toward the subject and the audience. In the written language, we do not have the advantage of hearing the author's voice; all we have are the words on the page. To interpret tone here, we must closely analyze the writer's style.

Tone and Word Choice

One of the elements of style that contributes to tone is word choice or diction. Writers are concerned about their choice of words because words are their medium—their means of communication. The French novelist Flaubert reportedly spent hours pondering the choice of the right word for a single sentence. Poets particularly choose their words carefully because poetry is a concentrated art form in which every word is significant. It is important for you as a reader, then, to understand the denotation and the connotation of words and to consider why writers choose particular words when they have so many other possibilities from which to choose. Knowing a word's denotation and its connotations may help you understand the writer's motivation.

The **denotation** of a word refers to the specific meaning or meanings that can be found in a good dictionary. For example, the word "run" may mean—among other things—to move quickly, to be a candidate in an election, to operate a machine, or to sponsor an event. Given the context or the way the word is used in a sentence, we would be able to decide which meaning the writer intended. In contrast, the **connotation** of a word—usually a noun, verb, adjective, or adverb—refers to the emotional overtones that become associated with it. Some overtones or extended meanings are shared by most members of a culture, but words also carry personal connotations that vary with each person. Let's examine the word "Christmas." Denotatively, it refers to the holiday commemorating Christ's birth on December 25, while the shared connotations generally relate to love, sharing, gift-giving, and family togetherness. However, each individual forms personal associations with this word that could vary from bills to depression and humbug.

In choosing words to convey their ideas, then, writers are aware of these two different types of meaning and take advantage of them. To be a critical reader, you, too, must consider the emotional meaning of a word as well as its dictionary definition. If you are unsure of the meaning of a word or if an author seems to be using a word in a new or different context, you must check a college-level dictionary to fully understand and appreciate the ideas being expressed.

Another aspect of word choice or style relates to the level of diction writers use to express their ideas. A **formal** level of usage employs standard English words that are often dignified and stately, and they are always used in grammatically correct ways. A **colloquial** level of usage refers to words and grammatical forms most frequently used in ordinary or familiar conversation, while **informal** usage refers to language use without strict attention to set forms and which could include some slang expressions. Authors are aware of these levels of usage and choose the one that is appropriate to the thoughts they wish to express or to the character they are developing.

Words may also be labeled as **specific** (factual), **concrete** (sensory), or **abstract** (general). For example, to say that John is seven feet tall is specific, that he has to stoop to get through a doorway is concrete, and that he is very tall is abstract. Since most writers strive to show rather than tell, they often choose specific and concrete words to convey their meaning; there are times, however, when they will choose to be general or abstract because it suits their rhetorical purpose.

Tone, Imagery, and Figurative Language

Tone or attitude can be quickly perceived by analyzing the images (the sensory pictures) the author uses to convey ideas. When the speaker in Robert Herrick's "To the Virgins, to Make Much of Time"[1] tells the young women to "Gather ye Rose-buds while ye may," the image of "Rose-buds" suggests the numerous potentially beautiful experiences that are possible when one is young. The wise, encouraging tone of the older speaker shows his knowledge of life and his desire to share the wisdom he has gained through time. In contrast, Marge Piercy in "A Work of Artifice" uses the image of a stunted bonsai tree to convey her feelings about the way various elements of society have limited women's potential. By putting the nine-inch bonsai next to the eighty-foot evergreen, she visually illustrates her angry tone or attitude toward the forces that dwarf a woman's development. The positive or negative nature of the images, then, is a good clue to the author's attitude toward the subject matter.

Authors also use figurative language—similes and metaphors—to convey tone. Again, the tone of these comparisons helps to reveal the author's attitude toward the subject of the work. When Wilfred Owen in "Dulce Et Decorum Est"[2] describes battle-weary soldiers as "Bent double, like old beggars under

---

[1] In *Master Poems of the English Language*, ed. Oscar Williams (New York: Washington Square, 1967) 141.
[2] THE COLLECTED POEMS of Wilfred Owen, edited by C. Day-Lewis. Copyright © The Owen Estate and Chatto & Windus Ltd., 1946, 1963. Reprinted by permission of Chatto & Windus Ltd. and New Directions.

sacks, / Knock-kneed, coughing like hags" (lines 1–2), the similes suggest that the ugliness and horrors of war have turned young men into impoverished, sick old men. The negative comparisons reveal Owen's scornful, critical attitude toward war as a destroyer of innocent young soldiers who are misled into believing that war is a glorious experience.

Shakespeare uses a metaphor to describe the constancy of true love in "Sonnet 116."[3]

> . . . [Love] is an ever-fixèd mark
> That looks on tempests and is never shaken. (lines 5–6)

By comparing love to a fixed star, Shakespeare emphasizes the unchanging nature of true love and its ability to withstand threats to its existence. By using a positive, uplifting metaphor for love, he reveals his admiration for the strength of this human emotion. It is possible, then, to identify the images, the similes, and the metaphors authors choose to convey their ideas, and from them, to identify the tone or attitude toward the subject.

Tone and Symbolism

It is also possible to infer an author's tone or attitude toward his subject from the types of symbols in the work. If the symbols are positive ones, open to positive, uplifting interpretations, then the tone is usually positive as well. If, on the other hand, the symbols are negative, then the tone is usually negative. Robert Herrick's use of "rose-buds" as a symbol for the beautiful things in life conveys a totally different tone from William Blake's symbol of the "sick rose" which conveys a negative tone toward the forces that work to undermine love.

Tone and Sentence Structure

Because words are put together to form sentences, sentence length and structure are other elements of style that affect meaning. The total number of words in a sentence or the number of different parts of speech (adjectives, verbs, adverbs) can help you determine if a writer's style is journalistic (brief and specific) or ornamental (lengthy and abstract) in a particular passage. Generally, the greater the number of adjectives, verbs, or adverbs, the more forceful and descriptive the style. Sentence structure—simple, complex, compound, compound-complex—can also be labeled to show how it affects such elements of style as rhythm, repetition, and variety. Even punctuation marks like commas, dashes, and exclamation points can help to convey an author's attitude toward his subject.

And so by combining all of these elements—word choice, denotation and connotation, usage levels, images, similes, metaphors, and sentence lengths and patterns—an author communicates a tone, an attitude toward the subject matter. Keep in mind, however, that an author's attitude may change in the course of the work, so be aware of this possibility as you analyze the tone.

Describing Tone

When we describe tone, we generally use adjectives that describe the different attitudes an individual is capable of expressing. The possibilities are endless, but some common attitudes include the following: hopeful, confident, genial, poignant, passionate, intimate, respectful, stoical, despairing, depressing, flippant, indignant, bored, sarcastic, cynical, condescending, hardboiled, critical, mocking, scornful, negative, angry, hostile, fearless, fearful, comic, humorous, playful, sympathetic, positive, negative, admiring, loving, serious, lighthearted, impassioned, solemn, caring, elevated, inflated, formal, informal, appreciative, touching, sombre, biting, heartfelt, bitter, caustic, stinging, scathing, and ironic.

---

[3] In *Master Poems of the English Language* 57.

❧ Analyzing Tone

One technique that will help you analyze and appreciate an author's choice of words is to use an un-abridged dictionary to find the precise meaning for each word and to locate other possible meanings that could add richness to the work. Another technique is to try substituting your own word or words in place of the author's.

Let's look at Walter Savage Landor's poem entitled "On His Seventy-Fifth Birthday"[4] to try these techniques and to examine other elements of style that produce tone, like word order, the use of comparisons through metaphors or similes, and imagery.

> I strove with none, for none was worth my strife.
> Nature I loved and, next to Nature, Art:
> I warm'd both hands before the fire of life;
> It sinks, and I am ready to depart.

Since this poem was written in 1850, some meanings have changed for the words that Landor chose to convey his ideas. If you check a college-level dictionary, such as *The Random House Dictionary of the English Language,* you will find that in the first line, Landor is using an obsolete denotation for the verb "to strive" meaning "to rival or vie." The obsolete meaning of the verb "to rival" is "to strive to win from, equal, or outdo." When Landor states that he did not try to "equal or outdo" anyone because no one was worth his "effort"—an archaic meaning of the word "strife"—he conveys a proud, somewhat arrogant tone. He implies that he did not have to prove himself or his talent by competing with others. In his own estimation, he stood above the crowd.

The word order in the second line is also significant. By putting the word Nature first, Landor emphasizes it and makes Nature seem even more important than the *I* that follows. Here the egotism in the first line takes second place to the forces and the power of the universe. By placing his second love—Art—last in the sentence, Landor also produces emphasis and conveys his pride in his appreciation of both natural and man-made beauty.

Landor's use of metaphor and his choice of imagery in the third line produce a sensuous tone. He describes life metaphorically as a "fire," and when he says that he "warm'd both hands before" it, the image suggests that he was fully and completely involved in life. One denotation of the word "fire" relates to one's passions, and "fire" usually carries the shared connotations of light and warmth. These combined meanings suggest that Landor sensuously enjoyed all the good things that life has to offer.

Through his word choices in the last line, Landor shows a positive attitude or tone toward the approach of death. The fire of life "sinks," suggesting decline but not destruction, and by choosing the word "depart" rather than the word "die," he acknowledges that death is not an end but a departure to another destination, to another level of existence. In fact, the last line is shorter than all the others to show that he is not afraid but "ready" for whatever the end of life will bring. Overall, then, the stylistic devices that Landor uses project the positive, self-satisfied tone of a man who is proud of his actions, his loves, and his philosophy of life.

Recognizing Irony

Out of all the possible attitudes an author may express toward his or her subject, it is absolutely essential to recognize the use of an ironic tone. Irony generally refers to words or situations in which there

---

[4] Walter Savage Landor, "On His Seventy-Fifth Birthday" *Structure and Meaning,* ed. Anthony Dubé, John Karl Franson, Russell E. Murphy, and James W. Parins (Boston: Houghton, 1976) 620.

❧

is some ambiguity because of two possible levels of meaning. Often the opposite of what is said or intended turns out to be the real meaning or situation.

There are at least four different types of irony: verbal, situational, dramatic, and cosmic. **Verbal irony** is used in speech when people respond with statements that have more than one possible meaning or interpretation. For example, when asked about a demanding, critical boss, an employee might respond, "He's a really nice guy." By the inflection placed on "really nice," most people would understand that the boss is really a miserable guy, so the meaning is the opposite of what is stated. Verbal irony can also be achieved through overstatement or understatement in which something is intentionally represented as more or as less than it really is. Andrew Marvell uses **overstatement** or **hyperbole** in his poem "To His Coy Mistress."[5] The speaker, in an effort to convince his mistress to make love, uses exaggeration as he tells her how he would use his time if it were unlimited: "An hundred years should go to praise / Thine eyes, and on thy forehead gaze" (lines 13–16). Here the overstatement of time helps to emphasize the actual shortness of time available to the lovers. W. H. Auden uses **understatement** at the end of "The Unknown Citizen," a poem critical of unthinking conformity. When he states that any questions about the unknown citizen's freedom or happiness are absurd, he is underplaying the citizen's conformity and thereby emphasizing it. Verbal irony, then, is often used to underscore ideas that the author wants to convey.

Verbal irony can also take the form of the **double entendre,** a statement that can be interpreted on two levels, the literal and the sexual. For example, when Connie in Joyce Carol Oates' "Where Are You Going, Where Have You Been?"[6] begins to fear for her life because of the threat that Arnold poses, "she felt her breath start jerking back and forth in her lungs as if it were something Arnold Friend were stabbing her with again and again with no tenderness" (314). The "jerking back and forth" and the "stabbing again and again with no tenderness" can be read strictly as Connie's physical response to fear or as images of the rape that Arnold seems to have in mind for her. The double meaning adds a level of suspense and terror to Connie's situation.

Situational irony occurs when a good end is intended and an evil one results, or vice versa. In Flannery O'Connor's "A Good Man Is Hard to Find," for example, the grandmother believes that she is doing a good deed by bringing the cat along on the family vacation so that it won't be left alone in the house. In reality, however, the cat, again with the help of the grandmother, causes the car accident that puts the family at the mercy of The Misfit, an escaped convict.

Dramatic irony occurs when the audience or the reader knows more about a situation than the characters in the work. An example occurs in Ring Lardner's short story "Haircut." The narrator is Whitey, the town barber, a simple, insensitive talker who is telling a customer about the supposedly accidental death of the town bully, Jim Kendall. As Whitey tells the story, the sensitive reader infers from the details Whitey recounts that Jim's death at the hands of the town simpleton was murder—not an accident. Whitey sees things in a limited way because of his limited intelligence and vision; the reader perceives the reality of the situation from his greater vantage point.

Cosmic irony is evident in Tennessee Williams' treatment of the Wingfield family in *The Glass Menagerie.* Their lives illustrate their futile efforts to escape their problems. Everything goes badly in Amanda's plan to marry off Laura. Tom resents being forced into playing matchmaker, and when the plan fails, the play ends in darkness. Life is presented as a series of no-win situations from which the family cannot escape. The cards are stacked against them, and all their hopes and dreams come to a tragic end. Cosmic irony suggests that the universe is oblivious to their efforts to control their destiny; fate rules all.

---

[5] In *Master Poems of the English Language* 202.
[6] In *The Wheel of Love and Other Stories* (New York: Vanguard, 1970). Used by permission of Vanguard Press, a division of Random House, Inc.

Functions of Tone

One important function of tone in a work is to convey the theme. Just as the real message in a verbal communication is determined by the tone in which the words are spoken, the theme in a written work is also determined by the author's tone. In James Thurber's "The Secret Life of Walter Mitty,"[7] for example, a reader would simply see Walter as a loser if it weren't for the author's humorous tone or attitude toward his hero. This tone is conveyed by his descriptions of Walter's dreams. In many of them, Walter imagines a sound that must please his aesthetic inner ear. He hears it while flying the Navy hydroplane: "The pounding of the cylinders increased; ta-pocketa-pocketa *pocketa-pocketa-pocketa*" (72). He hears it again as Captain Mitty is about to leave on a bombing mission: "... from somewhere came the menacing pocketa-pocketa-pocketa of the new flame-throwers" (79–80). Walter's fondness for this strange sound shows his pleasure in the simple things in life and illustrates his basically simple and unassuming character. Yet despite his simplicity, Thurber lets him triumph over his critical wife by giving him enough intelligence to keep his secret life a "secret." "Walter Mitty the Undefeated, inscrutable to the last" (81) is proof that the little man can be a hero in his own way, which is one of Thurber's themes in the work.

Another important function of tone is to communicate the author's emotional attitude toward his subject, thereby creating a mood or atmosphere within the work itself. As we said, the overall tone in "The Secret Life of Walter Mitty" is a comic one, but it also conveys Thurber's sympathy for Walter as he deals with his domineering wife. When she tells him that he's "not a young man any longer" (73) and that she's "going to take [his] temperature" (80) as soon as she gets him home, the reader's sympathy also goes out to him because Mrs. Mitty's tone really whittles away at his manhood.

In a totally different type of story, "The Lesson"[8] by Toni Cade Bambara, the emotional atmosphere shifts as the tone of the narrator shifts. The storyteller is Sylvia, a young black girl living in the ghetto, who begins her tale about a lesson she learned from Miss Moore in a confident and cocky tone because she believes that everyone else is wrong but she is "just right" (87). She thinks that she has a pretty good life in the ghetto until she is shocked into an awareness of the limits of her world by a $1,195 sailboat. As she realizes that she isn't in on this good life, her tone changes to one of anger. When this lesson about the division of wealth sinks in, Sylvia's tone becomes one which combines thoughtfulness and determination as she decides "ain't nobody gonna beat me at nuthing" (96). Sylvia's shifting tone is really Bambara's shifting tone as she communicates her theme about the injustices in our social system, her anger about them, and her determination to overcome them. As the involved reader perceives this theme and feels these same emotions, he may understand, perhaps for the first time, the frustrations of the poor in America. Tone, then, shapes the message or theme in a work and helps to create an emotional atmosphere that readers respond to as they become involved with the characters and their situations.

Writing about Tone: Step by Step

When preparing to write an essay which analyzes tone in a work of literature, try to keep these steps in mind:

1. Tone is more subtle in some works than it is in others, so try to choose a work in which the tone is more obvious because of the author's use of language: the choice of words, usage levels, imagery, figurative language, sentence structure, rhythm, repetition, irony, overstatement or understatement, and other appropriate elements of style.

---

[7] James Thurber, "The Secret Life of Walter Mitty" *My World—And Welcome to It* (New York: Harcourt, 1970).
[8] From *Gorilla, My Love* (New York: Random, 1972). Used by permission of Random House.

2. Read the work carefully and then describe the dominant tone with one or more descriptive adjectives. Circle those elements in the work that help to convey the tone and decide how they can be organized most effectively in your essay. If the work is short, for example, a one- or two-stanza poem, its tone could conceivably be discussed in an essay with one or two well developed body paragraphs. If the work is longer, look for places where it could logically be divided into parts. This division could be based on shifts in tone or on the types of elements conveying the tone, thereby creating separate paragraphs on word choice, on images and comparisons, on word order and sentence structure, and so on.

3. In the introduction, the thesis will consist of several parts:
   a. a statement identifying the tone through the use of descriptive adjectives;
   b. a statement identifying how the body paragraphs will be organized, e.g., around word choice, imagery, figurative language, repetition, style, character development;
   c. a statement identifying the functions of tone in the work: how it conveys the theme and/or how it conveys the author's emotional attitude and produces an emotional response in the reader.

4. The body paragraphs illustrate how the tone is conveyed in the work by using the literary analysis pattern of generalization, introductory material for a quotation, the direct quotation, and analysis. Proceed logically through the work, generalizing about tone and then supporting the generalization with quotations from the work. Follow this with in-depth analysis of how and why the tone is communicated through the elements you've quoted. As always, the analysis is the most important part of this pattern.

5. The conclusion is an in-depth discussion of the functions of tone that were identified in the thesis statement. Try to show how the tone shapes and communicates the theme and/or how it conveys the author's emotional attitude toward the subject and produces a similar emotional response in the reader.

The following diagram, model essays, and plan sheet will help you organize and write an essay on tone in a work of literature.

Diagram of the Structure of a Tone Analysis Essay

Title

Introductory Paragraph:

Open with interesting lead material.

Name the work and the author.

Briefly summarize the work, identify the dominant tone with one or two descriptive adjectives, and state how the body will be organized. ⎫

State the functions of tone in the work, i.e., how it conveys theme, how it communicates the author's emotional attitude, how it produces an emotional response in the reader. ⎭ Thesis

Body Paragraphs:

In body paragraph one, describe the opening situation in the work by identifying—where applicable—the character(s), their relationships, and their setting. Then support your statement about the tone by using the literary analysis pattern to explain the qualities in the work that convey it. Generalize first about the tone, introduce the quotation, and then directly quote the words, phrases, or sentences that convey the tone. Follow the quotation with in-depth analysis of how and why these stylistic elements produce the tone.

Begin all other body paragraphs with a topic sentence that identifies the dominant tone in the section of the work to be analyzed. Support the topic sentence by using the literary analysis pattern: generalization, introductory material for the quotation, the quotation itself, and analysis. Remember that analysis is an explanation of how the quotation illustrates and proves your generalization about tone; it explores all of the possible meanings that are both explicit and implicit in the quote.

Concluding Paragraph:

Start with a topic sentence which relates this paragraph to the functions of tone which were stated in the thesis. Each function is taken up in turn and is thoroughly explored and explained. This paragraph should be approximately five to seven sentences in length to insure a thorough discussion of the effect(s) of tone in the work.

Model Essay One

The first student essay illustrates the structure and the use of the literary analysis pattern in tone analysis by discussing tone in a short story.

The Power of Conformity

Are you tired of life in the fast lane? Would you like to leave the stress of big-city life and move to a small town where life would be idyllic and carefree? Actually, small-town life could take away your individuality and turn you into an automaton according to John Updike in his short story "A & P"[1] which takes place in a small town "north of Boston" (191). When three girls enter the store in bathing suits, Sammy, a nineteen-year-old clerk, uses the occasion to quit by protesting the manager's treatment of them. *Through his critical tone—which he expresses through Sammy— Updike communicates his theme that small towns create small-minded people. This can be seen in Sammy's attitude toward the people in the town, the shoppers in the A & P, and the store's manager, Lengel.*

Thesis Statement

Topic Sentence

Updike's critical attitude toward the townspeople is evident from the way Sammy describes their lifestyle. He says that the "town is five miles from a beach," but "there's people in this town haven't seen the ocean in twenty years" (191). The townspeople seem to be in a rut. Even though they live near the ocean, they never change their routine to include the pleasure and relaxation that the seaside could offer them. The boredom of their lives is reflected in the conservative nature of the town which includes "two banks and the Congregational church and the newspaper store and three real estate offices . . ." (191). It sounds like all the townspeople do is save money, go to church, read the newspaper to check up on their neighbors, and buy real estate, a conservative investment. Their lives have become so routine that even the city maintenance is repetitive. Sammy describes "twenty-seven old freeloaders [who are] tearing up Central Street because the sewer broke again" (191). Evidently the work crew makes the same mistakes each time and the same problem recurs, just the way the other citizens in the town keep following the same patterns in their dull, boring, and repetitive lives. Updike's portrayal of the lifestyle of the townspeople through his spokesman Sammy is highly critical because people lack flexibility and avoid any kind of change.

Topic Sentence

This same inflexible attitude is seen in the way the townspeople shop in the A & P. Through Sammy's critical comments, Updike points out how blindly following routine turns people into "sheep" (190). When the bathing-suit-clad girls are walking through the A & P, they upset the routine of the usual shoppers. Sammy describes the scene:

> The sheep pushing their carts down the aisle—the girls were walking against the usual traffic (not that we have one-way signs or anything)—were pretty hilarious. You could see them, when Queenie's [one of the girls'] white shoulders dawned on them,

[1] John Updike, "A & P" *Pigeon Feathers And Other Stories,* First ed. (New York: Knopf, 1962). Used by permission of Alfred A. Knopf, Inc.

kind of jerk, or hop, or hiccup, but their eyes snapped back to their own baskets and on they pushed. (190)

Sammy's "sheep" image aptly describes the shoppers, for sheep are dumb animals that follow each other to the point of jumping in the same place over a nonexistent obstacle. The shoppers can't believe that someone would walk against the traffic flow, and when they see Queenie's uncovered shoulders, their initial reaction is shock because that isn't done in such a conservative town. Despite their disbelief, however, they continue to shop because that is their usual pattern. They are so automatic in their actions that Sammy says, "I bet you could set off dynamite in an A & P and the people would by and large keep reaching and checking oatmeal off their lists . . ." (190). Even a disaster would not stop these robots from completing their assigned tasks. They are programmed to the point where all of their behaviors are unconscious. By describing these actions through the eyes of nineteen-year-old Sammy who has not yet become a total follower, a sheep, Updike helps us see how people can be shaped by their environment to the point where they lose their individuality and are able to see and do things only one way.

Topic Sentence   *The narrowmindedness of the townspeople is epitomized by the manager of the A & P, Lengel. Through Sammy, Updike is critical of the way Lengel treats the three unusual shoppers.* When he encounters the girls in their bathing suits, "he concentrates on giving them that sad Sunday-school-superintendent stare" (193). This image of Lengel projects his morally superior attitude and creates the feeling that any type of unusual behavior is sinful. In a small town, any deviation from the norm is noted and treated as an offense against the establishment. Lengel is precise in describing the behavior he expects of the girls: "'After this come in here with your shoulders covered. It's our policy.' He turns his back" (194). Policy is what Lengel lives by, and he refuses to consider any exception to it. His turned back is an image that symbolizes his closed mind. Sammy sees that Lengel uses policy as a means of power over others when he says, "Policy is what the kingpins want. What all others want is juvenile delinquency" (194). This implies that if people don't follow exactly what the policy-makers want, they are labeled as troublemakers or delinquents. Such a narrow-minded view of human behavior makes the people in this small town frightened of any change. That's why the shoppers who are watching the scene between Lengel and the girls act like "sheep" (194) and "scared pigs in a chute" (195). They are not capable of a reasoned judgment because they have been programmed to believe in conformity, and the slightest display of non-conformity disrupts their world. This is what Updike, through Sammy, is so critical of—the nonthinking acceptance of traditional norms and the immediate rejection or avoidance of anyone who does not follow them. Updike suggests an alternative to this policy-oriented behavior when he has Sammy say that "pee-pul" (196) are more important than policy. For small-minded followers, however, people are not always predictable but policy is, so it offers them security. The inhabitants of this small town in Massachusetts—a state where people were burned as witches if they were different from the norm—have truly become "sheep."

Restatement of Thesis

And so, through Sammy's critical tone in his comments about life in his small town and about the shoppers and the manager in the A & P, Updike communicates his theme that small towns can turn people into narrow-minded followers. When patterns of behavior become so established that they never change, people lose their ability to deal with life on a rational level. Conformity destroys the need for thought; to be accepted, all one has to do is follow the customs, norms, and traditions followed by everyone else. That's why Updike is so critical of life in this small town. Diversity and non-conformity are not crimes; they represent the richness of human experience. To close our minds to other possibilities is to become non-thinking robots who go through life blindly following "the kingpins" and their "policy." Sammy, an independent young man, feels the need to break out of this boring, stultifying atmosphere, and he does so by quitting his job at the A & P. He refuses to become like the others even though he realizes "how hard the world [is] going to be to [him] hereafter" (196). Sammy truly is Updike's hero in this town of thoughtless followers.

Anna Woods

Model Essay Two

The following student-written essay discusses the tone of Walt Whitman's poem.

When I heard the learn'd astronomer[1]

When I heard the learn'd astronomer,
When the proofs, the figures, were ranged in columns
    before me,
When I was shown the charts and diagrams, to add, divide,
    and measure them.
When I sitting heard the astronomer where he lectured
    with much applause in the lecture-room,
How soon unaccountable I became tired and sick,
Till rising and gliding out I wander'd off by myself,
In the mystical moist night-air, and from time to time,
Look'd up in perfect silence at the stars.

The Real Thing

Have you ever been bored in a lecture hall? If you have, you can relate to the situation Walt Whitman presents in his poem "When I heard the learn'd astronomer."[1] The speaker grows weary of the detailed mathematical theories the astronomer presents about the universe and finds pleasure

[1] In *The Columbia Anthology of American Poetry*, ed. Jay Parini (New York: Columbia UP, 1995) 214.

in leaving and being alone to contemplate the stars. *Through his use of repetition and word choice, Whitman communicates his change in tone from boredom to wonder and conveys his theme that one does not have to know astronomical theory to appreciate the beauty and perfection of the universe.*

The speaker begins the first four lines of the poem with the repetitious use of the opening word "When" to introduce immediately his bored attitude toward the information presented by the "learn'd astronomer" (line 1). In his lecture, he focuses on "the proofs, the figures" (2), the mathematical evidence formulated by scientists about the stars. Then when the astronomer brings out "the charts and diagrams, to add, divide, and measure them" (3), he loses the speaker. This dry, unexciting mathematical approach dulls his senses, and as the lecturer adds level after level of detail, the speaker's boredom increases. Even the *when* clauses increase in length, suggesting that all of this information is overwhelming to the speaker despite the fact that the astronomer is rewarded with "much applause in the lecture-room" (4). The speaker is blunt about his personal attitude toward the lecture when he states, "I became tired and sick" (5), bored with the scientific data on the nature of the universe.

The word choices in the second part of the poem show how the speaker's attitude changes from one of boredom to one of awe and wonder as he escapes from the lecture hall. He describes his leaving as a "rising and gliding out" (6), words which suggest a new beginning, a freedom of movement from boring surroundings into "the mystical moist night-air" (7). The word "mystical" hints at the supernatural aspects of the universe, and the word "moist" contrasts with the dry details presented by the astronomer. The night air revives the speaker, and in awe and wonder, he looks "up in perfect silence at the stars" (8). No longer looking at "charts and diagrams" (3) or listening to "proofs" (2), he is free to appreciate—in delicious silence—the glory and beauty of the magnificent stars. The speaker's tone now is relaxed and relieved as he enjoys the wonder of the outside world.

Whitman, then, uses the repetitious beginning of the first four lines to convey the boring tone of the astronomer's lecture and the connotative meaning of words in the last four lines to show his change of attitude as the speaker leaves the lecture and, in a state of wonder, basks in the glory of the stars. Through this change in tone, Whitman brings out the theme that the real beauty of the universe can be enjoyed by anyone who will step out into the night and quietly contemplate the star-filled sky. The speaker's presence at the lecture indicates his desire to learn about the scientific aspects of the universe, but overwhelmed by the details, he realizes that the actual experience of the stars is far better than any chart or diagram ever could be. He now knows that nothing beats the real thing.

Peg Murphy

Model Essay Three

As you read the following poem by John Donne, try to determine the speaker's tone, his attitude toward death. The student essay that follows illustrates tone analysis in a poem.

Holy Sonnet 10[1]

Death, be not proud, though some have called thee
Mighty and dreadful, for thou art not so;
For those whom thou think'st thou dost overthrow
Die not, poor Death, nor yet canst thou kill me.
From rest and sleep, which but thy pictures be,
Much pleasure; then from thee much more must flow,
And soonest our best men with thee do go,
Rest of their bones, and soul's delivery.
Thou art slave to fate, chance, kings, and desperate men,
And dost with poison, war, and sickness dwell,
And poppy or charms can make us sleep as well
And better than thy stroke; why swell'st thou then?
One short sleep past, we wake eternally.
And death shall be no more; Death, thou shalt die.

A Condemnation of Death

Thesis Statement

In "Holy Sonnet 10,"[1] John Donne describes his attitude toward death. Death has long been acknowledged as an event that man cannot escape, giving it supreme power over man's fate and invoking fear in the hearts of many. Donne, however, is unafraid. He mocks death; he taunts it with his own sense of immortality. *This mocking tone is conveyed through his choice of words and his descriptions of death's counterparts and companions. Donne's Christian theme of eternal life through death is emphasized by his attitude toward physical death, and his fearless attitude produces a similar attitude in the reader.*

Topic Sentence

Donne begins by speaking directly to death and attacking its power. One can hear the mockery and scorn in his voice as he says,

Death, be not proud, though some have called thee
Mighty and dreadful, for thou art not so;
For those whom thou think'st thou dost overthrow
Die not, poor Death, nor yet canst thou kill me. (lines 1–4)

Donne attacks death's pride and power by stating that those who appear to be dead are not; they continue to live on in another plane of existence. Therefore, the poet feels that he, too, is invulnerable. Because death is powerless, it has nothing to be proud of, and so Donne mocks this "mighty and dreadful" force by emphasizing his own supremacy over it.

Topic Sentence

To further mock death's powerful image, Donne compares it to pleasurable experiences: "From rest and sleep, which but thy pictures be, / Much

[1]John Donne, "Holy Sonnet 10" *John Donne: The Complete English Poems*, ed. A. J. Smith (New York: St. Martin's, 1974) 313.

pleasure; then from thee much more must flow . . ." (5–6). By equating death with "rest and sleep," Donne makes death seem desirable. If fleeting pleasure is gained from temporary states of being, then death which is a permanent state must give eternal pleasure. Death's fearful hold over man is mocked and scorned by placing it on a level with the positive value of pleasure. Donne again makes death desirable by stating that "our best men with thee do go" to find "rest" and their "soul's delivery" (7–8). Surely one cannot fear an event sought by "best men" who seek the comforts of "rest" and "delivery." In the first two quatrains, then, the poet destroys the image of death as a powerful figure by stating that those who appear to have been conquered by death still live, that death is powerless against him, and that death is even more pleasurable than the natural state of rest.

Topic Sentence   *The third quatrain also begins in a mocking, cutting tone as Donne enumerates those forces that control death:* "Thou art slave to fate, chance, kings, and desperate men . . ." (9). Here death's powerful image is weakened as the poet points out that it is a "slave" sent by commands from forces as ignoble as "desperate men." It has no power of its own but is controlled by others. This mocking tone becomes even more cutting as death's companions are described. It lives with "poison, war, and sickness . . ." (10). Surrounded by such loathsome and hideous events, death has nothing to be proud of; by association, it, too, becomes loathsome and hideous. To further undermine death's power, Donne equates it with the effects of the "poppy or charms" (11), suggesting that death is no more to be feared than the sleep brought on by drugs. Donne's question to death suggests that it has no reason to be proud: "why swell'st thou then?" (12). He has humiliated death by pointing out that it is controlled by others, keeps company with hateful companions, and is not even as powerful as opium.

Topic Sentence   *In the closing couplet, Donne's Christian attitude toward death clearly emerges:* "One short sleep past, we wake eternally . . ." (13). Here death is but a transitional stage that clearly leads to an eternal existence in heaven. To that life, there will be no end; therefore, Donne states, "Death, thou shalt die" (14). Death's dominion ends as man becomes part of the eternal existence of God.

Restatement of Thesis   *Through his mocking, fearless tone, then, Donne conveys his theme that death has no power over the Christian.* Those who believe in God "die not;" they "wake eternally." Death is a pleasurable event since it leads to the Christian's greatest pleasure: eternal life with God. It is obvious that Donne's attitude toward death is a fearless one. He is unafraid as he plainly taunts death: "nor yet canst thou kill me" (4). This attitude in the face of an event that has long been feared inspires the reader with courage and helps him to view death in a new light. Death is not the end but the beginning of a life without end, a life where death and all of its companions—"poison, war, and sickness"—cease to exist. Surely death is a reason for the Christian to rejoice!

Sally Boyle

Have you heard the theory that it's not what you wear but how you wear it that makes the real statement? The same is true with what you say because it's how you say it—the tone you use—that conveys your attitude, your meaning. If you watch your own use of tone—your word choice, your inflection, even your facial expression when you're speaking—you'll learn how effectively it can communicate your meaning. Tone can be a useful tool in many different situations.

❧ Tone Analysis Essay Plan Sheet ❧

Author: _____ Title: _____

Thesis: _____

_____

_____

_____

_____

Topic sentence: _____

_____

_____

Supporting quote: page or line _____

Supporting quote: page or line _____

Supporting quote: page or line _____

Topic sentence: _____

_____

_____

Supporting quote: page or line _____

Supporting quote: page or line _____

Supporting quote: page or line _____ ____

Topic sentence: _____

_____

_____

Supporting quote: page or line _____

Supporting quote: page or line _____

Supporting quote: page or line _____

Topic sentence: _____

_____

_____

Supporting quote: page or line _____

Supporting quote: page or line _____

Supporting quote: page or line _____

Topic sentence: _____

_____

_____

Supporting quote: page or line _____

Supporting quote: page or line _____

Supporting quote: page or line _____

Topic sentence: _____

_____

_____

Supporting quote: page or line _____

Supporting quote: page or line _____

Supporting quote: page or line _____

Concluding points: _____

_____

_____

_____

_____

_____

_____

_____

❧ Peer/Self-Evaluation of a Tone Analysis Essay ❧

Directions: Make specific suggestions about each part of the essay, pointing out particular areas that the writer could improve. Keep in mind the qualities of good writing: unity, organization, development, clarity, and coherence.

I. Introduction

Is the lead relevant and interesting?

Are the author's full name and the title of the work correctly spelled and punctuated?

Does the summary of the work lead into the thesis statement which identifies the tone and suggests how the body will be organized?

Does the thesis also list the functions of tone—the communication of the theme and/or the creation of the mood or atmosphere in the work—that will be discussed in the conclusion?

II. Body Paragraphs

Does the topic sentence identify the tone in the part of the work to be discussed in the paragraph?

Do the supporting quotations focus on the elements that produce the tone?

Do the analysis sections explain how and why the tone can be inferred from the quoted details?

Are the analysis sections adequately developed?

Are the body paragraphs unified and coherent?

III. Conclusion

Is a signal word included somewhere in the paragraph?

Are the tone and its functions rephrased at the start of the paragraph?

Is each function thoroughly explored and explained?

Is the clincher sentence relevant and effective?

IV. Expression

Are all the ideas expressed in complete sentences?

Are the sentences clear and correctly punctuated?

Are there any problems with subject-verb or pronoun-antecedent agreement?

Are all the words correctly spelled?

V. Overall Evaluation

Most effective part of the essay:

Least effective part of the essay:

List three specific actions which could be taken by the writer to improve this and future papers:

1.

2.

3.

Evaluator's name: _____ Date: _____

❧ Exercise on Tone ❧

> What tone or feeling is William Wordsworth expressing toward his view of
> London and the Thames River which he is describing from his vantage
> point on Westminster Bridge? Circle key words, images, and figures of
> speech to support your response.

Composed upon Westminster Bridge[1]

Earth has not anything to show more fair:
Dull would he be of soul who could pass by
A sight so touching in its majesty;
This City now doth, like a garment, wear
The beauty of the morning; silent, bare,
Ships, towers, domes, theaters, and temples lie
Open unto the fields, and to the sky;
All bright and glittering in the smokeless air.
Never did sun more beautifully steep
In his first splendor, valley, rock, or hill;
Ne'er saw I, never felt, a calm so deep!
The river glideth at his own sweet will:
Dear God! the very houses seem asleep;
And all that mighty heart is lying still!

Tone:_____

_____

Stylistic devices:_____

_____

_____

_____

_____

_____

_____

_____

---

[1] From *Literature: Options for Reading and Writing*, Second Ed. Ed. Donald A. Daiker, Mary Fuller, and Jack E. Wallace (New York: Harper, 1989) 601.

Writing an Extended Literary Analysis Essay

Overview

After you have learned how to analyze the elements of fiction and poetry and how to express your analysis in a well organized essay of 500 to 1,000 words, you have mastered all of the skills necessary for writing an extended analysis of a literary work. This type of paper may be required to show your competency as you near the end of a course or as you share what you have learned about a longer work or about several works by one author. Whatever the length of your paper, it should be organized into an interesting beginning with a precise thesis statement, a well developed body, and a logical conclusion.

Choosing a Subject for an Extended Essay

If your instructor does not assign the subject for your extended analysis, it is best to choose a work that you are familiar with and enjoy, one that you have thought deeply about, or one that has hung on in your mind because of its connections to your life experiences. When seeking a way into the work, consider the elements that make it unique and special. Some possibilities include an unusual plot structure, a different use of time with flashbacks or flashforwards, a change in attitude or tone, a unique use of point of view, in-depth characterization, strange or unusual settings, complex themes, archetypal symbols, or multiple images.

As you begin your thinking and planning by doing some free writing, branching/brainstorming, or clustering activities, look for ideas that relate to significant parts of the work so that you will have adequate content to analyze and discuss. If you are focusing on a single work, ask yourself as you review your notes if there are ideas that can be tied together through a series of causes or effects, through a series of examples that relate to a single literary element, or through a process of similar development.

If you are focusing on two or more works by different authors, look for situations, characters, settings, images, symbols, or themes that could be tied together in a comparison/contrast paper. If the works are by the same author, look for similarities in plot, characterization, point of view, symbols, style, or theme. Perhaps you can classify the types of situations, protagonists, or antagonists the author tends to create. You want to find a method of organization that will help you create a coherent and unified discussion your reader will be able to follow and understand.

❧ Planning an Extended Literary Analysis Essay

The length of an essay of literary analysis is determined in part by the length of the work or works being analyzed and in part by the specificity of the thesis. If, for example, you are analyzing setting in a short story, your essay will probably be shorter than one analyzing setting in a novel since adding length multiplies the complexity of the work. On the other hand, if your thesis in the essay on the novel is restricted to just one setting rather than all of the possibilities, then your essay may not be any longer than the paper on the short story. All of this suggests that if you are assigned an essay of 1,500 words or more, you must thoroughly develop your analysis of a shorter work or broaden your thesis to encompass enough aspects of the work to produce the desired length.

When you have decided on a logical way to develop your ideas, you are ready to formulate your thesis and its main supporting points. This sentence is the guiding principle of your essay; it guides your choice of supporting quotations and your analysis of them, and it guides your reader through the body of your essay as he or she follows the main points through to your conclusion.

❧ Comparing/Contrasting: An Organizational Approach

If you choose to focus your essay on just one literary element—character, theme, setting, point of view, symbolism, imagery, structure, or tone—the method of development and organization discussed in the specific chapter on that element will work for an extended essay assignment; you will, of course, have to develop the body of the paper more extensively through the use of additional quotations and more in-depth analysis. If, however, you choose to compare and/or contrast two authors, several works by different authors, or two or more works by the same author, you have several choices to make about how you can arrange your main points.

One of your choices is called the *subject-by-subject* approach because it focuses on one subject at a time. In this organizational pattern, you make all of your points about the first subject in the first part of your essay, use a transition to move the reader into the second subject, and then make the same points in the same order about the second subject.

An outline of this pattern would look like this:

> *Subject A (an author, work, or literary element)*
>
>   Point 1
>
>   Point 2
>
>   Point 3
>
>   Point 4
>
> *Transitional sentence or paragraph*
>
> *Subject B (an author, work, or literary element)*
>
>   Point 1
>
>   Point 2
>
>   Point 3
>
>   Point 4

This style can be effective in short papers, but it can sometimes be ineffective for longer ones because the essay tends to break into two separate discussions, and it demands that the reader keep in mind all of the points about the first work to appreciate the points you make about the second. These problems can be lessened, however, if you consciously try to tie the key similarities or differences together as they are revealed in the second half of the discussion.

Another organizational choice for comparison/contrast is labeled *point-by-point*. This approach is effective because it arranges the body of the essay around your main points of likeness or difference which function as the topic sentences or main divisions of your essay. Once the point is established, you discuss the first subject, use a transition to move the reader to the second subject, and then discuss that subject as it relates to your point.

An outline of this pattern looks like this:

Point 1

Subject A (an author, work, or literary element)

Transition

Subject B (an author, work, or literary element)

Point 2

Subject A

Transition

Subject B

Point 3

Subject A

Transition

Subject B

Point 4

Subject A

Transition

Subject B

You may keep your discussion of each main point in one paragraph, or you may present the first subject in one paragraph and then put the transition and second subject in the following paragraph. The choice you make will be determined in part by the length of your discussion; if you have a lot to say about each subject, use separate paragraphs to give equal emphasis to each one.

One important concept to keep in mind about the *point-by-point* organizational pattern is that it is *not* sentence-by-sentence. In *point-by-point*, you write only about the first subject in the first part of the discussion, and then after a transition, you write only about the second subject. Some students slip into sentence-by-sentence (sometimes called the ping-pong ball approach) by writing one sentence about the first subject and then one about the second, following this pattern throughout the entire paragraph. This bounces the reader back and forth between the subjects, involves a tremendous amount of repetition, and demands extensive use of transitions.

If you are writing a long essay of comparison/contrast, you will probably choose to use the *point-by-point* approach to order your discussion.

❧ Writing an Extended Literary Analysis Essay: Step by Step

As you prepare to write your essay, try to follow these steps:

1. Choose a work or several works that you know well because you have read them several times, have analyzed them in class discussions, or have read relevant criticism written by literary scholars. (Remember that if you use a critic's ideas as a starting point or as a way to develop your own ideas, you must document your sources.)

2. If you plan to use comparison/contrast as the organizing principle of your essay, be sure that you have a rhetorical purpose clearly in mind as you draft your essay. You may use comparison/contrast to show that one author/work/literary element is more, less, or equally effective as another, that similar subjects/themes/elements can be effectively presented from different points of view or in different genres, or that the similarities or differences help highlight the tone, the structure, or the theme in the work(s). Choose either the subject-by-subject approach or the point-by-point approach and stay with it throughout the essay, using appropriate transitions as you move from one subject to another.

3. The *introduction* should include an effective lead to gain the reader's interest, a tie-in to the work's or works' title and author which are stated, and a brief summary of the work(s) focusing on the aspect(s) to be dealt with in the essay. The thesis itself clearly states the main idea(s) to be developed or the points of comparison/contrast to be discussed in the body of the essay. By stating the main supporting points as part of the thesis, you can then indicate the major divisions in your essay through your use of the key words from the thesis statement.

4. The *body paragraphs* are built on the literary analysis pattern: topic sentence, introduction to the quotation, the quotation of relevant narration or dialogue, and in-depth analysis of how the quotation proves the topic sentence; this pattern is repeated by using a transitional word or phrase to begin the introduction to a new quotation, by quoting another relevant part of the work, and then by analyzing it in terms of the topic sentence. This pattern can be used more than twice in a paragraph (the more the better), and it can be adapted by sometimes including a quotation in the introduction to the quote or by using a quotation as part of the analysis section. A review of the body paragraphs in the model essays in this text will provide an overview of the flexibility of this pattern.

5. The *conclusion* will give your essay closure if you begin with a signal word (thus, therefore, and so), summarize by rephrasing your thesis and main points, stress the significance of the ideas you've discussed, and change the speed or tempo of your final sentences to create a sense of finality. This paragraph is important since it is your last chance to make an impression on the reader, and final impressions can be even more important than first ones.

The following diagram, model essays, and plan sheets will help you organize and write an extended literary analysis essay.

Title

Introductory Paragraph(s):

Open with interesting lead material.

Name the work(s) and the author(s).

Briefly summarize the work(s) by focusing on the ideas or on the literary element—character, setting, theme, point of view, symbolism, imagery, structure, tone—that you plan to analyze.

State the thesis and its supporting points that will be discussed in the body paragraphs.

Body Paragraphs:

Using the supporting points listed above, divide the body of the essay into major sections by using key words from the thesis to show the organization and development of your ideas.

The major sections can be broken down into several paragraphs by using the literary analysis pattern of generalization, introductory information for a supporting quotation, the quotation of relevant details, and thorough analysis to show how and why the quotation proves and supports the topic sentence and the thesis statement.

Let your paragraphing sense guide you in relation to breaking your discussion into coherent and unified paragraphs. Remember that when you introduce a new concept or subpoint or when your discussion extends more than three-quarters of a page, you should consider starting a new paragraph at some logical point.

Concluding Paragraph(s):

Include a signal word and then rephrase the thesis and its supporting points. Explain the significance or importance of the ideas you have discussed and finish with a strong last sentence (usually one that is longer or shorter than those you have already written) to give your essay a sense of closure and finality. If the body of the essay is extremely long, you may wish to write a longer conclusion by extending your discussion of the significance of your analysis, but be sure that you do not introduce any new ideas as you end your paper.

Model Essay One

This student essay compares the central characters in two of Flannery O'Connor's short stories. Notice the point-by-point organization and the use of transitions.

They Would Have Been Good Women If . . .

Thesis Statement

Topic Sentence

Topic Sentence

"'She would have been a good woman,' The Misfit says of the grand-mother in Flannery O'Connor's "A Good Man Is Hard to Find,"[1] "'if it had been somebody there to shoot her every minute of her life'" (133). In a similar fashion, one may assert that Mrs. Turpin in O'Connor's "Revela-tion"[2] would have been a good woman if there had been somebody there to smash her face every minute of her life. Both the grandmother and Mrs. Turpin are somewhat elderly women who come face to face with violence. On her vacation, the grandmother encounters a callous criminal, while Mrs. Turpin's conversation in the doctor's office ends when she is ferociously attacked by a disapproving teenager. *In both cases, these domineering and condescending women come to reconcile their views of society and religion.*

The grandmother's domineering ways are evident right from the start of the story. "A Good Man Is Hard to Find" opens with the grandmother's "seizing at every chance to change Bailey's mind" (117) about going to Florida: "'Now look here, Bailey, see here, read this,'" (117) commands the grandmother. This is a mother speaking to her son; however, both are ob-viously well into adulthood, and the grandmother's dictating tone of voice shows that she has never relinquished authoritative control over her son Bailey. The grandmother's repetition of these commands makes them seem commonplace. She shows no fear of opposition in giving her commands to him as she rattles "the newspaper at his bald head" (117), demonstrating absolute dominance. She wants things to run her way—not Bailey's.

Like the grandmother, Mrs. Turpin is immediately seen as a dominating force in "Revelation." When the Turpins enter the doctor's office and look for a seat, Mrs. Turpin quickly unleashes her authority as she commands, "'Claude, you sit in that chair there'" (488), giving him a push. Like the grandmother, Mrs. Turpin exhibits verbal dominance by her command and physical intimidation by her push. And Claude reacts to this "as if he were accustomed to doing what she told him" (488). However, where the grand-mother prided herself on being a lady, Mrs. Turpin seems to be more arro-gant about her dominance. The command she gives to her husband is said "in a voice that included anyone who wanted to listen" (488). This suggests that not only does Mrs. Turpin have powerful authority in her marriage, but that she also feels it is important that everyone present sees just how powerful she is.

[1] Excerpts from A GOOD MAN IS HARD TO FIND, copyright 1953 by Flannery O'Connor and renewed 1981 by Mrs. Regina O'Connor. Reprinted by permission of Harcourt Brace Jovanovich, Inc.

[2] Flannery O'Connor, "Revelation" *Everything That Rises Must Converge.* Copyright © 1964, 1965 by the Estate of Mary Flannery O'Connor. Reprinted by permission of Farrar, Straus, and Giroux, Inc.

The grandmother's domineering ways cause her to be rather condescending. When Bailey and his family are driving through Georgia, the grandmother exclaims, "'Oh look at the cute little pickaninny!'" (119). The grandmother's use of the terms "pickaninny" and "nigger" (119) reveals how completely she has accepted racist values. She also says that "'little niggers in the country don't have things like we do'" (119) when June Star points out that he has no britches. Of course, by "things" she means luxury items. Never would she think of "things" as enough food to sustain health or enough clothes or shelter. She regards a scene of wretchedness as picturesque and would like to "'paint that picture'" (119) not as a damning social indictment, but as a means of passive fun.

Whereas the grandmother demonstrates condescendence when she is given the opportunity, Mrs. Turpin continuously and relentlessly displays her egotistical patronizing. She lets everyone in the doctor's office know that she has "a little of everything" (494), and she frequently uses the term "niggers" (496). She also speaks of being tired of "'buttering up'" niggers (494) to do servant work for her. This type of phrasing shows that not only has she readily internalized racist values, but she has also become sickeningly complacent in her selfishness. And if this isn't enough, "sometimes at night [. . .] Mrs. Turpin would occupy herself with the question of who she would have chosen to be if she could not have been herself" (491). And she would have to choose between being a "nigger" or "white-trash" (491). This demonstrates Mrs. Turpin's remarkable obsession to wallow in self-satisfaction over being herself. She seems to associate divinity with being of the noble class and pities in a mocking way the lower classes who, to her, are spiritually deprived. Unfortunately, she cannot see her own spiritual deprivation in this extremely condescending attitude.

In fact, the grandmother and Mrs. Turpin are so self-righteous, they seem to think of themselves as extremely virtuous and religious. However, this notion changes as they both encounter tragedy, and at the conclusion of O'Connor's stories, both the grandmother and Mrs. Turpin experience new, powerful, mystical religious insights.

The grandmother demonstrates confidence in her knowledge of Jesus when she inquires of The Misfit, "'Do you ever pray?'" (129). The grandmother here could have kept insisting that The Misfit is a "good man" in a further effort to manipulate him to spare her, but by throwing this question at him, she suggests that maybe he is not a "good man" and implies that through her knowledge of Jesus, she could save him as evidenced by her statement, "'Pray, pray [. . .]. That's when you should have started to pray'" (130). Later, when The Misfit seems to show a hint of emotion, "the grandmother's head cleared for an instant" (132). This shows that the grandmother has transcended the state of sheer terror she was in and is now thinking on a new level: "'Why you're one of my babies,'" she cries. "'You're one of my own children!'" (132). Whereas previously the grandmother thought of The Misfit as a cold-blooded disgrace to society, she now sees him as one of her own children, one of her babies. This shows that she is now thinking in purely Christian terms, for in Christian terms, we are all brothers and sisters, children of God. This type of reaction is a far cry from what the grandmother shows us throughout the story, and only in fear of death does this insight pour out of her.

Topic Sentence

Mrs. Turpin, on the other hand, shows her arrogance and pride in her religious knowledge when she hears a familiar gospel song in the doctor's office and "supplied the last line mentally, 'And wona these days I know I'll wear a crown'" (490). Mrs. Turpin seems to feel supremely justified in being overwhelmed by the spirit of this song. She is very confident of her destiny with God and appears to even be self-sanctifying. However, after being attacked and called an "'old wart hog'" (500) from hell, Mrs. Turpin is very worried and distressed by this statement, and she ponders it for quite some time. Then, at the very end of the story, while standing at the pig-parlor, "a visionary light settled into her eyes" (508). In the same way as the grandmother, Mrs. Turpin has reached a transcendental state of mind and is now experiencing profound insights. And in her vision she sees "a vast horde of souls [. . .] rumbling toward heaven. There were whole companies of white-trash, clean for the first time in their lives, and bands of black niggers in white robes, and battalions of freaks and lunatics shouting and clapping and leaping like frogs" (508). Mrs. Turpin's spiritual vision is now unobstructed by her hypocritical values. She sees all the types of people that she had previously mocked and degraded, as well as people like herself, as part of some greater Oneness. Like the grandmother, she also comes to the Christian view that all humans are brothers and sisters, children of God. She realizes how meek and humble people should be before the Lord when she sees people like herself, and "even their virtues were being burned away" (508).

Thus Flannery O'Connor's characters of the grandmother and Mrs. Turpin convey a piercing theme about how pathetically ignorant one can become in a life of self-satisfaction. *They are good examples of people who become overbearing and condescending almost to the point of being evil. And it is a shame because we all are capable of being filled with the power, glory, and awe of God. This fact, however, has a great tendency to be forgotten unless there is a gun to one's head or a smack in the face to act as a reminder.* O'Connor's characters point to the need for a religious revolution against a secular world to attain true Christian values.

Restatement of Thesis

Frank Jones

Model Essay Two

Here is a student-written essay that analyzes the four major settings in Judith Guest's novel *Ordinary People.*

The Perils of Perfection

It is important for people to have high self-esteem, but there are many times in everyday life when certain events try to shatter our personal image. The way in which we handle ourselves in these situations builds character. However, just as this is not a perfect world, people do not always react in a perfect manner. In Judith Guest's novel *Ordinary People,*[1] the Jarretts portray the perfect family until a sudden tragedy shatters their world. Beth and Calvin have created the perfect home for their sons, Conrad and Jordan (Buck), but this perfect home has not shielded Buck from sudden death. Conrad survives the boating accident that has taken Buck only to face an emotional ordeal more tumultuous than the accident. *Through the effective use of setting, Guest shows us how Beth Jarrett's world of perfection affects the life and attitudes of her family and how her total control puts dangerous constraints on their emotions. These constraints extend to Conrad's school life and mental health. However, through the flexible and caring attitudes conveyed in T. C. Berger's office and Jeannine Pratt's home, Guest shows us the theme that people are more important than the quest for perfection. To achieve mental health and our own identities, we must allow our personal feelings and thoughts to surface and be acknowledged so they may be put in the proper perspective. At times, this cannot be accomplished alone, and caring friends may help us sort out our thoughts.*

Thesis Statement

Topic Sentence

The isolation created by Beth's perfection in her home reveals that an individual's quest for perfection can cause inner turmoil in the people surrounding her. As Conrad readjusts his life from the mental institution to the perfect house, he thinks the house is "too big for three people. Straining, he can barely hear the early-morning sounds of his father and mother organizing things, synchronizing schedules at the other end of the hall" (3). Even in the family's isolation, order and control prevail. The vast space allows Conrad to be alone with his thoughts, but his mind operates with knowledge that Beth's organization and control reign. He feels that he must stay in that same path of perfection that Beth and Buck have paved. Conrad thinks that "he wants to belong to this house again, needs to be part of these tall windows set low to the ground, walls half-hidden behind thick waxy rhododendron leaves [and] the cedar hedge in front [. . .]" (15). Beth's perfection even extends to the outside appearance of the house, and Conrad needs to find solace in this protected and private world. Not only does he need to hide in the organization of this home, but he also needs to be accepted into the house and into Beth's life.

[1]From ORDINARY PEOPLE by Judith Guest. Copyright © 1976 by Judith Guest. Used by permission of Viking Penguin, a division of Penguin Books USA Inc. All parenthetical page numbers refer to the text in this edition.

Beth's perfection has created a shroud of protection for her, and Cal and Conrad have been left out. No clutter is allowed to surface in this home, whether it be physical or emotional. Conrad has learned from early childhood that order needs to prevail in Beth's home to gain her acceptance. As Beth was tending to her babies, this was made evident as she would become "tense with fury as she scrubbed the fingermarks from the walls; she bursting suddenly into tears because of a toy left out of place, or a spoonful of food thrown onto the floor from the high chair" (83). Conrad was conditioned to know that perfection and order were the only things Beth could accept. Physical and emotional turmoil and mess would not be tolerated in her life, and therefore, they could never appear. Emotion was shown only when control was lost in her external world. Other emotional baggage was left hidden in the depths of her mind. As Beth and Calvin discuss his conversation at a cocktail party about Conrad's psychiatric visits, Beth declares, "'I thought your blurting it out like that was in the worse possible taste'" (65). These are things not even discussed openly at home, let alone at a cocktail party with other people. These topics produce disorder and a messy display of feelings. Admission of disorder indicates loss of perfection and control. It is obvious that Beth's personality controls this home. The only expression allowed to Cal and the boys is hidden in the basement, the only room that Calvin "had designed [. . .] himself; the three of them had finished together" (130). Here, expression is allowed to the males where it could be hidden from the casual visitor and could not contradict the elegance and formality in the rest of the house. Their expression has been kept separate from her perfection.

The tense world of perfection extends to Conrad's and Buck's school life and promotes the downfall of Conrad's mental health when he is left to carry on the successes without Buck. Conrad's pressure had escalated, and several events indicated his initial downfall: poems to his English teacher about "violence and war" (18); a quiz being returned "marked 'incomplete'" (69); notices from Mr. Knight indicating "a straight-A student dropping to D's and E's in three months' time" (105). The pressure and extended isolation encouraged his depression and guilt which led to the suicide attempt and admission to the hospital. On his return, Conrad's isolation is even more pronounced, as indicated during swimming practice with Coach Salan's achievement-oriented attitude and the apprehension of the other boys. During a confrontation with Salan, Conrad is asked, "'Did I ask you before if they gave you shock out there?'" (21). Salan is treating Conrad as if he is some kind of freak and not part of the team. He embellishes on Conrad's lack of special skills and pushes for total physical achievement. This attitude prevails throughout the locker room, as the conversation among the swimmers emphasizes achievement and recalls Buck's swimming prowess.

Conrad's only escape is in choir, where he can attain control yet still escape his subconscious thoughts and is given internal release through song. Conrad feels that "choir is the one time of day when he lets down his guard; there is peace in the strict concentration that Faughnan [the choir director] demands of all of them, in the sweet dissonance of voices in chorus" (19). Here, he remains autonomous but is surrounded by people striving for the same goal. There is union in their quest for perfection, and the feelings of isolation dissipate during this time.

Topic Sentence

Through the relaxed setting in T. C. Berger's office, a contrast to isolation is achieved there, too. The atmosphere encourages openness and a release of feelings that Conrad cannot experience in his home or at school. As Conrad approaches Berger's office, "a scene of total disorder confronts him" (36), and the disorder continues in Berger's office. Conrad approaches the disorder with apprehension, but Berger's acceptance of it sets the mood. Conrad does not find a tense, disgruntled person, but someone who is flexible enough to still perform in the midst of mess. This is evident as he greets Conrad: "'Yeah. You look like somebody Crawford would send me. Somebody who's a match for my daring wit and inquiring mind'" (36). Berger shows his attitude toward life through his acceptance of disorder and through the light-hearted manner he projects. The mess will be there later to deal with; the people in the room come first. Berger verbalizes this attitude as he tells Conrad, "'I'm not big on control. I prefer things fluid'" (41). During Conrad's visits, he learns to feel comfortable in these surroundings, and a sense of camaraderie with Berger helps him to relax enough to reveal the emotions he tries to control.

Topic Sentence

Conrad slowly realizes that sharing his thoughts makes things better than maintaining control. During one of their sessions, "Berger sits like a plump guru, legs folded under him. There are flecks of powdered sugar dotting the front of his sweater" (125). Conrad's mother would have been in a tirade over speckled powder sugar, but this man continues his concentration on Conrad. He emphasizes that people are more important than perfect surroundings. Control and perfection create isolation. Berger stresses that communication is needed when he tells Conrad, "'Let him [the person inside] talk. Let him tell you what you did that was so bad'" (207). He is telling Conrad that mess is being contained in his mind, and it must be released so the thoughts that are junk can be discarded. Through Berger's caring attitude, Conrad finds the depths of his guilt and learns to be accepting and flexible. In isolation, these thoughts were buried; in companionship, these thoughts are allowed to surface and be confronted.

Topic Sentence

Similarly, the setting in Jeannine Pratt's home creates comfortable awareness and companionship for Conrad. In Berger's office, the mess and dim lighting allow Conrad to release his inner thoughts. However, in Jeannine's home, life prevails. When Conrad visits Jeannine, "she ushers him into the small, tidy living room, where a small boy sits cross-legged on the couch, watching television" (153). The same casual atmosphere of Berger's office prevails, but here there is order. As "he gazes about the room, [he sees] plants everywhere" (154), which suggests life in this home—light, airy life. The home is arranged so as not to promote isolation as his home does, and it holds the order that Berger's office denied. In this atmosphere, he finds companionship, comfort, and love. After Jeannine and he experience physical love, she reveals a time in her life when she was involved with the wrong crowd, when she "'smoked [. . .] took pills [. . .] junked around. Sometimes we needed money and kids stole stuff'" (230). In her confidences, Conrad realizes that he is not alone in his dark moments. People who are not in the mental hospital also experience times when they get lost in themselves. He also realizes that he can find understanding and love in this girl and that he is no longer alone. He finds that "he is in touch for good, with hope, with himself, no matter what" (233). Through the friendship of Berger, he has allowed his thoughts to surface, and through Jeannine's companionship and love, his mind has come to accept what he cannot change.

Restatement of Thesis

Thus Guest's use of setting communicates the theme that the need for perfection can produce isolation. Through the perfect Jarrett home and Conrad's achievement-oriented academic life, she shows the tension created in an individual. These settings communicate the perils of isolation and introverted tendencies. On the other hand, through the casual and caring atmosphere in Berger's office and Jeannine's home, Guest stresses the importance of communication, sharing, and acceptance. Through these activities, we can find ourselves and, as Conrad finally did, we can also make peace with ourselves.

Mary Beninato

Model Essay Three

Here is an extended explication of a sonnet written by William Wordsworth.

It Is a Beauteous Evening[1]

It is a beauteous evening, calm and free,
The holy time is as quiet as a Nun
Breathless with adoration; the broad sun
Is sinking down in its tranquility;
The gentleness of heaven broods o'er the Sea:
Listen! the mighty Being is awake
And doth with his eternal motion make
A sound like thunder—everlastingly.
Dear Child! dear Girl! that walkest with me here,
If thou appear untouched by solemn thought,
Thy nature is not therefore less divine:
Thou liest in Abraham's bosom all the year,
And worship'st at the Temple's inner shrine,
God being with thee when we know it not.

Wordsworth: God Is in Nature and in the Child

Have you ever had the pleasure of witnessing a beautiful sunset? The English poet William Wordsworth had such an experience, and it inspired a Petrarchan sonnet entitled "It Is a Beauteous Evening."[1] *Through his use*

Thesis Statement

[1] William Wordsworth, "It Is a Beauteous Evening" *The Norton Anthology of English Literature*, ed. M. H. Abrams, 5th ed. (New York: Norton, 1987) 1439.

of poetic devices, Wordsworth communicates the theme that the spirit of God dwells in both nature and the child.

Topic Sentence   *The immediate setting of the poem is a calm and quiet evening which draws the poet into deep thought, a kind of solemn meditation.* The object considered is nature at the time of sunset:

> It is a beauteous evening, calm and free,
> The holy time is quiet as a Nun
> Breathless with adoration; the broad sun
> Is sinking down in its tranquility;
> The gentleness of heaven broods o'er the Sea: (lines 1–5)

In his description of the scene, Wordsworth sees all of nature in religious-meditative terms which reflect his own contemplative mood. He calls evening a "holy time" (2) because it is "calm and free" (1). This calmness suggests a state of worship, a state which is free because it is not limited by human considerations and is open to all men. Evening is also the time of vespers or evensong. Because the evening possesses the attributes of quietness and holiness, Wordworth compares it to "a Nun / Breathless with adoration" (2–3), an act of praise in which one contemplates God's perfection and worships it. The nun's breathlessness describes a state of self-suspension resulting from the loss of the self in a meditative experience, and it also defines the outer limits of this meditative state. She is so completely immersed in God that her vital systems seem to be suspended.

Topic Sentence   *The image of the "broad sun" (3) suggests that its largeness and circularity are especially prominent.* The sun itself has often been seen in religious terms: its circularity represents a kind of mystical union. The sun and sea will achieve a unity when the setting is complete—a unity similar in kind to the unity of the soul and God in adoration or meditation. The "sun / Is sinking down" (3–4), an act which suggests submersion and reinforces the nun's submersion in the spirit of God. It may also refer to kneeling, the probable position of the nun as she adores. The sun possesses a "tranquility" (4) as does the nun in her quiet state of adoration. Since the setting sun will be followed by a rising sun, an image of new life, setting may be seen as a creative act which precipitates the coming of new life.

Topic Sentence   *This implicit creative spirit in nature is reiterated in the image of the heavens.* "Heaven," brooding "o'er the sea" (5), may be seen as its lover. "Gentleness" (5) is a quality usually characteristic of a lover, and it is here attributed to heaven. Heaven has religious denotations, and "broods o'er" (5) may describe the pensive-meditative state of the nun or connote a physical act of love, the object of which is the natural element, the sea.

Topic Sentence   *The result of this creative act between heaven and the sea is its eternal sound:*

> Listen! the mighty Being is awake,
> And doth with his eternal motion make
> A sound like thunder—everlastingly. (6–8)

The "mighty Being" (6) may be either the sea or more likely the spirit of God which permeates it and all of nature. The sea is "awake / . . . with . . . eternal motion" (6–7), and this contrasts with the images in the first five lines which suggest a kind of static immobility. "Awake" (5) may also suggest a supernatural quality of the godhead—that being its eternal existence. While the motion of the sea produces "a sound like thunder" (8) from the waves crashing against the beach, it is the motion of God through the universe which creates that movement and the beauty and harmony of nature that exist specifically here in the "beauteous evening" (1). As the sea's motion is eternal, so is the force which creates and sustains it: God.

Topic Sentence

Structurally, the octave is one sentence though composed of several independent elements. In the beginning of his analysis of the object of meditation, Wordsworth concentrates on the sights of nature, but he then moves to the thunderous sound of the sea and sets up the contrast between it and the quiet evening, the tranquil sun, the gentle heaven, and the receptive and yielding sea. There is also the contrast in the octave of the physical appearance of outward nature and the reality for the poet of the indwelling spirit of God. Lines six through eight fulfill the expectations set up in the first five lines because they explicitly refer to this spirit of God which has been implicit in the other images. In line six, the word "Listen!"—an imperative spoken to someone—prepares the reader for the presence of the listener addressed in the sestet. The caesura created by the dash which precedes the last word of the octave is dramatically effective. "Everlastingly" (8) is a grand and awesome word; its five syllables and the pause almost demand that it be spoken in a grand and awesome manner. The word gives an air of solemnity to the entire octave besides reinforcing the eternal aspects of God's presence in nature.

Topic Sentence

The sestet reaffirms all the sentiments of the octave but telescopes them into the person of the child:

> Dear Child! dear Girl! that walkest with me here,
> If thou appear untouched by solemn thought,
> Thy nature is not therefore less divine:
> Thou liest in Abraham's bosom all the year,
> And worship'st at the Temple's inner shrine,
> God being with thee when we know it not. (9–14)

The implication is that the "Dear Child" (9), the poet's daughter who is present, should respond to the holy time and become like the evening itself—nun-like—but she appears "untouched by [the] solemn thought" (10) of the poet which is complemented by the reflective natural setting of the sonnet. The verb "appear" (10) prepares for the poet's distinction between appearance and reality. He will penetrate the appearance of the child's unconnectedness with the rest of the scene and speak to the reality of her relationship with God and the rest of nature.

Topic Sentence

The statement "Thy nature is not therefore less divine" (11) is an incomplete comparison which may be filled in by all of the previous elements of the poem: not less divine than the poet's or than nature's as it exists in the evening, the sun, the heavens, and the sea. A kind of divinity seems to permeate all of creation, nature as well as man. Because the child cannot match the contemplative mood of the other elements, however, that does not mean she has been excluded from partaking of that creative spirit which flows through the universe. The colon at the end of line eleven sets up the expectations that the poet will explain why the child's nature is also divine.

Topic Sentence

This divinity is present because the child "liest in Abraham's bosom all the year" (12). She is filled with an unconscious sympathy for all of nature, not merely the grandiose and solemn. Her unconscious sympathy is conscious worship. Wordsworth uses the image of contact with Abraham's bosom to apply to the present existence of the soul of the child, suggesting a continuous cycle of spiritual life.

Topic Sentence

The words "all the year" (12) may imply that the poet does not feel his closeness to the divine power during all the seasons or in all of nature's guises and that because the child's communion is continual rather than sporadic and momentary, it is also superior. Hence the child, a worshipper at the "inner shrine" (13) of the soul, contrasts with the poet who worships at the outer shrine of nature. The soul is here seen as the temple or dwelling place of this spirit of God which sustains all of creation. While God's presence in the soul of the child is not visual, as it may be in the sights and sounds of nature, it is nonetheless as real.

Restatement of Thesis

And so Wordsworth's meditation on natural beauty leads him to affirm the existence of a divine presence that he can also perceive in the nature of his daughter. In his view, God is present in the beauteous evening and in the child because His eternal spirit dwells in all of His creations. For us, too, "The mighty Being" comes alive through the poet's use of imagery, through the power of the pictures in his words.

Mary McHale

JUST ONE MORE THING

Why is it that many of us are put off by length? When we are assigned a five-hundred-page novel or given a major writing assignment, many of us choke. However, if we keep in mind that the same concepts of reading and writing apply regardless of the length of the assignment, we won't feel so threatened; in fact, we'll feel empowered because when we know how to handle the "small" assignments, we can handle the "big ones" as well.

❧ Extended Literary Analysis Plan Sheet ❧

Author: _____ Title: _____

Thesis: _____

_____

_____

_____

_____

Topic sentence: _____

_____

_____

Supporting quote: page or line _____

Supporting quote: page or line _____

Supporting quote: page or line _____

Topic sentence: _____

_____

_____

Supporting quote: page or line _____

Supporting quote: page or line _____

Supporting quote: page or line _____

Topic sentence: _____

_____

_____

Supporting quote: page or line _____

Supporting quote: page or line _____

Supporting quote: page or line _____

Topic sentence: _____

_____

_____

                Supporting quote: page or line _____

                Supporting quote: page or line _____

                Supporting quote: page or line _____

Topic sentence: _____

_____

_____

                Supporting quote: page or line _____

                Supporting quote: page or line _____

                Supporting quote: page or line _____

Topic sentence: _____

_____

_____

                Supporting quote: page or line _____

                Supporting quote: page or line _____

                Supporting quote: page or line _____

Concluding points: _____

_____

_____

_____

_____

_____

_____

_____

❧ Peer/Self-Evaluation of an ❧ Extended Literary Analysis Essay

Directions: Make specific suggestions about each part of the essay, pointing out particular areas that the writer could improve. Keep in mind the qualities of good writing: unity, organization, development, clarity, and coherence.

I. Introduction

Is the lead relevant and interesting?

Are the author's or authors' full name and the title(s) of the work(s) correctly spelled and punctuated?

Does the summary of the work(s) focus on the ideas or the literary element(s) that will be analyzed in the essay?

Does the thesis clearly state the main points that will be discussed in the body paragraphs?

II. Body Paragraphs

Do the topic sentences contain key words from the thesis to connect the body paragraphs to the thesis points?

Do the body paragraphs follow the order of the points stated in the thesis?

Are the supporting quotations properly introduced and relevant?

Are the analysis sections adequately developed?

Are the body paragraphs unified and coherent?

III. Conclusion

Is a signal word included somewhere in the paragraph?

Are the thesis and its supporting points rephrased?

Is the significance of the thesis clear to the reader?

Is there a speed change between the last two sentences?

Is the final sentence an effective clincher?

IV. Expression

Are all the ideas expressed in complete sentences?

Are the sentences clear and correctly punctuated?

Are there any problems with subject-verb or pronoun-antecedent agreement?

Are all the words correctly spelled?

V. Overall Evaluation

Most effective part of the essay:

Least effective part of the essay:

List three specific actions which could be taken by the writer to improve this and future papers:
1.

2.

3.

Evaluator's name: _____ Date: _____

Writing Literary Research Papers

Overview

A research paper includes your ideas about a topic as well as those you quote or paraphrase from primary or secondary sources. This type of paper, frequently assigned in college classes, can be easy to write if you follow a series of logical steps that begin with planning and research and end with drafting and documentation.

✵ Writing a Literary Research Paper: Step by Step

Now that you have learned how to use the literary analysis pattern in the essays you have been writing, you are well equipped to produce a well organized and well supported research paper. Although your research paper will probably be longer than your other essays, it will still be organized into three parts: an introduction, a body, and a conclusion. Your paper will be well supported because in addition to the quotations from the work(s) you are analyzing (a primary source), you will be supporting and developing your ideas with information taken from secondary sources, material written about your subject, including critical studies, biographies, historical accounts, social commentaries, and introductions or afterwards to texts. Doing research requires that you spend time reviewing and studying relevant works by scholars, and by "standing on their shoulders," you can contribute to that body of scholarship through your own thinking and writing. When you are able to combine your insights with those of others, the sense of accomplishment you experience is a lasting one. Years from now, you will remember the topics of your research papers when other written assignments have been long forgotten.

Literary research does not differ significantly from other forms of research that you have done. The following steps provide a review of the process combined with specific recommendations related to researching a literary topic.

Choosing Your Research Topic

If you are free to choose the topic for your research paper, you may want to consider one of the following possible approaches:

- an analysis of a particular author's philosophy, style, tone, psychology, themes, or influences in one or in several works;

- a comparison or contrast of two authors, works, characters, styles, or literary periods;
- an analysis of an author's development through several works;
- a refutation of a critical study on a work;
- a comparison of two or more critical studies of a single work;
- a discussion of additional insights the author of a critical study overlooked or omitted;
- a review of the source or idea for a single work or for several works by one author;
- a study of the social, economic, or political influences on an author or on specific works;
- an examination of any work in terms of its characters, setting, symbolism, point of view, themes, style, structure, imagery, humor, or tone.

You may want to examine some of the literary journals to see the different types of critical approaches that are possible in literature. If you pick up the current copies and scan the table of contents, you can see the topics scholars are examining in their research. Your library probably has many of the following journals available for your use either in paper, on microfilm, or on a database:

American Literature
American Quarterly
Chaucer Review
College English
Comparative Literature
Critique—Studies in Modern Fiction
English Literature in Transition
Essays in Criticism
Explicator
Kenyon Review
Literary Review

Modern Fiction Studies
Modern Language Notes
Nineteenth Century Literature
Notes and Queries
PMLA
Shakespeare Quarterly
Studies in English Literature
Studies in Short Fiction
Twentieth Century Literature
Victorian Studies
Yale Review

Once you choose a topic, be sure to narrow it to workable proportions to avoid being too general or too limited in your approach. The required length of your assignment is the best guide to use in determining the scope of your topic.

Building Your Bibliography

You can begin compiling your bibliography by looking up your subject in the online catalog, checking particularly for major works of criticism—either books by one author or edited collections of critical essays published by university presses. Once you have the works in hand, check the table of contents and the index to see if they contain material relevant to your topic. Pay particular attention to any bibliographies included in the texts; they can guide you to additional sources. Try to find books with the most recent publication dates since they will most likely include references to earlier scholarship on your topic.

Indexes can be used to locate journal articles that contain current scholarly opinion and most likely include a bibliography. Check the beginning of each work for directions on its use, and be sure to copy relevant entries carefully and completely when using the following indexes:

Bibliographic Index
Book Review Index
Essay and General Literature Index
Humanities Index
International Index
MLA International Bibliography
MLA Abstracts

The *MLA International Bibliography*, available in both paper and CD-ROM versions, is especially useful in literary research because it lists scholarly books and articles published each year on modern languages, literature, folklore, and linguistics. The front of the volume contains a table of contents and a guide for users that presents an overview of how to use the index, how to read the citations, how to use the subject index, and how to conduct a search. Also included, of course, is a list of the abbreviations used for the periodicals cited; it illustrates the broad range of study and investigation that this reference work indexes and makes accessible to students and scholars alike. As with any index, you should begin with the most recent volume and work backward to the year the work or works you are researching were written.

Works which include prepared bibliographies are also useful. You may want to consult *The Year's Work in English Studies* if you are writing on an English author or *American Literary Scholarship* if your focus is on an American writer. Other valuable sources are *A Research Guide for Undergraduate Students: English and American Literature; Bibliography of Women and Literature; Recent Studies in Myths and Literature 1970–1990: An Annotated Bibliography; Articles on Twentieth Century Literature; Guide to American Poetry Explication; Poetry Explication;* and *Twentieth Century Short Story Explication.*

Electronic Research and the Library

In addition to print materials, libraries now have technology that allows you to search electronic databases to find material on your subject. Here is a brief description of some of the services that are available:

Academic Search Elite from EBSCO Information Services provides full text for over 1,530 academic, social sciences, humanities, general science, education, and multi-cultural journals. In addition to the full text, this database offers indexing and abstracts for over 2,880 journals. Full-text backfiles go back to January of 1990, while indexing and abstract backfiles go back to January of 1984.

MagillOnLiterature also from EBSCO is an online reference system accessible via the Internet. It offers a variety of proprietary full-text databases and popular databases from leading information providers. The comprehensive databases range from general reference collections to specially designed subject-specific databases for public, academic, medical, corporate, and school libraries.

Expanded Academic ASAP from the Gale Group accesses scholarly journals, news magazines, and newspapers in one easy-to-use interface. The database covers a wide range of disciplines including journals in the humanities, social sciences, and science and technology that can be searched by subject or by key words. It provides full-text coverage of 1,300 journal titles and citations/abstracts for 2,300 additional journal titles. The database coverage is from 1980 to the present.

NetFirst from OCLC FirstSearch contains references to over 105,000 of the best Web sites. It takes Internet research a step beyond that of the Internet search engines by abstracting each site, organizing each site by subject, and weeding out sites with less useful content.

Periodical Abstracts also from OCLC FirstSearch includes articles from over 2,040 titles from 1987 to the present on a wide range of subjects including business, current affairs, economics, literature, psychology, religion, and women's studies.

ProQuest from ProQuest Information and Learning Company contains over 2,000 periodicals—nearly 1,000 of them in ASCII full-text or full-image formats—in a wide range of subject areas. The database can be searched by keyword, publication, subject, or phrase. Each type of search provides direct access to the full database. Searches can be restricted by date and also to full-text articles and peer-reviewed journals. The database coverage is from 1986 to the present.

Discovering Authors is a CD-ROM database containing information on frequently studied authors, including biographies, excerpts from critical essays, a bibliography of the author's works, and references to additional sources, and all can be printed for your review.

Your library may have these electronic sources or others like them, and the easiest way to learn their use is to sit down and try them. Most systems contain easy-to-follow on-screen instructions, so it will not take you long to generate pages of possible sources. Keep in mind, though, that while databases make research faster, you must still be selective by reading the articles carefully to determine if the information is reliable and relevant to your topic.

Electronic Research and Your PC

Through your online access service provider, your own personal computer can open library doors around the world. Search engines, also called "crawlers" or "spiders," automatically visit web sites on the Internet and create catalogs of web pages. When using a search engine, you need to be as precise as possible in the wording of your topic to avoid having to sift through literally thousands of web pages. A quick review of the search tips provided by the search engine will save you time and help you locate the precise information you need for your research. Type your subject and keywords in the query box, click search, and the search engine will return the results in seconds. AltaVista, one of the largest search engines on the web because of the number of pages indexed, and Google, highly rated for the best overall search process, are favorites with many researchers. Other search engines include AOL Search, Direct Hit, Excite, HotBot, Inktomi, Lycos, MSN Search, Netscape Search, and Northern Light.

Web directories are compiled by editors who place the submitted web sites into appropriate categories. The oldest web site directory is Yahoo, which is well respected as the web's most popular search service. Another growing directory based on user submissions is LookSmart, which provides browsable listings for both MSN Search and Excite.

By using a search engine or a directory, you can access web sites relevant to your specific topic. If you find a web page containing material you wish to use in your essay, you will have to document it like any other source material. Each entry generated by a search engine or a directory includes a URL (Uniform Resource Locator) or an electronic address which must be cited as part of the documentation process. To check the current guidelines for documenting such information, you can use Yahoo to access the Modern Language Association of America's web page by typing Modern Language Association in the search box, initiating the search, and then clicking on the hyperlink *MLA Style*. The world of research and documentation is at your fingertips.

Doing Preliminary Reading

Besides reviewing the books, articles, and web pages you have located, you can also consult some specialized reference works that could be useful for your preliminary reading on your subject:

African American Writers
American Writers: A Collection of Literary Biographies
British Writers
Cambridge Guide to Literature in English
Cambridge Guide to World Theatre
Cassel's Encyclopaedia of World Literature
Contemporary Authors
Contemporary Literary Criticism
Critical Survey of Drama
Critical Survey of Poetry
Critical Survey of Short Fiction

Crown Guide to the World's Great Plays from Ancient Greece to Modern Times
Latin American Writers
Literary Research Guide
McGraw Hill Encyclopedia of World Drama
Nineteenth Century Literary Criticism
Oxford Companion to American Literature
Oxford Companion to Canadian Literature
Oxford Companion to Classical Literature
Oxford Companion to English Literature
Penguin Companion to American Literature
Penguin Companion to Classical, Oriental, and African Literature
Penguin Companion to English Literature
Penguin Companion to European Literature
Short Story Criticism
Twentieth Century Literary Criticism

As you evaluate your reading, do you find that you agree with the writers and their analyses, or are you in disagreement with a particular critic and his theories on the work? Have you discovered a new idea that you could trace throughout the work? Have you learned additional facts that deepen your understanding of the work? Choosing one of these approaches will help you use your research in your thinking rather than in just reporting what others have said. Be sure to mark those sections that you want to return to later to take notes.

Formulating Your Thesis and Taking Notes

After you have finished your preliminary reading and have decided on a research approach, you can formulate a tentative thesis and begin to develop your position on your topic by writing down your own thoughts and opinions first. Doing that will help you avoid total dependence on your sources. You want to be original in your thinking—not just a human copy machine that duplicates others' words and thoughts. When you have finished with this step, you can begin to take notes from your sources to support your thesis.

Taking notes on cards can simplify the matter of organization because you can arrange and rearrange them easily according to your thesis points, especially if you record only one quotation or paraphrase per card along with the source. Remember, too, that you can put your own ideas on a card as they arise during the note-taking process so that you will not forget them later. Some researchers work with xerox copies of materials they want to use in their papers. They can then highlight information they may want to use without recopying it, and by using a numbering system, they can indicate which point in the thesis the information will support.

Whatever note-taking approach you use, be sure you have the page number, the name of the work, and all other relevant information so you can correctly identify the sources of your quotations and ideas. Also, be sure to use quotation marks around anything that you directly copy so that you can avoid any hint of plagiarism. Remember that any ideas you take from a source for a direct quotation, a summary (a brief restatement of an idea) or a paraphrase (a rewording of an excerpt) must be documented with a textnote and a works cited entry.

Writing a Draft of Your Paper

After you have organized your notes around your thesis points, you can begin to rough out a first draft of your paper in terms of its three major parts—the introduction, the body, and the conclusion. Your main goal should be to get your ideas down on paper to see how they fit together, to see if your research effectively proves your thesis.

An **introduction** to a literary study usually includes references to research that has already been done on the topic. If you summarize critical studies or include important biographical or historical data, you can use that information as background or as a point of departure that can lead nicely into your particular approach to the topic and to your thesis, the main organizing principle in your essay. Consider ways to divide the thesis into main points or major parts that will function as the major divisions in your paper and that can be identified by key words or sub-headings in the body of the essay.

In the **body paragraphs,** remember to use the literary analysis pattern (topic sentence, introductory material for a quotation, the quotation itself, and analysis of it) when working with your sources. One place where quotations from secondary sources work well is after the analysis sections you write to analyze the quotes from your primary source. Generalize about your research; introduce a relevant quotation, paraphrase, or summary; comment on the significance of its content; and then add your own ideas and views on the topic under discussion. Use your research to back up your interpretation or as a springboard to a counterpoint.

Two places where the use of quotations is questionable in body paragraphs are as topic sentences or as final sentences in a paragraph. Without a clearly stated topic sentence, the reader is left to guess at the point the quotation is supposed to support, and if a quotation ends a paragraph, the reader is again forced to guess at the significance or relevance of the quoted excerpt. Your own words should start and end the paragraph.

Be sure to include the source of your references in the text of your draft so that you will have an easier time documenting your sources. Incorporate as much evidence as you can without turning your essay into a series of quotations tied together with brief transitions. Your own ideas should dominate the paper.

As you **conclude,** briefly summarize your main points and explain the conclusions you have reached as a result of your research. The significance of your findings and of your new insights can be emphasized in the last few sentences by your style and by the content of your clincher sentence. Be sure to take the time to polish your ending in a long paper, for if your reader's concentration has waned at all, here is the chance to remind him of the importance of your research and your scholarly attitude toward it.

Revising Your Draft

As you know, the purpose of revising any piece of writing is to improve its clarity and its coherence, and these qualities are especially important in a research paper. Working the material from your sources smoothly into your essay requires an awareness of your style and that of the author you are quoting or paraphrasing. To review various stylistic techniques for incorporating quotations, read the first part of Chapter Three once more, and for suggestions on revising, see page 29 in Chapter Two.

Documenting Your Research

Since the *MLA Handbook for Writers of Research Papers*—the style sheet usually used in literary research—discusses three different styles of notes, including footnotes, endnotes, and textnotes, be sure you follow the guidelines recommended by your instructor. Regardless of the form you follow, you will have to prepare a Works Cited page, an alphabetical list of the sources used in the preparation of your paper. Chapter Three includes models that you can use to help you with this part of the research process. The Works Cited page is important because it provides your reader with sources that he or she may wish to consult for further information on your subject.

Typing Your Manuscript

Again, be sure to follow your instructor's directions concerning the format for your manuscript. If you are not given specific instructions, you may want to follow these guidelines established by the Modern Language Association for research papers.

- Type or print your paper on white medium-weight paper only.
- Leave one inch margins on both sides and at the top and bottom of the paper.
- Place your last name and the page number on all the pages (including the Works Cited page) in the upper right-hand corner three lines from the top; then skip three more lines to begin the text.
- A title page is not required for a research paper. At the left margin, one inch (six lines) from the top of the page, type or print your name, your instructor's name, the course, and the date on separate lines, double-spacing between them. Double-space again and center the title, and then double-space once more between the title and the first line of the text.
- Do not quote or underline your title or type it in all capital letters; capitalize the first word, all other principal words, and the first word of the subtitle if one is present.
- Double-space throughout the paper (even long quotations) and throughout the Works Cited page.

Proofreading the Final Copy

Proofreading your final copy is an essential step in the writing process. You do not want the time and energy you put into researching and writing your paper to be overlooked by your instructor because you overlooked the process of proofreading. Here are some guidelines you can follow for any written assignment:

- Read your work carefully on-screen, and be sure to use your spell-checker before printing a hard copy of your paper. (Remember that a spell-checker will not find correct spellings of words that are used incorrectly, e.g., *there* for *their*).
- As you check the hard copy, read slowly and aloud with a pen in hand to mark areas that need to be changed or corrected.
- Do more than one reading. If you allow some time to pass (an hour, a day, several days—whatever your deadline permits) between readings, your memory of the work will have faded, allowing you to see problems you may have overlooked in previous checks.
- After making your changes and corrections, print two final copies: one for your instructor and one for your records. In the unlikely event that your paper is misplaced or lost, you will have no problem producing its replacement.

When your paper is returned, be sure to study your instructor's comments and recommendations; they are designed to help you master the process of expressing your ideas accurately, clearly, and professionally.

The following diagram and model papers will help you organize and write an effective research paper on a literary topic.

Diagram of the Structure of a Literary Research Paper

Title

Introductory Paragraph(s):

Open with interesting lead material.

Introduce the broad topic of your research, including the name of the work(s) and the author(s).

Cite previous works or research studies that relate to your topic.

Identify your point of departure from these works or studies.

State your thesis—the point you intend to prove with research from primary and secondary sources—and list its main supporting points.

Body Paragraphs:

Using the logical points of division suggested by your thesis, separate the body of the paper into main parts or sections. As you begin each main part, use key words from the thesis to show the development and organization of your ideas.

Support your topic sentences by using the literary analysis pattern of generalization, introductory material for your evidence, a quotation, summary, or paraphrase from a primary or secondary source, and thorough analysis to show how and why the quotation, summary, or paraphrase proves and supports your topic sentence and your thesis statement.

Concluding Paragraph(s):

Include a signal word and then summarize the main points of your discussion. State the significance of your findings and your contribution to the body of knowledge about the subject of your research. End with a speed change and a strong clincher sentence to give your work a sense of finality.

Erica Walsh
Professor McKeague
Composition II
November 18, 20--

<u>The Old Man and the Sea</u>: A Lesson in Courage

The skill that Santiago, the old Cuban fisherman in Ernest Hemingway's novella <u>The Old Man and
the Sea</u>, exhibits as he struggles to catch a giant
marlin in the ocean waters off Cuba is extraordinary. As he beats off the sharks in a futile effort
to save his prize, "he is undefeated, he endures,
and his loss therefore, in the manner of it, is
itself a victory" (Young 125). <u>By the way Hemingway</u>

Thesis Statement

<u>presents Santiago's interactions with the marlin
and the Mako shark, he reveals the old fisherman's
love and respect for nature and brings out the theme
that despite his losses, a man's spirit can remain
undefeated.</u>

Topic Sentence

<u>As Santiago interacts with and relates to the
marlin, he reveals his love for the great fish he
has caught.</u> After he has hooked "the biggest fish
that he had ever seen" (Hemingway 63) and has
struggled with it for more than twenty-four hours,
he addresses the marlin and says, "'Fish,' [. . .]
'I love you and respect you very much'" (Hemingway
54). Despite the discomfort and pain Santiago has
experienced in his battle with the fish, he still
cares deeply about him. He admires his beauty and
respects his strength, acknowledging that the marlin
is a noble antagonist. Even though Santiago knows
that his skill and intelligence will enable him to
kill the fish, he shows respect for the marlin's
inherent qualities when he thinks, "Never have I
seen a greater, [. . .], or a calmer or more noble
thing than you, brother" (Hemingway 92). Santiago
admires the marlin's power and strength and his

determined efforts to escape. Engaged in the longest and greatest battle of his life, the giant fish still seems to be "good for ever" (Hemingway 92). Recognizing his kinship with his catch, Santiago sees him as a brother, an equal. According to critic Philip Young, "Santiago's respect for his foe, the marlin, which is love, actually as for a brother, is surpassed by Hemingway's respect for both that fish and Santiago himself, and for the whole of life which this battle epitomizes [. . .]" (131). Santiago reveals the depths of Hemingway's love for nature and those who reverence it and his admiration for those who struggle courageously against unconquerable odds. Santiago's battle suggests that life is a game that man cannot win, but he can conduct himself humbly and courageously while he is being destroyed.

Topic Sentence   As Santiago battles the Mako shark that attacks the dead marlin after he has tied it to his skiff, he acknowledges his respect for the shark's courage and determination. When he pierces the heart of the marlin and its blood mixes with the sea, he sees the first shark approaching: "he knew that this was a shark that had no fear at all and would do exactly what he wished" (Hemingway 101). The shark hones in on his prey and is determined to share in Santiago's prize catch. The shark is not afraid of the fisherman or of anything else that stands in the way of the food he seeks. When Santiago thinks about the Mako shark's role in the ocean, he realizes that it is similar to his own: "He lives on the live fish as [I] do. [. . .] He is beautiful and noble and knows no fear of anything" (Hemingway 105-106). The shark, too, is a fisherman, always in search of food to satisfy his tremendous appetite. Santiago acknowledges and admires the qualities that make the shark a sleek feeding machine. Realizing that he is in the shark's territory, Santiago knows that he will have to fight to keep his prize: "Thus, when the [shark comes], it is almost a thing expected, almost as a punishment which the old man brings upon himself in going far out 'beyond all people'" (Burhans 50). Even as he battles this powerful force that fights to keep the marlin for himself, Santiago respects his opponent's determination to fight to the death to carry out his instinctive feeding ritual. The shark is as relentless as Santiago is courageous.

Topic Sentence   Through Santiago's epic struggle to bring in his prize marlin through the shark-infested waters, Hemingway brings out the theme that a man's spirit can remain undefeated despite his losses. After the sharks have destroyed half of the marlin, the old man is still determined to battle them, saying, "'I'll fight them until I die'" (Hemingway 115). Even though he is struggling with fatigue and physical pain, he is willing to expend his last ounce of energy to defend his catch. He is not going to give up in the middle of a battle; he is going to see this struggle through to its conclusion--even if he dies doing it. He realizes that more sharks will come, but he tells himself, "'A man can be destroyed but not defeated.' [. . .] 'Don't think, old man,' [. . .]. 'Sail on this course and take it when it comes'" (Hemingway 103). Santiago realizes that he and his marlin may be destroyed by the hungry sharks, but as long as he does not give up, he can never be truly defeated. His instinct is to give his all to preserve his trophy fish, so he will not let himself think about any other option. He has chosen a response, a course, and he will deal with whatever it brings his way. Therefore, he stays his course and prevails:

> With the huge skeleton tied to his skiff, he had brought the proof of his victory home. His courage and endurance are

> registered with awe among his fellow fish-
> ermen--'There has never been such a fish'
> --and he goes to sleep dreaming of those
> images [of lions] from his youth of brave
> indomitable power [. . .]. (Baker 130)

Despite the fact that only bones remain as proof of his great accomplishment, Santiago is undefeated, and his lion-hearted spirit is ready to begin anew his struggle with the natural forces that shape his life as a fisherman. His sleep and his dreams will renew his spirit and bring him back again to the sea that he loves.

Restatement of Thesis

And so Hemingway's use of the ocean waters off Cuba as the setting for his novella is very effec-tive. "There is [an] extraordinary vividness of the background--the sea, which is very personal to Santiago, whose knowledge of it, and feeling for it, bring it brilliantly and lovingly close" (Young 125). Moreover, Santiago's attitude during his struggle with the marlin and the loss of his catch to the sharks transforms this sea story into a message of hope and inspiration for all who struggle with life. As Hemingway himself put it, "'I've always preferred to believe that man is undefeated'" (Hotchner 73). Santiago illustrates that belief perfectly.

Works Cited

Baker, Sheridan. Ernest Hemingway: An Introduction and Interpre-
    tation. New York: Holt, 1967.
Burhans, Clinton S., Jr. "The Old Man and the Sea: Hemingway's
    Tragic Vision of Man." Hemingway and His Critics. Ed.
    Carlos Baker. New York: Hill, 1961.
Hemingway Ernest. The Old Man and the Sea. New York: Macmillan,
    1962.
Hotchner, A. E. Papa Hemingway. New York: Random, 1955.
Young, Philip. Ernest Hemingway: A Reconsideration. University
    Park: The Pennsylvania State UP, 1966.

Joyce Carey
Professor McKeague
Composition II
25 October, 20--

Counterpoint in <u>The Great Gatsby</u>

When <u>The Great Gatsby</u> was published in 1925, it was hailed as a "critical triumph" (Hoffman 1). It was also a popular success because it dealt with the role of money, the Manhattan underworld, love, and the American Dream (Hoffman 8). Since its publication, the novel has been analyzed and re-analyzed by the critics over the past three-quarters of a century. One such analysis appeared in the <u>English Journal</u> in October of 1966. Its author, James M. Mellard, contends that counterpoint is the major technique Fitzgerald uses in <u>The Great Gatsby</u>. <u>He demonstrates his thesis by discussing "the counterpoint in characterization, setting (including symbol and scene) and narrative structure" (853), but his choice of contrasts is sometimes superficial when other possibilities are considered.</u> He focuses on Tom Buchanan and Jay Gatsby, Myrtle Wilson and Daisy Buchanan, Dr. T. J. Eckleburg and Owl-eyes, and the "green light at the end of Daisy's dock" (859).

<u>In choosing to point out the counterpoint which exists between Tom Buchanan and Jay Gatsby, Mellard discusses the obvious differences which usually exist between a protagonist and an antagonist.</u> The first contrast he discusses--Tom's life being anticlimactic while Gatsby's deals in futurity (854)--is actually not a difference at all. What Mellard has failed to recognize is the underlying sameness of their lives: neither lives in the present. He states that Tom lives in the glory of his "past achievement" while Gatsby, though rooted in the past, be-

Thesis Statement

Topic Sentence

lieves he can recapture it at some future time (854). Both of them, however, are unrealistic about the present: Tom believes that physical strength and a white heritage make him superior, and Gatsby believes that wealth will make his dream come true.

Topic Sentence

The second item of counterpoint that Mellard discusses is also not a valid one. While he is correct in saying that Tom's energy is physical and Jay's spiritual (854), he has not seen that both these sources of motivating power are corrupt and hence essentially alike. Both Tom and Jay lack intellectual energy. Both are equally distant from the rational energy which should be the source of human actions. While being superficially different, both physical and spiritual energy are equally ineffective for dealing with a rational world. How ineffective is shown by the fate of the two men: Gatsby is killed by Wilson (Fitzgerald 142), and Tom flees from the scene to "let other people clean up the mess . . ." (Fitzgerald 158). Neither is capable of facing reality.

Topic Sentence

A third area of counterpoint which Mellard notes is that Gatsby is "profoundly kind" while Tom is cruel (854). It would be more accurate to state that Tom is "profoundly" cruel (witness his treatment of Daisy, Myrtle, and George), while Gatsby's apparent kindness might be questioned in terms of its end. His kind gestures toward the guests at his parties are designed to enhance his image as "the son of some wealthy people in the Middle West" (Fitzgerald 60). And the kindness that Gatsby shows toward Nick may easily be seen as an attempt to smooth the path which could bring him and Daisy together. Mellard's choice of the words "profoundly kind" to describe Gatsby is an inaccurate one; superficially kind would be more precise but would lessen the strength of his argument. Because the cruelty of Tom and the kindness of Gatsby exist on completely different levels, they cannot be accurately described as true counterpoints.

Topic Sentence   The importance of counterpoint in character could have been more validly demonstrated if Mellard had compared Nick and Gatsby rather than Tom and Gatsby. Mellard admits the importance of Nick and his moral development in the novel (853), but he relegates him to a position of observer and judge of Tom and Gatsby (854). Actually, Nick learns an important lesson through his interaction with Gatsby and the "foul dust [that] floated in the wake of his dreams" (Fitzgerald 8). Nick reveals himself at the beginning of the novel as a conservative with a historical heritage (Fitzgerald 8). Gatsby, on the other hand, is a dreamer whose heritage is rooted in "romantic possibilities" (Fitzgerald 98). As a part of his heritage, Nick possesses values which grow and develop in the course of the novel; Gatsby, however, is generally without conscience about the means he uses to achieve his dream. Though from an established family, Nick is relatively poor, Gatsby rich. Gatsby is a mysterious figure who is characterized by a "romantic readiness" (Fitzgerald 8). Nick, in contrast, is an ordinary fellow with a realistic attitude toward the present (Fitzgerald 99). Gatsby "does not pass from innocence to experience" (Chase 300), while Nick gains an insight into himself and moral worth as a result of that summer of 1922. After this experience, he "is ready at last to [go] home" (Piper 329) to "the warm center of the world, the Middle West" (Fitzgerald 9), to pick up his life.

Topic Sentence   Nick, then, is the real counterpart of the major qualities of Gatsby which Mellard notes. Gatsby, he says, deals with futurity because of his attempts to recapture the past (854). Nick is the true juxtaposition to Gatsby because he deals in the reality of the present: "'Can't recapture the past?

Why of course you can'" is Gatsby's answer to Nick's realistic statement, "You can't repeat the past'" (99). If Gatsby is motivated by spiritual energy as Mellard contends (854), Nick's energy is rational. Because Nick is reason, he can learn, and because Gatsby is sheer will, he is broken and destroyed by life. "Nick's discovery is that the power of will without the direction of intelligence is a destructive power [. . .]" (Hanzo 294). Gatsby believes that he can recapture the past simply by willing it to be so, but he does not realize the complexity of human motivation and of human relationships.

Topic Sentence
Mellard's discussion of the counterpoint between Myrtle and Daisy is accurate, but he omits one important contrast. Both women are found out in their relationships with other men and forced to make a choice. Daisy chooses to remain with her husband (Fitzgerald 145) and thus destroys Gatsby's dream. Myrtle chooses her lover, and in an attempt to give herself to him, she is killed (Fitzgerald 122). Though different choices, both actions end in death: Myrtle's--because she is physical--on the physical level, and Daisy's--because she is Gatsby's dream--on the symbolic, spiritual level. These deaths demonstrate that neither the physical nor the spiritual level is sufficient for life. Fitzgerald seems to be saying that only when the rational level is combined with the spiritual level can man successfully deal with his problems.

Topic Sentence
Mellard is taken in by obvious similarities when he juxtaposes the "owl-eyed" man with the eyes of Dr. T. J. Eckleburg (856). In this discussion, Mellard deviates from his original position by stating that Eckleburg's "eyes are really Nick's" and that "the good doctor's function seems hardly distinguishable from Nick's own" (856). He is actually, then, juxtaposing Nick and Owl-eyes, and while it is true that the judgments made by them are at

opposite poles, that alone does not make them counterpointed characters.

Topic Sentence The true counterpart of Owl-eyes is Wolfsheim, Gatsby's business connection. His name suggests an animal of prey that uses others for its own ends. Wolfsheim's predominant characteristic is his sentimentality, while Owl-eyes' is intellectuality. He is impressed by Gatsby's library (Fitzgerald 45). This fact and his name suggest a wisdom and an intelligence which separate him from the others who frequent Gatsby's parties. Because he did not even know Gatsby personally, his presence at the funeral points up the absence of Wolfsheim and the other guests. Owl-eyes' realistic epitaph, "'the poor son-of-a-bitch'" (154), contrasts with Wolfsheim's final words which sound as if they might have been solemnly pronounced by a preacher: "'Let us learn to show our friendship for a man when he is alive and not after he is dead'" (151). The intellectual party-goer realizes that Gatsby's life was an empty illusion, while the underworld "gonnegtion" does not want "'to get mixed up in [Gatsby's death] in any way'" (151). They represent truly opposite points of view about human relationships.

Topic Sentence Mellard states "that there is no counterpoint for the green light at the end of Daisy's boat dock" which he says "is associated with the Grail itself [. . .], the quest, the quester, and the possibilities of the American Dream [. . .]" (859). There is, however, an obvious counterpoint that he has missed: "Gatsby's gorgeous car" (59). It is "a rich cream color, bright with nickel, swollen here and there in its monstrous length with triumphant hat-boxes and supper-boxes and toolboxes, and terraced with a labyrinth of windshields that mirrored a dozen suns" (60). If the green light symbolizes the American dream, then the cream color car symbolizes the materialism that destroys and replaces that dream. It destroys on the physical level, for it kills Myrtle, and it destroys on the spiritual level, for when Daisy discovers how Gatsby got his money, she turns to Tom and Jay's dream is destroyed. It is this materialism which created the wasteland of the twenties and which even now prohibits the fulfillment of the American dream.

Restatement of Thesis

And so while the fundamental thesis expounded by Mellard is sound, he has too often chosen the obvious when more meaningful counterpoints could have been found. Gatsby has a more valid counterpoint in Nick than in Tom, and while Daisy and Myrtle make different choices concerning their marriages, both come to unhappy ends. Moreover, Owl-eyes is Wolfsheim's counterpart, just as Gatsby's car is a fitting counterpoint to the green light on Daisy's dock. Like Jay Gatsby, Mellard's vision is good, but his means are suspect.

Works Cited

Chase, Richard. "The American Novel and Its Traditions." The Great Gatsby: A Study. Ed. Frederick J. Hoffman. New York: Scribner's, 1962. 297-302.

Fitzgerald, F. Scott. The Great Gatsby. New York: Scribner's, 1925.

Hanzo, Thomas. "The Theme and the Narrator of The Great Gatsby." The Great Gatsby: A Study. Ed. Frederick J. Hoffman. New York: Scribner's, 1962. 286-96.

Hoffman, Frederick J., ed. The Great Gatsby: A Study. New York: Scribner's, 1962.

Mellard, James M. "Counterpoint as Technique in The Great Gatsby." English Journal 50 (October 1966): 853-59.

Piper, Henry Dan. "The Untrimmed Christmas Tree: The Religious Background of The Great Gatsby." The Great Gatsby: A Study. Ed. Frederick J. Hoffman. New York: Scribner's, 1962. 321-34.

Deborah Wilhelm
Professor Noteboom
American Literature
5 May 20--

Dreiser's <u>An American Tragedy</u>:
The Protagonist As Victim

Dreams of success have long occupied the hearts
and minds of Americans. It is assumed that every
individual is entitled to rise as high in the social
order as his aspirations will allow. But the American Dream does not always have a happy ending.
Theodore Dreiser, in his classic novel <u>An American
Tragedy</u>, depicts this dark side of the American
Dream as he portrays Clyde Griffiths' journey from
poverty-stricken childhood to the brink of success
and finally to his death in the electric chair.
As critic Donald Pizer observes, "The tragedy of
Clyde Griffiths, crudely put, is that of a seeker of
sex and beauty who is destroyed by weaknesses within
himself and his society as he attempts to fulfill
his quest" (24). Dreiser himself was intimately
acquainted with such a dream. At age sixteen he
escaped a life of incredible poverty by running away
to Chicago. As one biographer states, "'Burning with
desire,' he dreamed of 'the mansions that should
belong to [him]! [. . .] The beauties who should
note and receive [him]'" (Lydenberg 39). _Although
the novel is heavily biographical and autobiographi-
cal,_ Dreiser's primary motivation is not simply to
tell a story but to instruct the reader to choose
his dreams carefully, or like Clyde Griffiths, become a victim, not only of the materialistic society
in which one lives, but also a victim of one's own
desires.

Thesis Statement

Page one of the novel finds Clyde on the low-
est rung of the social ladder--a victim from birth.

Topic Sentence

The son of street preachers, he yearns to be a part of the glamorous world and to wear a "high hat, bow tie, white kid gloves and patent leather shoes. [. . .] And once he [. . .] was able to wear such clothes as these—well, then was he not well set upon the path that leads to all the blisses?" (Dreiser 29). When Clyde moves to Lycurgus to take a menial position in his uncle's collar factory, a move which he hopes will propel him into the world of the rich, it becomes painfully clear that despite his blood ties, he is still considered inferior to his New York relations. Dreiser writes that "he was merely being permitted to look into a world to which he did not belong; also, that because of his poverty it would be impossible to fit him into [that society]" (223). Throughout the work, Dreiser uses Lycurgus as a symbol of the "stratification between the rich and the poor," and he describes this division as "sharp as though cut by a knife or divided by a high wall" (249-250). However, not only are the classes separate in this New York town, but they are also kept that way through what critic John McAleer describes as an Emersonian self-reliance that had been perverted by predators (3) and what Donald Pizer calls the strong climbing to success on the backs of the weak (219). Born into the underprivileged class, Clyde is a victim of the prevailing social order and will so remain.

Topic Sentence

<u>Clyde is also at the mercy of the community's standard of morality</u>. Seen by the narrow-minded townspeople of Bridgeburg as a representative of the ruling class who had misused one of their own country girls (Roberta), he is condemned by public opinion even before the trial begins. The jury was "with but one exception, all religious, if not moral, and all convinced of Clyde's guilt before ever they sat down" (Dreiser 638-639). He is slaughtered for a sin which was no more serious than that of engaging in

"illicit sexual pleasure" (Grebstein 316). Further-more, Clyde himself is hindered by moral conscience, as evidenced by his treatment of and feeling for Roberta. He is intensely attracted to her, but once he has forced her to give up her virginity, he loses much of his desire for her and casts her aside as a fallen woman. It seems that Clyde is governed in his thinking, if not his actions, by the same moral framework as the country folk of Cataraqui County. By viewing her as somehow tainted, he shuts her out of his life and thus gives up the one woman with whom he could have shared a true, deep love.

Topic Sentence   <u>Having no well-developed philosophy of love</u>, <u>Clyde substitutes lust in its stead</u>. Like Dreiser, his creator, Clyde is driven by a blazing desire for sex and a fear of being sexually weak (Warren, <u>Homage</u> 105). Exceptionally handsome and well-dressed, Clyde easily attracts the opposite sex. Even Sondra, put off by his pennilessness, is "drawn to him because she senses in him an animal spontaneity" (McAleer 136). But, as the novel progresses, it becomes clear that Clyde's sexual desire is his bane: "His was a disposition easily and often intensely inflamed by the chemistry of sex and the formula of beauty. He could not easily withstand the appeal, let alone the call, of sex" (Dreiser 239). Thus, he gets Roberta pregnant just at the moment when Sondra begins to take a personal interest in him. Hooked on the horns of this dilemma, he finally chooses to do away with Roberta and, in so doing, pays the ultimate price.

Topic Sentence   <u>That Clyde could not find a more suitable means of release from this dilemma demonstrates his ineptness</u>. As the author himself argues, "The truth was that in this crisis he was as interesting an illustration of the enormous handicaps imposed by ignorance, youth, poverty and fear as one could have found" (Dreiser 384). Initially ignorant about the use of contraceptives, he later tries to secure a miscarriage drug for Roberta but doesn't know where to seek aid or what questions to ask once he does find a helpful druggist. Neither he nor Roberta can afford to pay for a doctor-performed abortion. A strong case can be made for Clyde's extreme selfishness in his treatment of Roberta, but many critics also find a current of sentimentality and tenderness in his responses. John McAleer states that it is because Clyde pities Roberta that he sleeps with her despite his waning interest (135-136). Although Warren prefers to call this "covert self-pity," this act of charity results in her pregnancy. Because Clyde lacks the "negative virtue of cruelty," he is unable to simply break off his relationship with Roberta and later to fully plan and execute her murder (Hussman 132). It is, in fact, this push-pull between what his conscience directs and his deepest desires demand that causes his inability to act during the most critical moments in his life (Pizer 243). His lack of action after the car accident in Kansas City, his inability to flee in the face of certain apprehension by Mason's sheriffs, and even his indecision as to his own guilt as he is being strapped into the electric chair all confirm this "palsy of the will--of courage" (Dreiser 491).

Topic Sentence   Although Clyde's own temperament helps ensnare him in his lethal predicament, it is his single vision of Sondra as the embodiment of the fulfillment of his every desire that finally seals his fate. More than just a beautiful debutante or a ticket to the beautiful life, she is a fusion of all his material and spiritual desires. He worships her, this "goddess in her shrine of gilt and tinsel" (Dreiser 314). Pizer asserts that Clyde has rejected traditional religion for a "different kind of heaven to which he pledges his soul" (238). So enamored of her is he, and so sacred seems she, that even his usual sexual desire is tempered, and he treats her not as a fully-fleshed human, but as a "perfect object." The things that surround her become a kind of iconography, and Twelfth Lake becomes a heaven on earth where this saint and her devotee carry out the rituals of dancing, swimming, and boating (Pizer 253). In pursuing Sondra and his illusive dream, Clyde forfeits a life of contentment with Roberta; in blindly following Sondra's shining star, he sacrifices Roberta's life as well as his own.

Dreiser, through Jephson, philosophizes during the trial: it was "a case of being bewitched, my poor boy--by beauty, love, wealth, by things that we sometimes think we want very, very much, and cannot ever have" (681). With this simple statement, Dreiser sums up the message of An American Tragedy. But the novel is so much more than just a bitter criticism of the American Dream. Warren maintains that Dreiser grasped the essence of American urban society more strongly than any other writer. He contends that man is "not merely set against the machine of society or the universe; he is himself a machine, and is set against the machine that is himself" (Homage 130). For Clyde, battered by society, limited by his temperament, and driven by his desires, the American Dream turns into a nightmare. How ironic, then, that Dreiser, in repudiating the American Dream, finally had the Dream come true for him.

Restatement of Thesis

Works Cited

Dreiser, Theodore. <u>An American Tragedy</u>. 1925. Afterword by
    Irving Howe. Scarborough, ON: NAL, 1981.

Grebstein, Sheldon. "<u>An American Tragedy</u>: Theme and Structure."
    In <u>Critical Essays on Theodore Dreiser</u>. Ed. Donald Pizer.
    Boston: Hall, 1981.

Hussman, Lawrence. <u>Dreiser and His Fiction: A Twentieth-Century
    Quest</u>. Philadelphia: U of Pennsylvania P, 1983.

Lydenberg, John, ed. <u>Dreiser: A Collection of Critical Essays</u>.
    Englewood Cliffs: Prentice, 1971.

McAleer, John. <u>Theodore Dreiser: An Introduction and Interpreta-
    tion</u>. New York: Holt, 1968.

Pizer, Donald. <u>The Novels of Theodore Dreiser: A Critical
    Study</u>. Minneapolis: U of Minnesota P, 1976.

Warren, Robert. "An American Tragedy." In <u>Dreiser: A Collection
    of Critical Essays</u>. Ed. John Lydenberg. Englewood Cliffs:
    Prentice, 1971.

---. <u>Homage to Theodore Dreiser: On the Centennial of His
    Birth</u>. New York: Random, 1971.

Jennifer L. Gadd
Professor Noteboom
Introduction to Fiction
1 November, 20--

"God Bless Us, Every One!":
Dickens' "A Christmas Carol" as Social Gospel

When Charles Dickens' "A Christmas Carol" was
published shortly before Christmas in 1843, there
followed in London a tremendous outpouring of sea-
sonal goodwill. Thackeray referred to the story as
"a national benefit," and another contemporary con-
gratulated Dickens on having "fostered more kindly
feeling and prompted more positive acts of benefi-
cence, than can be traced to all the pulpits and
confessionals in Christendom" (McKenzie 123). Such
was the sentiment in 1843, that Dickens' charming
tale of personal transformation inspired individual
acts of generosity. By 1870, when Charles Dickens
gave his last public reading of the "Carol," however, the Victorian landscape was changing. In reaction to the violent abuses of power committed by the
wealthy entrepreneurs of a burgeoning Industrial
Age, who justified their lack of decency and compassion with the questionable theories of Social
Darwinism, the latter half of the nineteenth century

Thesis Statement gave rise to an infant labor movement. The reform
sought by workers was undergirded theologically by
what became termed "social gospel." It can be shown
that Dickens' "A Christmas Carol" can be interpreted
in light of this "social gospel."

Topic Sentence Dickens was by no means insensitive to the
plight of the poor and downtrodden of society. He
was born on February 7, 1812, in Portsea, England.
His parents were spoiled and irresponsible, regularly attempting to live beyond their means. The

result was a continual financial problem, for which
the young Dickens often found himself responsible.
His parents sent him to work at a blacking factory,
wrapping and labeling pots twelve hours a day.
Shortly thereafter, his father was sent to
Marshalsea Debtors Prison, leaving twelve-year-old
Charles to support the family. The pretentiousness
of his parents, their willingness to let a child pay
their debts, and the shame and humiliation he was
forced to bear on their behalf made Dickens a cham-
pion of the poor and neglected, as one discovers
reading his works. The wounds of his sorry childhood
were deep and permanent (MacKenzie 6-16). The
MacKenzies write, "It had forged an indissoluble
bond of sympathy, even of identity, with the home-
less, the friendless, the orphans, the hungry, the
uneducated, and even the prisoners of London's
lower depths" (17).

Topic Sentence

The "social gospel" of the late 19th Century
was, as stated, a reaction to the abuses of Social
Darwinism. With the convenient excuse of "survival
of the fittest," wealthy businessmen and entrepreneurs assured themselves a cheap labor source and
maximum profits. Indeed, critic Eugene Black states,
"Labor was a commodity, viewed, treated, and responding as such. [. . .] [The] work force was a
ledger item, like money, raw cotton, or coal" (12).
Ebenezer Scrooge represents the prevailing attitude
of business in Victorian England. If the reform
movement was acclaiming a "social gospel," then
Scrooge was acclaiming a "social law." When solici-
tors for charity ask him for a Christmas donation,
he inquires whether the prisons, Union workhouses,
the Treadmill, and the Poor Law were not still in
effect. Upon hearing that they were, Scrooge replies, "'I'm very glad to hear it'" (Dickens 19). As
for his contribution above and beyond the letter of
the law, Scrooge asks to be put down for "'nothing'"

(Dickens 20). As an employer, Scrooge begrudges his clerk his Christmas holiday:

> 'You'll want all day tomorrow, I suppose?' said Scrooge.
>
> 'If quite convenient, sir.'
>
> 'It's not convenient,' said Scrooge, 'and it's not fair. If I was to stop half-a-crown for it, you'd think yourself ill-used, I'll be bound?'
>
> The clerk smiled faintly.
>
> 'And yet,' said Scrooge, 'you don't think me ill-used, when I pay a day's wages for no work.'
>
> The clerk observed that it was only once a year.
>
> 'A poor excuse for picking a man's pocket every twenty-fifth of December!' (Dickens 23-24)

It was in response to such dehumanizing working and societal conditions that reformers such as Robert Owen propounded theories based on a more benevolent paternalism.

Topic Sentence <u>Owen believed that circumstances, rather than nature, were the true determining factors in the formation of human character</u>. In order to improve society in any meaningful way, the quality of the lives of individual people must be improved. Owen further believed that since an out-of-control Industrialism was responsible for much of the social disharmony of his time, an effective solution to society's ills would naturally require cooperation by all segments of that society. To Owen, the end result of this cooperation would be a just community (Paul 735-736). Owen tested his theories on a small scale in rural areas and then joined the factory reform movement to exercise benevolent paternalism on a wider scale (Glen 564-565). From a theological standpoint, the central doctrine of Victorian "social gospel" is its belief that the kingdom of God could and would be realized on earth (Davis 81). Social gospel proponents saw their work as building this emerging Christian society.

Topic Sentence

The cornerstone of this sought-after society is the paternal figure. In "A Christmas Carol," Bob Cratchit is the model father. The fact that Bob is present at all is a departure, and a vital one, from the commonplace separation of families in the Industrial Age. In his paternal benevolence, Bob imparts the values of the social gospel to his family. He chides his family for speaking ill of Scrooge on Christmas, thereby modeling forgiveness. In an act of caretaking and sharing, Bob finds his son Peter a job and loans him his own shirt. Towards his invalid son Tiny Tim, Bob is solicitous and gentle. The entire Cratchit family is representative of a stage of human development beyond Scrooge (Davis 82). They have found a way, despite hardship, to transcend the competitive ethic of laissez-faire capitalism to create a higher ethic of family and community, based on love, self-sacrifice, and compassion. That the Cratchits commemorate the holiday season and enjoy each other's companionship in spite of their great poverty exemplifies model behavior. Each family member, from youngest to oldest, shares in the Christmas dinner preparations. The richness of this meal is an obvious comparison to their standard fare. The crowning glory of their feast is the dessert, the plum pudding:

> 'Oh, a wonderful pudding!' Bob Cratchit said, and calmly too, that he regarded it as the greatest success achieved by Mrs. Cratchit since their marriage. Mrs. Cratchit said that now the weight was

off her mind, she would confess she had
had her doubts about the quantity of
flour. Everybody had something to say
about it, but nobody said or thought it
was at all a small pudding for a large
family. It would have been flat heresy to
do so. Any Cratchit would have blushed
to hint at such a thing. (Dickens 70)

The family unit, led by a dominant and loving father
who models and imparts valued virtues, was, for the
proponents of the social gospel, the model of the
Christian kingdom (Davis 81). What Bob was to the
Cratchit family, Ebenezer Scrooge and his wealthy
colleagues in business and industry were to be to
society.

Topic Sentence   Dickens' themes of gentleness and generosity
being human virtues are part and parcel of the
tenets of the social gospel. To be benevolently
paternalistic, wealthy businesspeople and industrialists would have to exhibit gentleness and
generosity, not only to their employees, but to
society-at-large, recognizing each person's inherent
value and status as a human being. In "A Christmas
Carol," it is Scrooge's nephew, Fred, who attempts
to explain to his uncle this principle, using the
Christmas season to highlight a sentiment which
should, of course, be felt and practiced year-round:

'But I am sure I have always thought of
Christmas-time, when it has come round--
apart from the veneration due to its
sacred name and origin, if anything belonging to it can be apart from that--
as a good time; a kind, forgiving, charitable, pleasant time; the only time I
know of, in the long calendar of the year,
when men and women seem by one consent to
open their shut-up hearts freely, and to

think of people below them as if they really were fellow-passengers to the grave, and not another race of creatures bound on other journeys.' (Dickens 17)

The themes of kindness and charity are favorite ones for Dickens, who himself worked in a rat-infested factory as a child. Critic Charles McKenzie writes, "Harshness and injustice to the unfortunate poor always stimulated him to anger" (148). Religion, for Dickens, was only as good as the fruits it produced. He was more interested in actions of mercy and charity than in words of piety. (Dickens reserved his most vicious, scathing characterizations for religious hypocrites: Mr. and Miss Murdstone, Bumble, Pecksniff, Miss Barbary, Mrs. Gargery, and Pumblechook are only a few.) In terms of his social gospel, Dickens was also little interested in heavenly rewards for good works. It was the effects of kindly acts of benevolence and charity on this <u>earthly</u> kingdom that were paramount.

Topic Sentence

<u>The turning point in "A Christmas Carol," of course, is Scrooge's transformation from "covetous old sinner"</u> (Dickens 14) <u>to benevolent paternalist.</u> He can only take on this new role, however, after he begins to see himself in their plight, not only as a <u>cause</u> of their plight, but as sharers in a common humanity (Hardy 41-45). For this reason, the Ghost of Christmas Past shows Scrooge the abused and abandoned little boy he was, and in truth, still is (Hardy 44-46). Once he allows himself to feel compassion for himself, he can feel it for others. When the Ghost of Christmas Present shows him Ignorance and Want, the degraded and dehumanized children of humanity, he is mortified at their plight and wonders if there is no one to care for them. The Ghost throws Scrooge's own words back in his face: "'Are there no prisons? Are there no workhouses?'" (Dickens

84). Scrooge's conversion spurs him to action. According to critic Barbara Hardy, "The typical conversion of the great Victorian novel is not a religious conversion, but a turning from self-regard to love and social responsibility" (39). The transformed Scrooge becomes a symbol of the social gospel's ideal businessperson by becoming a surrogate father to Tiny Tim and benefactor to the whole Cratchit family. Scrooge becomes representative of the ideal employer by taking a paternal interest in his employee's "affairs." "In the process," writes one critic, "[Scrooge] restores fatherhood to the secular city where God has died, and the father has disappeared. His good works will become the healing spring to transform the city into the kingdom of God on earth" (Davis 87).

Topic Sentence

Although Charles Dickens intended for the theme of personal transformation to be a part of the "Carol's" Christmas message, the "social gospel" theme of benevolent parternalism transforming society must have been a satisfying interpretation for him as well, given his childhood experiences and keenly developed sense of justice. His literary work in the mid-nineteenth century was, in a sense, a precursor of the social gospel movement of later in that century, and Dickens was a supporter of its tenets and ideals. Critic Charles McKenzie states, "The religion he admired was the religion whose faith was manifested by its works of mercy and charity" (150). In "A Christmas Carol," Bob Cratchit and his family are the ideal fundamental unit of the Victorian era. Bob, as a dominant and loving father, imparts the values of kindness and charitable generosity to his family. These same values, according to proponents of the social gospel, should be exhibited by wealthy businesspeople and industrialists in their role as benevolent paternalists. The transformed Scrooge is the model of this role.

Restatement
of Thesis

Thus Dickens' "A Christmas Carol" can be interpreted in light of the "social gospel" of the later
19th century. Dickens felt strongly enough about the
importance of social reform to warn that a "govern-
ing class that does debar the populace from the
means of humanization . . . makes conditions ripe
for an outbreak of mad and savage disturbances"
(Davis 200). His words were to prove prophetic in
the labor movements of the early 20th century.
"A Christmas Carol" reveals Dickens' desire for a
humanizing influence on an increasingly industrial
society and his vision of a world in which everyone,
not just Tiny Tim, would declare, "God Bless Us,
Every One!"

Works Cited

Black, Eugene C. <u>Victorian Culture and Society</u>. New York:
    Walker, 1974.

Davis, Paul. <u>The Lives and Times of Ebenezer Scrooge</u>. New
    Haven: Yale UP, 1990.

Dickens, Charles. <u>Christmas Stories</u>. New York: World, 1946.

Glen, Robert. "Owenite Socialism." <u>Victorian Britain: An
    Encyclopedia</u>. 1988 ed.

Hardy, Barbara. "The Change of Heart in Dickens' Novels." In
    <u>Dickens: A Collection of Critical Essays</u>. Ed. Martin
    Price. Englewood Cliffs: Prentice, 1969.

MacKenzie, Norman and Jeanne. <u>Dickens: A Life</u>. New York: Oxford
    UP, 1979.

McKenzie, Charles H. <u>The Religious Sentiments of Charles
    Dickens</u>. New York: Haskell, 1973.

Paul, Donna Rice. "Socialism." <u>Victorian Britain: An
    Encyclopedia</u>. 1988 ed.

The following essay incorporating research is reprinted from the literary journal *Studies in Short Fiction* Spring 1988: 155–157. It is used by permission of the author and of *Studies in Short Fiction.*

Who Is Ellie? Oates' "Where Are You Going, Where Have You Been?"

Understandably enough, most of the attention generated by Joyce Carol Oates' "Where Are You Going, Where Have You Been?" *(Epoch,* Fall, 1966; collected, *The Wheel of Love,* 1970), has focused on the characters of 15-year-old Connie and her seducer/killer, Arnold Friend. Friend in particular has inspired a series of essays which delineate his resemblance to the devil,[1] and, curiously enough, Tom Quirk's study of Friend's real-life prototype, Charles Howard Schmid of Tucson, has enhanced rather than qualified the earlier discussions of Friend's allegorical ramifications.[2] Virtually no attention, however, has been paid to Friend's laconic accomplice, Ellie Oscar, a character whose appearance, personality, and behavior suggest he is the incarnation of the darker side of the admitted idol of Friend's prototype: Elvis Presley.

Consider Ellie's appearance. The first things Connie notices about him are the lock of hair "that fell onto his forehead" and his "sideburns" (p. 40), both of which call to mind Presley, whose trademark appearance was much imitated by his "cool" male admirers in the late 1950s and early 1960s. Equally significant is Ellie's attire: "His shirt collar was turned up all around and the very tips of the collar pointed out past his chin"; further, his shirt was "unbuttoned halfway to show his chest" (p. 45)—elements which even years after Presley's death in 1977 are still immediately associated with "the King." Other elements are also reminiscent of Presley. Ellie's omnipresent radio—without which he "grimaced, as if . . . the air was too much for him" (p. 50)—reminds us that the phenomena of Presley and the transistor radio were not only simultaneous but also symbiotic: each owed its popularity to the other, and both helped to usher in the hollow, illusory netherworld of adolescence so brilliantly limned in "Where Are You Going?" Likewise, the equally omnipresent sunglasses, that "told nothing about what [Ellie] was thinking" (p. 45), suggest not only Elvis's cool persona, but also the increasingly secretive, mysterious life he was leading at Graceland, his Memphis mansion, by the mid-1960s.

Presley was no killer, but certain aspects of his personality are clearly evident in the murderous Ellie. Chief among them is an apparent ambivalence in sexual identity and motivation. The points of Ellie's shirt look "as if they were protecting him" (p. 45); that unbuttoned shirt reveals not intimidating pectorals, but a "pale, bluish chest" (p. 45); and those sideburns give Ellie "a fierce, embarrassed

---

[1] Joyce M. Wegs, " 'Don't You Know Who I Am?': The Grotesque in Oates's 'Where Are You Going, Where Have you Been?' " *Journal of Narrative Technique,* 5 (January 1975), 66–72; Marie Mitchell Olesen Urbanski, "Existential Allegory: Joyce Carol Oates's 'Where Are You Going, Where Have You Been?' " *Studies in Short Fiction,* 15 (Spring 1978), 200–03; Joan D. Winslow, "The Stranger Within: Two Stories by Oates and Hawthorne." *Studies in Short Fiction,* 17 (Summer 1980) 263–68.

[2] Tom Quirk, "A Source for 'Where Are You Going, Where Have You Been?' " *Studies in Short Fiction,* 18 (Fall 1981) 413–19.

look" (p. 40). The ambivalence evident in Ellie—vulnerable and aggressive, "fierce" and "embarrassed"—was in many ways the key to Presley's own immense attraction. As *Newsweek* columnist Jack Kroll noted at the time of Presley's death, a close observer could perceive "an almost androgynous softness and passivity in his punk-hood persona. Elvis and his revolution were vulnerability disguised as bravado."[3] The man who sang saccharine teen love songs such as "Teddy Bear" (1957) and "Good Luck Charm" (1961) also sang the hard-driving "[You're the] Devil in Disguise" (1963) and "Hard-Headed Woman" (1958); in his personal life, Presley collected Teddy bears—and guns. This bizarre combination of a child-like, almost effeminate innocence, plus an insistently adult, male aggressiveness is quite evident in Ellie, whose very name (clearly a sweet-sounding, juvenile, feminine diminutive of "Elvis") neatly disguises—at least for the nonce—his role as an accomplice in rape and murder. It is not for nothing that the demonic Arnold—posing as Connie's "Friend"—would have as his accomplice a man with the chillingly ambivalent "face of a forty-year-old baby" (p. 46). Ellie *seems* passive: he never gets out of the golden car, and he says very little; but that seeming passivity is undermined by the facts that there is no real need for him to help Arnold (the control over Connie is absolute) and that his only words are an ominous suggestion presented as a helpful offer: "'You want that telephone pulled out?'" (p. 50). As with Elvis, Ellie projects an ambivalent sexual/motivational message which leaves his intended victim—a sexually mature but inexperienced adolescent girl—unsure of whether to perceive him as innocuous or sinister, and that unsureness renders her far more vulnerable than if he seemed only threatening.

And that is Oates's point. As Marie Mitchell Olesen Urbanski suggests, "the recurring music. . ., while ostensibly innocuous realistic detail, is [,] in fact, the vehicle of Connie's seduction [;] and because of its intangibility, not immediately recognizable as such."[4] More to the point, Tom Quirk argues that the dedication of "Where Are You Going?" to Bob Dylan

> is honorific because the history and effect of Bob Dylan's music had been to draw youth away from the romantic promises and frantic strains of a brand of music sung by Buddy Holly, Chuck Berry, Elvis Presley and others. It was Bob Dylan, after all, who told us that the "times they are a changin'," and one of Oates's aims in her short story is to show that they have already changed. It is the gyrating, hip-grinding music of people like Elvis Presley, whom Schmid identified as his "idol," which emanates from Ellie's transistor radio, the "hard, fast, shrieking" songs played by the disc jockey "Bobby King" rather than the cryptic, atonal folk music of Bob Dylan.[5]

---

[3] Jack Kroll, "The Heartbreak Kid" *Newsweek*, August 29, 1977, p. 49.

[4] Urbanski, 201.

[5] Quirk, 417–18. The same blend of vulnerability and aggressiveness which is evident in Ellie and Elvis may be seen in the disc jockey, "Bobby King," whom both Connie and Arnold admire, and whose voice Arnold acquires (46). The name "Bobby" suggests a non-threatening, little-boy persona, while "King" (perhaps another veiled reference to Presley) suggests the enormous power wielded by males associated with rock music.

And what more forceful way to suggest the dangerous illusions and vacuousness generated by "the romantic promises and frantic strains of a brand of music sung by . . . Elvis Presley" than to have an Elvis-figure participate in the rape and murder of an innocent 15-year-old girl?

Alice Hall Petry
Rhode Island School of Design

JUST ONE MORE THING

Do you remember the excitement of getting your first library card? Most of us have happy memories of going to the library and bringing home those wonderful books to read and share. If you can recapture those feelings and transfer them to your research assignment, you'll find that it isn't a major hurdle designed to trip you up. It's an opportunity to become an expert, someone Webster defines as "a person with a high degree of skill in or knowledge of a certain subject." Reading widely—but selectively—about your specific subject can help you think in new ways about your topic and give you insights that you can share with other scholars. If you think of this assignment as digging for gold, you'll probably discover a wealth of ideas.

❧ Literary Research Paper Plan Sheet ❧

Author: _____ Title: _____

Reference(s) to past research: page _____ from _____

page _____ from _____

Thesis: _____

_____

_____

_____

_____

Topic sentence: _____

_____

_____

_____

Supporting quote: page _____ from _____

Supporting quote: page _____ from _____

Supporting quote: page _____ from _____

Topic sentence: _____

_____

_____

_____

Supporting quote: page _____ from _____

Supporting quote: page _____ from _____

Supporting quote: page _____ from _____

Topic sentence: _____

_____

_____

_____

    Supporting quote: page _____ from _____

    Supporting quote: page _____ from _____

    Supporting quote: page _____ from _____

Topic sentence: _____

_____

_____

_____

    Supporting quote: page _____ from _____

    Supporting quote: page _____ from _____

    Supporting quote: page _____ from _____

Topic sentence: _____

_____

_____

_____

    Supporting quote: page _____ from _____

    Supporting quote: page _____ from _____

    Supporting quote: page _____ from _____

Topic sentence: _____

_____

_____

_____

    Supporting quote: page _____ from _____

    Supporting quote: page _____ from _____

    Supporting quote: page _____ from _____

Topic sentence: _____

_____

_____

       Supporting quote: page _____ from _____

       Supporting quote: page _____ from _____

       Supporting quote: page _____ from _____

Topic sentence: _____

_____

_____

       Supporting quote: page _____ from _____

       Supporting quote: page _____ from _____

       Supporting quote: page _____ from _____

Topic sentence: _____

_____

_____

       Supporting quote: page _____ from _____

       Supporting quote: page _____ from _____

       Supporting quote: page _____ from _____

Concluding points: _____

_____

_____

_____

       Supporting quote: page _____ from _____

❧ Peer/Self-Evaluation of a Literary Research Paper ❧

> **Directions:** Make specific suggestions about each part of the essay, pointing out particular areas that the writer could improve. Keep in mind the qualities of good writing: unity, organization, development, clarity, and coherence.

I. Introduction

Is the lead relevant and interesting?

Are the author's full name and the title of the work correctly spelled and punctuated?

Does the brief summary of the work lead into the research topic that will be analyzed in the essay?

Are previous research studies cited that relate to the research topic?

Does the thesis clearly state the main points that will be discussed in the body paragraphs?

II. Body Paragraphs

Do the topic sentences contain key words from the thesis to connect the body paragraphs to the thesis points?

Are the supporting quotations from the primary source(s) properly introduced, relevant, and textnoted?

Are the quotations, paraphrases, and summaries from the secondary sources properly introduced, relevant, and textnoted?

Are the analysis sections adequately developed?

Are the body paragraphs unified and coherent?

III. Conclusion

Is a signal word included somewhere in the paragraph?

Are the thesis and its supporting points rephrased?

Is the significance of the thesis clear to the reader?

Are the speed change and the clincher effective?

Are the Works Cited entries correctly formatted?

IV. Expression

Are all the ideas expressed in complete sentences?

Are the sentences clear and correctly punctuated?

Are there any problems with subject-verb or pronoun-antecedent agreement?

Are all the words correctly spelled?

V. Overall Evaluation

Most effective part of the essay:

Least effective part of the essay:

List three specific actions which could be taken by the writer to improve this and future papers:

1.

2.

3.

Evaluator's name: _____ Date: _____

Taking Essay Examinations in Literature

Overview

Many instructors give essay examinations in literature classes to determine if learning has taken place because essay tests require students to think critically about a literary work and to shape and form their ideas by expressing them in writing. Mastering certain skills will enable you to do well when you face this type of writing about literature.

Taking Essay Examinations: Step by Step

Essay examinations are designed to test your understanding of a literary work. Writing is thinking, and when you formulate your response, you are making the material your own by verbalizing what you already know and by discovering new insights as you develop your ideas.

Effective preparation begins long before the exam itself. Success is based on a careful reading and re-reading of the assigned material, attendance at all lectures and seminars, detailed note taking, adequate study time, the development of possible questions and responses, and analysis of the test questions.

Reading the Material

In Chapter One, you will find a detailed discussion of how to read literature. The recommendations include a quick general reading and then a more specific one to note important details. If you complete the course readings in this way as they are assigned, you will be able to understand and participate in your instructor's discussion and analysis of the works in class, for understanding is essential to the essay writing process. Rereading and rethinking the works right before test time will help you recall relevant points and even key words and phrases that you can include in your essay response.

Attending Class

Class attendance is another important factor in doing well on tests. Being there helps you pick up clues about what your instructor thinks is important in a particular piece of literature. While all teachers expect more than a repetition of their ideas in your essay, a brief reference to a point they have emphasized will let them know that you heard and understood their lectures. Discussion sections where there is an exchange of ideas with your instructor and other students can give you additional insights that you may be able to incorporate into your essay answers.

Taking Notes

While most students attend lecture/discussion classes regularly, many believe that they will remember the ideas raised in class, so they fail to take notes, and if they do, they tend to be general and brief. I'm sure you have heard the statistics about memory retention: one typically forgets 30% of what was heard within the first hour, 50% within six days, and 80% within thirty days.[1] Obviously, taking good notes is a must.

Once you become familiar with your instructor's teaching style, you should recognize his or her method of emphasizing certain points. It may be tone, volume, repetition, extended development, or even the words "Write this down!" An effective way to do that is to paraphrase your instructor's ideas; that way you are "processing" them by expressing them in your own words. With practice, you can learn to write quickly and even develop your own shorthand to pick up more speed.

Arranging Adequate Study Time

Most instructors announce test dates early enough to allow students adequate study time. Once the date has been set, you should begin the studying/reviewing process. Waiting until the day or night before the test can be dangerous because unexpected events like overtime at work or unannounced company at home can spoil your plans. A few hours each day spread over a week's time are more effective than an eight-hour cramming session.

You might also consider studying with a classmate, for the old saying "Two heads are better than one" works well with test preparation. Studying with another member of the class gives you the chance to review class notes together and to talk about and quiz each other on the works you have studied. If you carry out these activities routinely throughout the course, your understanding of the material and your ability to do well on tests will increase greatly.

Developing Possible Test Questions and Responses

When you are rereading the assigned material and your class notes, pay special attention to the points that your instructor stressed in lectures and discussions. Has he or she emphasized recurrent themes or ideas, the historical background of works, the influence of writers on others, differences in style, or certain characters, settings, or symbols in specific works? When you discover a point of emphasis, you can formulate questions that would elicit that information. For example, if you had extensive notes on the differences between Restoration and Romantic poetry, you could construct the following questions:

Compare and/or contrast the qualities of Restoration and Romantic poetry.

and

Discuss the causes of the differences in Restoration and Romantic Poetry.

By turning the material in your notes into possible questions or by working with study questions that your instructor distributes before the test, you can begin to formulate possible essay responses. If your study time allows, you should write out a complete answer, including as many details from the work as possible to support your response. If your time is limited, you can at least write out a brief outline of your answer so you can decide on the main points you would want to cover. By studying in this question-answer way, you are learning how to organize, develop, and express your ideas, and this type of active preparation will help you gain confidence and avoid test anxiety that can lead to panic and poor grades.

---

[1] *Cyclopedia of Education*, ed. Paul Monroe, Ph.D. (New York: Macmillan, 1968) 192.

Analyzing the Test Questions

When you receive the test, be sure to read the instructions carefully. They contain details about how many questions you must answer, the point value assigned to each, and the required length. All of these factors are affected by the amount of time allowed for the test. With that point in mind, choose the questions (if you have a choice) that you feel best prepared to answer. If point values vary, plan to start with the questions carrying the most number of points. Before beginning to write, it's a good idea to reread the directions and the questions to be certain that you haven't missed essential information.

As you are rechecking the questions, circle or underline the key words and the major points you have to cover. Keep in mind that different key words require certain types of development because they require you to think in specific ways about your topic. Be sure that you understand the key term and that your answer reflects it.

Here are some of the most common terms used in questions on essay exams:

analyze:	break an idea or concept down into its component parts.
compare:	point out the likenesses shared by the topics.
contrast:	point out the differences between the topics.
define:	explain the meaning of the term or concept.
demonstrate:	explain or illustrate with the use of details and examples.
describe:	tell what something is like through the use of examples and specific details.
discuss:	state your ideas in detail on the given topic.
explain:	state details and examples to clarify the topic.
examine:	describe in detail the subject, situation, idea, or concept.
illustrate:	use examples to clarify the term, idea, or concept.
justify:	demonstrate that the situation, idea, or concept is right or valid.
list:	enumerate points, ideas, or concepts related to the topic.
prove:	cite evidence (facts, details) to support the general statement.
show:	use examples to illustrate the topic.
trace:	show how a subject, concept, or situation develops or changes over time.

Also, be sure to note the number of points or parts in the question and to respond to each one. A typical question might read like this: Explain Wordsworth's view of the commonplace and demonstrate how it is reflected in two of his poems. Obviously this question calls for a two-part answer that asks you first to explain a theory and then to show how it appears in two specific works. You will want to follow the order of the points and to separate the points into paragraphs.

After you have done your analysis of the questions, you are ready to begin your planning and essay writing.

Writing Your Response

As always, before you start to write, you should make a brief outline of the points you plan to include in your answer. Writing them out will give you a chance to put them in the best possible order for better continuity and coherence. Just be sure that you are directly answering the question that is asked.

Beginning with a thesis statement or topic sentence is essential for organization and clarity. This sentence should be clearly related to the question; in fact, most questions can be turned into effective opening sentences. For example, the question, compare and contrast the character of the Duke in Browning's "My Last Duchess" with the monk in his poem "Soliloquy of the Spanish Cloister," can be reworded as The Duke in "My Last Duchess" and the monk in "Soliloquy of the Spanish Cloister" are similar in their immense jealousy and pride, but they differ in the ways they express these qualities. This opening sentence actually answers the question and lets the reader know what points you plan to develop. It will also help you keep on track as you provide supporting details.

To fully develop your answer, you need to supply specifics from the work itself. In responding to the question on the Duke and the monk, you would want to mention the Duke's jealousy of those the Duchess smiled at, such as the painter of her portrait and the white mule she rode on the balcony. In discussing his pride, you would surely mention his feelings about his name and his refusal to stoop for anyone. When comparing the monk's jealousy of Brother Lawrence, you would mention his feelings about Lawrence's garden and his personalized goblet. The monk's pride is seen in his belief that he is superior to Brother Lawrence because of the manner in which he places his knife and fork in the shape of a cross and drinks his orange juice in three sips to honor the Trinity. These superficial acts show the monk's superficial spirituality and emphasize the sinfulness of his pride.

The second part of the response—the contrast between the Duke and the monk—would focus on how these men express these character flaws. Here you would want to mention how the Duke's jealousy and pride lead him to order the Duchess's death and how they shape his dealings with the Count's emissary. The duke is really telling him what behavior he expects from his next Duchess. He is open about his deeds and desires because of his power and position. In contrast, because the monk is supposed to be a religious man, he must be sly and secretive in the expression of his jealousy and pride; therefore, he sneaks around cutting Brother Lawrence's lillies and planning to tempt him with heretical texts from the Bible or his own corrupt novel. Including these kinds of details and incidents in your response will reveal your knowledge of the works and your ability to support your generalization with specific evidence from the text.

Staying on the Subject

Some students believe that the number of words is important to their grade. However, instructors want quality—not quantity—so don't pad your answers with irrelevant material. If you get off the point, you will waste valuable test time and make your instructor think that you are trying to bluff your way through the course. Remember that unity and coherence are important qualities in any piece of writing.

Paragraphing Your Response

In organizing your answer, be sure to paragraph to make your discussion easier to follow. For example, in your essay on the Duke and the monk, you could put all of your points about the Duke in one paragraph and your points about the monk in another (subject-by-subject organization), or you could paragraph around the points of likeness and difference and discuss both characters in the same paragraph (point-by-point organization). In essays that do not call for comparison/contrast, put each major point or idea in a separate paragraph. You may want to skip several lines between paragraphs and between essays just in case you recall additional details to support your answer. Remember that paragraphing logically makes your essay easier to read and evaluate—qualities your instructor will surely appreciate.

Watching the Time

Whenever you take a test, you have to be time-conscious in order to complete all of the required test items. Try to allow a set amount of time per question so that the development of your essays does not vary drastically. If you should run short of time, at least make a brief outline of other points you would have covered so that your instructor will know what you would have said if time had been available. In that case, he or she might award a few extra points, and you surely want all the points you can get.

Revising and Proofreading

All good writers reread their work before putting it in the hands of the reader to make sure that their meaning is clear. In the rush of ideas in a test-taking situation, it is easy to omit words or punctuation marks and to make spelling or usage errors. Any of these problems could make your ideas difficult to follow. If you can set aside five minutes at the end of the test to make required changes to improve correctness, clarity, and coherence, your instructor will see your revisions and appreciate your efforts to improve your response.

Analyzing the Results

When the test is returned, it is essential that you study your instructor's comments so you will learn how he or she evaluates essay examinations. Most instructors will explain why you lost points by listing things you should have covered, but if no explanation is given for your score, talk with your instructor about your grade and ask his or her advice about how to prepare for future tests. With the information you gain from your instructors, from this chapter, and from the experience of taking essay exams, you will quickly become a more confident and competent test taker.

Model Essay Answers to Test Questions

Here are some student-written responses to questions taken from essay examinations. Notice especially the opening and closing sentences and the amount of specific information included in each paragraph.

1. Contrast the American husband and the Italian innkeeper in Hemingway's "Cat in the Rain."

The differences in the American husband, George, and the Italian innkeeper are best illustrated in their differing attitudes toward the American wife.

The American husband seems uninterested in pleasing his wife. Her desire to help the cat crouched under the table in the rain is unimportant to him. He seems more interested in his reading than in helping her with the rescue. When she is unsuccessful and returns disappointed to the room, he does not share her disappointment but returns to his reading. As her unhappiness about the cat spills over into her unhappiness in general about her short hair and her lack of things of her own because of living in a hotel rather than a home, he is totally unsympathetic and cold as he tells her to "shut up" and read rather than talk to him. He is cold and uncaring about her needs and desires. The American husband is the person controlling their rootless existence, and he is totally unconcerned about his wife's lack of fulfillment.

The Italian innkeeper, on the other hand, is very anxious to please the American wife. He obviously respects her since he bows whenever she passes his office. The innkeeper's attention makes her feel special (something she doesn't feel from her husband), and when he realizes she is trying to help the cat caught in the rain, he thoughtfully sends the maid to keep her dry with an umbrella. This act makes the wife feel important because of his concern for her and her needs. When the innkeeper learns the attempted cat rescue has failed, his thoughtfulness comes through again when he sends the maid with a cat to her room to please her. He seems to understand her feminine need to nurture and protect the cat which illustrates her need for something to love.

Overall, the young, insensitive American husband fails to recognize the importance of little things in the life of his wife, something the older, sensitive Italian innkeeper values and appreciates.

Melanie Marren

2. Analyze Hawthorne's use of dark/light symbolism in "Young Goodman Brown."

Hawthorne's use of dark/light symbolism in "Young Goodman Brown" is very effective. Goodman starts his journey at sunset and says good-bye to his Faith. The sunset is symbolic of the last light of the day or the dying of the day, suggesting the dying of Goodman's faith. He continues down a dark, dreary, gloomy path into the forest where he meets the devil. The darkness here represents the evil Brown will face, and the devil is symbolic of Brown's dark side (alter ego).

Goodman's next encounter with light is when he looks up at the stars to the heavens. This last bit of light symbolizes his remaining bit of faith, but a black cloud sweeps by and covers the stars, symbolizing that his desperate attempts to fight off evil are not possible. The next light Goodman sees is a red light from the burning trees. This light flares up to cast light and then down to cast shadow. This struggle between the light and dark is symbolic of Goodman's inner struggle between good and evil. Finally when Goodman awakens in the early morning sun, the light symbolizes his new beginning or new realization that evil exists in all men. Thus the dark/light symbolism brings out Hawthorne's theme in the work.

Denise Gobeille

3. Discuss the narrator's loss of innocence in Joyce's "Araby."

In "Araby," the narrator's journey represents the archetype of loss of innocence and the gaining of knowledge. He is infatuated with Mangan's sister, and his actions are controlled by this. He watches her each morning, fantasizes about love, does poorly in school, and dreams about buying her a present at Araby, a bazaar. When his uncle is late and the narrator is forced to take the late train, his journey to experience has begun. He is alone in the deserted train to suggest that the journey from innocence to experience is one each individual makes alone. He also must enter the bazaar through a more expensive entrance, suggesting that one pays dearly for experience.

When the narrator finally enters the bazaar, he sees two men counting money; this represents materialism, and his fantasies about the romantic aspects of the fair begin to crumble. As he listens to the conversation of the young woman and her two admirers, he begins to see the phoniness in their relationship and probably realizes that his relationship with Mangan's sister is equally artificial. When the young woman treats him coldly, he feels foolish and embarrassed, and when the lights are turned off in the hall and he gazes into the darkness, his loss of innocence is complete; he has been initiated into the harshness of adult reality. The narrator's journey has taken him from his innocent views of love to the reality that he had been living in a world of illusion.

Denise Gobeille

4. Justify Hemingway's use of the African jungle as the setting for "The Short Happy Life of Francis Macomber."

The African jungle is an excellent choice of setting for Francis's change from a coward to brave man because the jungle is a total change from his usual setting and it introduces him to two role models from which to learn courage.

Francis, a wealthy American, has lived in a world where he could hide from his fear of the unknown, his fear of losing his wife, his money, or his life. His fears are interior until he faces the charging wounded lion in Africa, and that incident causes him to face the fact that fear rules his behavior. The lion is real, and that makes Francis's fear real.

The jungle setting also teaches Francis how to deal with his fear through the example of the wounded lion and Wilson, the white hunter. Even though the lion is wounded, it is determined to use its last ounce of strength to face the thing that threatens it. It faces death head on and even continues to crawl after half of its head is blown off by Wilson who stood firm in front of its charge while Francis ran in fear. Wilson is used to facing danger because the African jungle is his world. He is older, experienced, and he has mastered his fear of the biggest unknown—death. His example shows Francis that living in fear is not really living at all, and when he realizes that, he is able to stand firm and fire at the charging wounded buffalo.

Francis's moment of courage is like the lion's and Wilson's, for he will never again run from life's dangers or conflicts. In the African jungle, he has become a man.

Melanie Marren

5. Compare and contrast Frost's poems "Home Burial" and "West-running Brook."

The basic similarities between "Home Burial" and "West-running Brook" by Robert Frost are that they are two easy-to-read poems that deal with conversations between husbands and wives who are discussing their differences. One of Frost's favorite themes is the "principle of contraries," which he brings forth in both of these poems. The basic problem in "Home Burial" is that the husband and wife are dealing differently with the emotions they feel over the death of their child. He displays his grief through his actions; she displays hers through her emotions and attitude toward the death. They judge each other harshly, refusing to see or unable to realize that they are both grieving, though differently. They are contraries, and they are unable to realize it. However, "West-running Brook" answers this problem as the husband and wife in that poem realize that they are contraries and welcome the fact. They believe that their differences breathe life into their relationship as the boulder in the brook turns the water back onto itself, revitalizing the flow. Frost believes that contrariness is good and should be welcomed and embraced.

Marsha Horder

6. In Joyce Carol Oates' story "Where Are You Going, Where Have You Been?" what role does music play in Connie's life and in her relationship with Arnold Friend?

Music played an important role in Connie's life and daydreams, and Arnold's interest in the same music appealed to her. Whenever Connie went to the drive-in, the music in the background gave her pleasure and gratification. It made her feel good, and that was reflected in the look of joy on her face. Whenever she would daydream about boys, her fantasies were based on the way love was described in songs, and even in the background of her dreams, there was always the pounding beat of the rock music she enjoyed so much.

Connie's view of love is based on the illusions created by the song lyrics, so when Arnold arrives and is listening to the same rock station she is, she is attracted to him. She even thought that Arnold's voice sounded like the voice of the disc jockey Bobby King. When Arnold talked to Connie about going for a ride with him, he sounded like he was reciting the words to a song, and he even tapped his fists together in time to the music. Arnold personifies the type of lover that Connie has been dreaming about, and even after she realizes that he is older than he claims to be, she is still mesmerized by his clever approach which includes words taken from a song about a girl rushing into her boyfriend's arms. Arnold uses music to help seduce Connie, and as she leaves with him, he calls her his sweet blue-eyed girl which is probably a line from another love song because Connie has brown eyes.

Music, then, was the basis for Connie's fantasies of love, and through Arnold's manipulation, it becomes the basis for her seduction.

Jim Boyle

7. What social expectations of women does Marge Piercy attack in "Barbie Doll," "A Work of Artifice," and "What's That Smell in the Kitchen?"

In "Barbie Doll," Piercy attacks the social expectation that all women will have Barbie doll figures. She shows how difficult that is for women by describing the life of a young girl who does not fit the mold because of her big nose and fat legs. From her earliest years, this girl is trained for her role as wife and mother through the makeup and toys she is given, but when she is told by a classmate that she does not look like Barbie, her whole life is shattered. She overlooks her strong points and concentrates only on her flaws. When she snaps and mutilates her body, killing herself because she cannot measure up to society's expectations, the people at her wake say she looks beautiful because the undertaker has replaced her nose and her legs are not visible in the coffin. The emphasis that society puts on appearance for women is the true killer of this young woman.

In "A Work of Artifice," Piercy shows how the powerful forces of society and traditional views shape a woman's existence and how she is expected to conform without complaint. Piercy uses the metaphor of a bonsai tree which is shaped and pruned to keep it small, thus preventing it from reaching its natural height and greatness, to show how society keeps women from achieving their potential. The gardener, a representative of the male world, tries to convince the tree that it is naturally inferior and should be grateful that it is allowed to grow at all. When Piercy compares the tree more directly to women, she states that society begins early to keep women inferior by physically restraining their development as in China and by mentally undermining their potential by telling them they have less brainpower so they should expend all of their energy trying to be beautiful to please the men in their lives.

The social expectation that women are the cooks and men are the kings waiting to be served is attacked in the poem "What's That Smell in the Kitchen?" According to Piercy, the women in America are rebelling against their role as cook by burning the food that they should be serving with a smile to their hungry husbands. Because society expects women to be happy with this subservient role, they cannot openly complain, so they covertly declare war on their husbands and attack them where it hurts the most—in their stomachs. If the way to a man's heart is through his stomach, he should be getting the message that something is wrong. Women are tired of being tied to the kitchen, and they are taking their anger and frustration out on the food they serve. They have seen their lives turn into drudgery—the way gourmet dinners turn into unappetizing leftovers—and they are mad enough about it to begin fighting back.

And so in these poems, Piercy attacks the social expectations that women are supposed to look like dolls, are supposed to be happy even though they are not given the opportunity to reach their full potential, and are supposed to stay in the kitchen like a servant. Piercy's feminism is truly evident in her work.

Sue Peterson

8. Explain why *The Sun Also Rises* should not be seen as simply a textbook illustration of "lost generationism" in the twenties. Discuss specific characters to support your answer.

The Sun Also Rises cannot be seen simply as a book on the lost generation because all of the characters in the novel are not part of this lost generation. Characters such as Brett Ashely, Robert Cohn, and Mike Campbell are wastelanders. They are incapable of true emotions, and they move aimlessly through life. They don't appreciate the world around them.

However, other characters such as Jake Barnes, Bill Gorton, and Pedro Romero are not members of the lost generation. They are quite aware of what is going on around them, especially Jake Barnes. Even though Jake is physically impotent, he is in no way emotionally impotent. With such a physical handicap as his, it would have been easy to end it all; however, he took life head on and grew emotionally in other areas as a result of his injury. His love of nature is another example of his mature emotional side. Not everyone takes time to look around at the awesomeness of nature, but both Jake and Bill realize this awesomeness. Pedro Romero is another example of one who is not a wastelander. For a young man, he is very mature and sure of himself. A good example of his maturity is the way he behaves when Brett tells him to leave; he leaves quietly and pays the check. This is a total contrast to the way Cohn behaves when Brett leaves him; he acts like an over-emotional, immature child.

After looking at these characters and their actions and emotions and seeing how different they are, it is clear that *The Sun Also Rises* cannot be labeled as a textbook on the lost generation.

Sharon Sierawski

A Note on Taking Open-Book Exams

In an open-book exam on literature, you are required to use quotations from the text to support your response. Some students feel that taking this type of exam is a breeze because they have the material they need right in front of them. As a result, they fail to prepare adequately by carefully rereading the text or by marking key incidents and important sections of narration or dialogue.

Actually, the open-book exam is very challenging since you can lose valuable time looking through the work for that quote you half remember but can't locate, and your response is often judged more critically and specifically by the instructor.

The suggestions made in this chapter about essay exams in general should be followed carefully when you prepare for the open-book exam, but you should give special attention to the construction of possible test questions and responses. That way you can mark the text with clue words to help you find relevant supporting quotations for your response. Remember that the topic sentence, the introduction to the quotation, the quotation itself, and the analysis of the quotation form the pattern to use as you construct the body paragraphs of your response. Following a transition, you can add a second pattern—introduce a second quotation, quote it, analyze it—to support the topic sentence effectively.

If you prepare thoroughly using thought processes like analysis (breaking down your notes into possible test questions) and synthesis (putting your ideas together in the form of an essay answer), you will be able to write strong and to-the-point test responses quickly and confidently.

❦ Self-Evaluation of Preparation for Essay Exams ❦

Completing this worksheet will help you identify study topics for essay examinations.

1. List the main topics your instructor covered in lecture and discussion sections:

2. Which topics in the above list did your instructor spend the most time analyzing and discussing?

3. From the above topics, formulate as many possible test questions as you can based on the information in your text and in your notes.

4. Based on the information given by your instructor about the test, e.g., time allowed, number of questions you must answer, and point value, select several of your test questions and prepare an outline of your response.

5. If time permits, write out a complete response to the questions that you think your instructor is most likely to ask.

6. List any areas of weakness in your own writing that you need to be aware of as you write and proof-read your responses:

7. List any "pet" areas—either positive or negative—that your instructor tends to focus on when grading your essay responses:

8. Be honest about your preparation for the test by completing the following chart:

Material read: _____ all _____ most _____ half _____ none

Class attendance: number of absences _____

Class note taking: _____ all _____ some _____ none

Study time: number of hours _____

Number of sample test questions written: _____

Number of sample responses written: _____

This Is Not the End

✵ The Future Outlook

Now that you have learned about the elements of literature and how to write about them, you should be able to understand and appreciate any work of literature: those assigned in other classes you take or those you choose to read for your own pleasure and enjoyment. Even films and television dramas will have more meaning for you when you consider characterization, setting, point of view, symbolism, imagery, structure, tone, and theme.

In addition to writing about literature, you have really learned to write about anything you have read and then must analyze in writing. The basic process is usually the same: generalize about the content, introduce a supporting quotation, quote a section of the work to support and illustrate your generalization, and then analyze/explain the quotation by expanding and exploring its specific content and relevance to your general point. This formula, which you have been practicing this semester, is effective because the specific support for your generalizations comes from the work itself. And since you have been practicing your writing, it's probably safe to say that your skill level has increased. The more you write, the more skillful you will become in expressing your ideas clearly and accurately.

As you continue your education and as you enter the working world, remember that you will often be judged on how you express yourself in writing. This course and other writing courses you will take are a beginning—a good foundation for the writing you will do in the future. And if you remember the organizing principles of introduction, body, and conclusion and the analysis pattern of generalization/introduction to a quotation/quotation/analysis, you will surely be judged as a good writer who knows how to organize and present ideas logically and effectively.

Write on!

Index

321

"Writing about Literature: Step by Step" Instructional CD-Rom

The CD-Rom included with this book gives you the opportunity to complete the exercises, the detailed essay plan sheets with specific instructions on each part of the essay, and the peer/self-evaluation forms on your computer and then print them for your instructor. Also included are additional information and exercises on critical thinking; writing, editing, and evaluating effective introductions, body paragraphs, and conclusions; documenting research sources; and analyzing character, point of view, poetry, structure, and style. All of these learning activities—designed to help you apply what you have learned—can be printed for class and saved for future reference.

The CD-Rom is dual platform and self-executing. Insert it into your computer and choose the "User's Guide" icon for further instructions.